Åsne Seierstad was born in 1970 and studied Russian, Spanish and the History of Philosophy at Oslo University. She worked as a correspondent in Russia between 1993 and 1996, and in China in 1997. In 1999 she reported on the war in Kosovo for Norwegian television. She spent a year in Afghanistan from the autumn of 2001, reporting for a number of major Scandinavian newspapers. In spring 2003 she reported on the war in Iraq from Baghdad, and in 2004 published *A Hundred and One Days*, her compelling journal of the war and its after-effects.

Åsne Seierstad has received numerous awards for her journalism. *The Bookseller of Kabul*, published in 2003, is one of the bestselling Norwegian books of all time and has been translated into thirty-seven languages.

With Their Backs to the World

Portraits from Serbia

Åsne Seierstad

Translated by
Sindre Kartvedt

BASIC
BOOKS

A Member of the Perseus Books Group
New York

Books published by Basic Books are available at special discounts for
bulk purchases in the United States by corporations, institutions, and
other organizations. For more information, please contact the Special
Markets Department at the Perseus Books Group, 11 Cambridge Center,
Cambridge MA 02142, or call (617) 252-5298 or (800) 255-1514,
or e-mail special.markets@perseusbooks.com.

A CIP data record for this title is available from the Library of Congress
ISBN-13: 978-0-465-07602-4 ; ISBN-10: 0-465-07602-5
British ISBN: 1-84408-214-8
06 07 08 09/ 10 9 8 7 6 5 4 3 2 1

For Frøydis and Dag

Contents

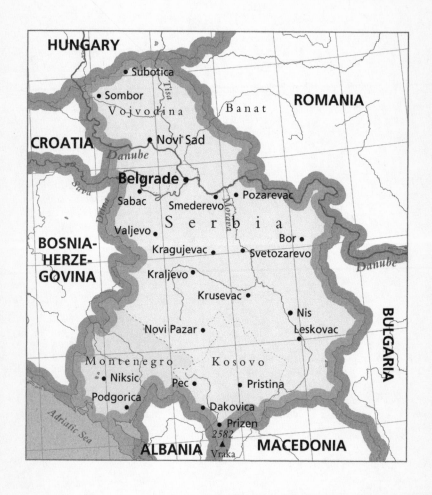

Foreword

'I had come to Yugoslavia to see what history meant in flesh and blood.'

Rebecca West, *Black Lamb and Grey Falcon*, 1941

This book grew out of three visits I made to Serbia between 1999 and 2004. When I decided to write it, the Serbs had just lost their fourth war in eight years. The war in Kosovo seemed to be over, and with it the apparently never-ending sequence of skirmishes, battles, massacres, torture, plunder and killings that made up the nightmarish wars of the Balkans during the 1990s. An ongoing inferno that left around two hundred thousand dead, millions of refugees, and tore societies to pieces.

But now these wars were over, they said. Were they really? Is it ever that simple?

In March 1999 Kosovo Albanians flooded across the borders of Macedonia, Montenegro and Albania, in order

to escape the Serbian soldiers or their Serbian neighbours –
following NATO's bombing raids. I was covering the conflict for the Norwegian Broadcasting Corporation, NRK.
The refugees told of Serbian atrocities, burned villages and
murdered relatives. Of being hunted by their neighbours
like wild game.

Seventy-eight days later it was the Serbs who fled – in
the thousands. The Albanians took their turn at the wheel
of the Balkan cycle of bloody violence. Now it was their
chance to slaughter, burn and pillage, and their vengeance
was commensurate with the cruelty they had been subjected to. Soon Serbs told the same stories that the
Albanians had recounted only weeks earlier – of being
hunted by their neighbours.

I couldn't stop wondering about the Serbs, these out-
casts of Europe. This people that started one war after the
other, and lost them all.

I read everything I could get my hands on about
Slobodan Milosevic's power strategies and war machine,
about the fractured opposition, about the oppression. But
I found little that really told me who they were, these
people who – virtually overnight – found themselves cast
as warmongers and butchers. I wanted to know how they
lived, what they talked about, what they cared about.

'You only want to have your prejudices confirmed,'
people said when I asked them to tell me who they were.

'How can you understand what's going on when we
can't even understand it ourselves?' asked one.

'How can you expect us to answer questions when we
are all walking around in a coma?' was the reaction from a
young art student.

While I went looking for answers, Milosevic tightened
his grip. 'The regime won't leave without a bloodbath,'

suspected Zarko Korac, from the political opposition, in a restaurant in Belgrade one spring evening. 'Blood will flow,' he assured me when I suggested that people seemed apathetic and not at all that ready to fight. He pointed to the beer-drinking crowd around us: 'This is what Sarajevo looked like the night before the war broke out.'

Eventually I found thirteen individuals and one family, and followed them during the winter and spring of 2000. These people together made up a picture, a mosaic of sorts. Or rather, as my neighbour Peca suggested, a *muckalica*: a classic Serbian dish that consists of meats and vegetables, chopped into spices and oil and left to simmer for hours.

In my *muckalica* their names are Grandpa Bora, Mira, Rambo and Branko. They might be Titoists or nationalists, Yugonostalgic or anti-nationalists. They are students, rock stars, refugees and poets.

One scorching-hot summer day in 2000 I left Belgrade. By the end of September the book was published. The story was over. Or so I thought.

Two weeks after publication I returned to Serbia, carrying fourteen copies for the people who had shared their lives and thoughts with me for half a year. Elections had just been held and I barely made it through customs – journalists were no longer allowed entry. I convinced the guards that I was only there to visit friends.

The next day all hell broke loose. Not the bloodbath that Korac had predicted, but a minor October revolution nonetheless. Half a million people gathered in front of the parliament on the morning of 5 October, to protest at Milosevic's refusal to recognise the opposition's candidate, Vojislav Kostunica, as the rightful winner of the election. They came from all over the country, on tractors, bulldozers, mopeds and buses. I managed to get a seat on top of a forklift from Cukarica. 'I'm not leaving my spot until Milosevic is gone,' said the burly farmer next to me. And together we watched this mass of humanity storm the parliament. The last gasps of Milosevic's regime consisted of a cloud of tear gas and a few rounds of gunfire.

Hundreds of thousands of people were committed to staying in Belgrade until the President was overthrown. If they weren't in Belgrade, they watched it unfold on TV. That morning Radio-televizija Srbije spewed its usual propaganda. Around noon the screens went black – the building that housed the broadcast was on fire after being stormed by demonstrators. The bosses escaped through the back doors and the journalists took over. That evening Vojislav Kostunica made his first appearance on the government's channel. Under his name it read: 'President of Yugoslavia'.

Many of my friends were not yet convinced. 'It's too easy. Serbia can't turn around in a few hours.'

I realised that the book wasn't finished. I had to write more: about the winners who had lost and the losers who had won. Again I visited all those who made up the pieces of my mosaic. What were they thinking now?

The second edition of the book followed the events up to the final night of the Milosevic era – to his arrest on 1 April 2001, when Serbia changed face.

'He built a web of wickedness. He manipulated us for thirteen years. He starved the whole country with his madness for war, and turned the rest of the world against us,' Prime Minister Zoran Djindjic told me that sunny spring day. We sat in the back of his black limousine, just hours after Milosevic had been arrested.

'Under a bad leadership Serbs are capable of committing

the most terrible atrocities; under good leaders we can do great deeds. It's like a field – if it's not cared for, the weeds will take over. But if you tend it, water and feed the seeds, you will reap a bountiful harvest,' he continued. 'Serbs are lazy, we lack discipline and have no capacity for self-criticism. Our primary flaw is that we believe we are stronger and better than anyone else.'

The Democratic Party's new Prime Minister explained to me how his country could be repaired and reconstructed. 'We need to reshape ourselves so we can once again fit into the rest of the world. We've taken part in every war and conflict in the Balkans in this century and allowed ourselves to be led by insane ideologues, demagogues and lunatics. After the Second Word War we got Tito; after the Wall came down we got Milosevic.'

After the fall of Milosevic Serbia got Djindjic. He was bursting with initiative and courage, and looked forward to the day when he could put his former enemy in front of a court. This professor of philosophy wanted to guide Serbia back to Europe and turn both its face and its chest to the world. He came down hard on members of the old regime and their Mafia ties, began a process of reform within the military and health sectors and attempted to innovate in education, business and agriculture. By the end of June 2001 one of his dreams had come true: Milosevic was sent to the UN's International Criminal Tribunal for the former Yugoslavia.

After 11 September 2001 the world seemed to forget about the Balkans. The reporters who used to cover the region left for other, bloodier parts of the world, but all the while Serbia stayed on its crooked course. The political factions that once were united against Milosevic's rule fell into a debilitating, fratricidal battle for power. Three times election results were declared invalid because not enough people bothered to vote. While the democratic parties and their leaderships squabbled, the nationalists – Milosevic's ideological successors – grew in popularity.

Zoran Djindjic's popularity fell proportionally. His tough reforms made people nostalgic for better days. The Mafia wanted a return to the system they knew, and could control. On 12 March 2003 the Prime Minister was assassinated on his way into the government building.

Only in death did Djindjic receive the love of the Serbian people. But without him Serbia stalled.

Once more I realised that this story was not over. Like the rest of the world, I had turned my attention to other wars in other hemispheres, leaving Serbia to stumble and drop out of sight and mind. But in the spring of 2004 I once again sought out my old friends to learn what they'd been through over the past three years.

'We can no longer pretend that Serbia is going forward,' I read before leaving. 'Ultranationalism is a deciding factor in politics, the economy is in a deep crisis, government institutions are weak and the security services are becoming a political tool,' concluded the report from the renowned International Crisis Group.

Apathy reigned. People who once took to the streets for liberty grew disillusioned when the new rulers hardly seemed to differ from the old. International aid kept decreasing and political support had almost vanished. While the EU helped build roads through Slovenia, Serbia was left to the weeds, as Djindjic had predicted. After deciding that Vojislav Kostunica's new government didn't provide 'satisfactory cooperation' with the Hague Tribunal, the United States cancelled a promised aid package of $100 million and rejected all aid to Serbia from the World Bank and the International Monetary Fund.

The issue of the Hague Tribunal was closely tied to a larger and more complex matter: the issue of guilt. Ever since the tribunal for war crimes in the former Yugoslavia was formed in 1993, it had been a sore point for many. The tribunal came into being in large part because the states and nations that once made up Yugoslavia were unable, or unwilling, to put their own war criminals on trial. In fact, the accused were often portrayed, and hailed, as national heroes. This happened in Croatia, in Bosnia and most certainly in Serbia.

It was – and is still – always 'the others' that commit war crimes against 'us'. The fog of victimisation is impenetrable in the Balkans. Everything – from the battle against the Turks on the Kosovo plains in 1389, where the Serbian martyr Tsar Lazar renounced the worldly kingdom for that of heaven, to the massacres of Serbs during the Second World War and the expulsions from Krajina in Croatia and Kosovo in the 1990s – serves the mythology of victimisation. To resist the efforts of the tribunal has become a way to display patriotism. 'Why us? Why us?' ask the citizens in Serbia, in Croatia, in Bosnia. 'It was the others who attacked us. We just defended ourselves.'

In the parliamentary elections of 2003 the Radical Party and Serbia's Socialist Party won a third of the votes. The leaders of these two parties, Vojislav Seselj and Slobodan Milosevic respectively, are on trial in The Hague. In the presidential election of June 2004 the Democrat Boris Tadic was declared the winner, closely followed by Tomislav Nikolic, an ultranationalist who still raves about a Greater Serbia. The country is split between those who want to fashion ties to Europe and the forces that still feed off the myth of past greatness.

In this divided Serbia, in the spring of 2004 I sought out my old friends, whom I'd now known for five years. I was curious to see how they had adapted to yet another new reality. My meetings with them were profound – I was touched to see how some of them managed while others failed.

With sadness I realised that the title I had chosen four years earlier, *With Their Backs to the World*, was still apt. In fact, more so than ever.

Oslo, 4 July 2004

Important Characters

Slobodan Milosevic
President of Serbia 1989–97 and leader of Serbia's Socialist Party (SPS). President of Yugoslavia 1997–2000. Arrested on 1 April 2001 and extradited to The Hague that year. Has been charged with genocide and crimes against humanity by the International War Crimes Tribunal in The Hague. He is defending himself at the trial.

Zoran Djindjic
Prime Minister of Serbia 2001–3. Assassinated on 12 March 2003. After two decades as a leading figure of the Western-minded opposition he masterminded the demonstrations that eventually brought down Milosevic. When he assumed power he attempted to introduce a market economy and other reforms.

Vojislav Kostunica
President of Yugoslavia 2000–3. Resigned when Yugoslavia was dissolved and the union between Serbia and

Montenegro came into being in 2003. Succeeded Zoran Zivkovic as Prime Minister of Serbia in the spring of 2004. A centrist politician with nationalistic leanings, he strives to temper the process of reform.

Vojislav Seselj
Ultranationalist who holds a doctorate in political science and leads the Nationalist Party. Commanded various para-military groups during the Balkan wars of the 1990s and is now in The Hague, charged with war crimes. His party's popularity is still growing in Serbia.

Vuk Draskovic
Leader of the Serbian Renewal Movement. A nationalist author during the 1990s, he briefly entered into an alliance with Milosevic, only to resign his post as Vice-Prime Minister during the Kosovo war of 1999. Has survived several assassination attempts. At present Foreign Minister of Serbia and Montenegro.

Boris Tadic
Leads the Serbian Democratic Party (SDS) and was elected President of Serbia on 26 June 2004. Desires closer ties to the West and a market economy.

Ratko Mladic
General who was military commander of the Bosnian Serbs during the Bosnian war of 1992–5. Charged by the Hague Tribunal with genocide and crimes against humanity. Mladic led the attacks on cities and villages in Bosnia and was responsible for several massacres, including Srebrenica. As of August 2005 he is still at large.

Radovan Karadzic

Political leader and President of the Bosnian Serbs during the early 1990s. President of the Bosnian Serb administration in Pale. Like Mladic, he is wanted by the Hague Tribunal and as of August 2005 he is still at large, protected by Serb nationalists in Bosnia.

Alija Izetbegovic

Muslim leader in Bosnia. President of Bosnia-Hercegovina 1990–6. Died in 2003.

Franjo Tudjman

President of Croatia 1990–9. Died in 1999.

Hashim Thaci

Former political leader of Kosovo's liberation army, the KLA, and now a politician in Kosovo.

Hunchbacks for Milosevic

'The early bird catches the worm.'

Serbian proverb

Each morning around six o'clock a whistle sounds between the houses of Borisav Vojnovic and Nikola Randelovic. This means that the coffee is ready. Strong Turkish coffee with three spoonfuls of sugar, and a quick shot of *rakija*. Already the workday is well under way in the village of Stanjinac, in the mountains of southern Serbia. Borisav has been up since five, feeding his two cows, the sheep, his lamb, the chickens and the rooster. By now he's already had a chat with Suba and Sredana as he fed them, fetched their water and carried out the droppings that are still steaming in the frosty morning air. He's taken care of Bonka the sheep and played with her lamb, which has no name because it will be butchered in June.

'The animals come first,' he says. So it's only after an

hour's caring for them that it's finally time for coffee and *rakija* – one day at Borisav's, the next at Nikola's. Borisav has marked his days on his calendar. This morning it is Nikola who makes his way across the courtyard on two wooden canes. He struggles up the stairs to Borisav's house. The two men greet each other and sit down. The *rakija* is gone in one gulp. 'Nosegulp' is what Borisav calls it; having the aroma of the liquor burn through your nostrils is as important a part of it as to feel the effect in the rest of your body.

There's a pleasant exhalation following the strong drink – a *travarita*, from *trava*, Serbian for 'herbs'. Borisav has made it himself, from plums, and seasoned it with kantarion, gentian, yarrow and sage. Over coffee the men talk of the corn to be sown and the potatoes to be planted. And of course of the animals. At the beginning of May Suba will calve, and her calf has already been named Kompjuter, because that's what Borisav will buy for his grandson with the money he gets when he sells it. The old men talk of sowing times, and even if this April morning seems to promise lovely, sunny weather, Borisav recalls the freezing night of 14 May 1952, when the entire village lost its crop. 'Never let an early spring fool you,' he says, and asks me to call him Deda Bora – Grandpa Bora. 'Everyone your age does,' he explains.

His living room is furnished with the bare necessities: a table, a few chairs, a cabinet, a chest and a sofa. On the walls there's a calendar and a framed picture of Slobodan Milosevic. The picture is from the late 1980s and a bit faded – Milosevic looks young and energetic. Southern Serbia is Milosevic's stronghold and the majority of his supporters are, like Deda Bora and Nikola, well beyond the age of retirement. 'Milosevic is the best president for

Serbia. He protects and defends us against those who want to sell us out,' says Deda Bora, referring to the political opposition in Serbia.

Like most Serbs, Deda Bora has seen his standard of living fall dramatically over the past ten years, the decade that Milosevic has been in power. Incomes are a fraction of what they were and savings vanished during the hyper-inflation of 1993. Deda Bora knows the answer: 'You can't get rich and fight a war at the same time.'

'Perhaps Milosevic shouldn't have started all these wars?' I suggest.

The old man is crestfallen. 'Serbia never started any wars. We've been attacked; first by the Slovenes, then by the Croats, then by the Muslims – of course we had to defend ourselves,' he explains. 'But we will rise again, just like we rose up after the Second World War. Since when didn't the Serbs rise up when they've been down?'

Nikola nods. 'Nobody can beat us.'

Still, Deda Bora's greatest hero remains Tito. Not even Milosevic measures up here. 'Under Tito nobody dared touch us, nobody interfered in our affairs and we worked with other nations on an equal footing. We never lived so well, never before and never since,' he says and admits that Milosevic does have one flaw. 'Tito was a diplomat; Milosevic is not.'

Like any good Titoist, Deda Bora is an atheist. This makes the picture on the bedroom wall a bit of a mystery – it's Leonardo da Vinci's painting of the Last Supper, with Jesus and the disciples.

'Jesus?' exclaims Deda Bora. 'That's not Jesus, that's Tsar Lazar, who perished on the field of Kosovo in 1389. The painting depicts the meal before the battle. That guy to the left, in yellow? That is Vuk Brankovic, who betrayed

Tsar Lazar to the Turks. And that one who whispers in Lazar's ear, that's Milos Obilic. He said, "You have a traitor at your left knee." But Lazar didn't listen to him and lost the battle.'

There is no room for doubt in Deda Bora's account, despite the fact that this is indeed a reproduction of Leonardo's *The Last Supper*. But throughout this countryside devoted to Tito, the myth of Tsar Lazar's sacrifice replaced Jesus Christ. The Last Supper became the secret meal. Judas became Vuk Brankovic. The disciples became Serbian soldiers.

In the bedroom another picture captures my attention. A half-naked woman lounges on a chaise longue in a baroque hall. Behind her the curtains flutter in a large window overlooking a beach with palm trees. Fat, naked babies hover around the woman. 'Verica put that one up. She was really fond of kids,' says Deda Bora and leaves the room. Borisav and Verica married when they were seventeen; their parents had proposed this when they were kids. And that's how it came to be, even if Verica's parents never lived to see it. They were killed by Bulgarian fascists when Verica was twelve. She watched them being shot in their own courtyard in 1942, accused of helping the Partisans. 'There was something special about Verica. I don't know what it was, but she was different from all the other girls. I just knew that it'd be us.'

Deda Bora sinks down by the kitchen table.

'We lost the first four ones,' he says, and the knuckles of his fists turn white. 'The doctors couldn't tell us why they never lived to see a month.' Verica was sure that she was cursed, and tried every cure there was. When her fifth child was born, on a cold day in December 1956, she wrapped it up, put the infant out on the road and hid behind some bushes. After a while a man came upon the child, picked it up and took it home with him. Verica followed him but didn't show herself until he had carried her son into his house. It was said that a curse like that would be broken when someone else brought the baby home. The boy grew up and was given the name Najden, which means 'found'. He is their only child, and today this grown man of more than a hundred kilos is a colonel in the Yugoslav army. 'It wasn't until it was clear that he would survive and grow up that we started living again,' says Deda Bora. 'By then we'd lived through seven years of babies dying.'

Verica went to her grave believing that the man on the road saved her son's life. Deda Bora is not so sure. 'I only believe in the things I can see,' he says. 'That's why I don't believe in God either.'

It's been three years since Verica died. She was in pain for a long time but never complained. By the time she got herself to a doctor it was too late. As Borisav talks about her tears form in his eyes. 'If it wasn't for the animals I'd be really lonely. I talk to them every day, and they talk back. Besides, I've got my neighbours, even if they keep disappearing on me – either they die or they go to some flat in the city. But having neighbours doesn't really help; I'm alone in my house, that's what's so hard. I don't like to eat by myself and I never drink coffee alone. Coffee alone isn't coffee.'

Borisav Vojnovic is (in 2000) in his seventieth year. His whole life he has lived in this village, Stanjinac, in the mountains near the border with Bulgaria. The village consists of three clusters of houses, a few kilometres apart, totalling a little more than a hundred small farms. The scenery is idyllic, with plains and rolling hills looking out over a deep, verdant valley. Violets grow by the side of the road. The cherry trees bloom and the apricot trees have large, pink buds. But this vision of paradise runs only so deep. Stanjinac is dying. Most of the fields are fallow now and the vines wither as nobody cares for them. Sometimes you still see someone in a field with a horse and plough, but it's heavy work in the clay earth. Most of the people in the village are over sixty. Every morning you see these sagging, hunched backs move towards the fields, each with a hoe in their hands. They straighten up as best they can when they stop and greet someone. 'It's as if the earth pulls them down itself,' Deda Bora says of the hunchbacks. 'It wants us back. The youngest man in the village is around forty, and a bachelor. It's too late for him,' says Deda Bora. 'He's already like an old man.'

There is one kid in the village, the grocer's. In the 1960s there were hundreds of kids running around the court-yards and fields here. When I ask how many people live in Stanjinac, Deda Bora begins to count: 'Smilja, Violeta, Milica, Bina, myself, Branka, Tihomir, Smira – that's eight – the other Tihomir, Nadica, Perica, Bogdana, Mara, Bora, and Nikola . . .'

Deda Bora is who you talk to when something needs taking care of. Today it's Tihomir's harrow that won't work. We walk a bit down to his house. Deda Bora points and tells of trees, fields and houses. 'That tree is more than five hundred years old,' he'll say. 'Whenever someone gets married, they have to visit it – they believe it's good luck.'

Once at Tihomir's, Deda Bora sits down on a stool, his glasses balanced on the tip of his nose, wrenches ready at his side. Tihomir stands and watches while Bora fiddles with the engine. Grandpa Bora is one of the sprightliest people in these parts and looks like a young lad next to his neighbour, who's around eighty. Yet even he still works his own lands, hunched back or not.

Deda Bora gets the machine to work and proceeds to turn the entire piece of land for Tihomir, since he's there already. Tihomir's wife offers coffee and corn cakes and shows off pictures from her granddaughter's wedding. Her furrowed hand proudly displays a photo of her grandchild in a shining white wedding dress. The photo is kept in a clear plastic bag so it won't get dirty or dusty as it makes its way around the table. The sparkling granddaughter poses with her grandparents. They come up to her shoulders: the grandmother in a headscarf and best shoes, her grandfather in his suit. While the bride flirts with the camera, Baba and Deda – Grandma and Grandpa – simply stare into the lens, deadly serious. That their granddaughter, or any of Bina's and Tihomir's other grandchildren, would ever take over the farm is out of the question. 'There is no future for this village,' says Deda Bora. 'In twenty years there'll be nobody left.'

As we stroll home from Tihomir and Bina's, we pass several abandoned houses. We stop to watch a man who ploughs a field below the road. Both man and horse have to stop constantly, and sweat pours off their bodies. Deda Bora sighs and walks on. He was the second man in the village to buy a tractor, in 1980. 'That was one of the greatest days of my life,' he notes.

At two o'clock it's lunchtime. Pickled bell peppers, home-made cheese, beans and bread. Bora complains of his lack of appetite. 'You should have seen me back when Verica was alive – I was big and strong. Now I'm just fading away. I can't eat meat any more; I've lost too many teeth.'

The food tastes of fresh air and sunshine. Deda Bora is famous for his cheese, which he sells in the village. 'You take ten litres of milk, add a tablespoon of salt for each litre, and let it boil for six minutes,' he explains, finding the clock he uses to measure the time. To show me how long six minutes is, he sets the clock. 'Then you add two tablespoons of eighty-proof vinegar and boil it for another six minutes. Then you pour it all into a cloth and put it under a large, flat stone for pressure. Then you just wait until it's done. Takes about a day and a night. You could do this yourself, when you get back to Norway,' he suggests.

After lunch it's time to feed the animals again. I offer to carry the heavy buckets of water, but the farmer refuses any assistance. 'Anyone who's gone to school doesn't have to work around here,' he says, as if this rule ought to be known far and wide. So I sink into the hay in the barn and let the April sun warm me while I listen to Bora talk to his animals downstairs.

When he was eight Borisav went to work as a shepherd. He's been a farmer, tailor, salesman, soldier, musician, Tito-propagandist and miner. As a newlywed seventeen-year-old he spent three years in the military, then worked a few years for Agitprop, the People's Front's department for agitation and propaganda under Tito. 'Anything that had to be done had to be done through Agitprop. I travelled around the countryside and taught; about Tito and his politics, and about how people could get more out of their fields. The last part was the most important because you didn't need to agitate much for Tito; everybody supported him anyway.' After his years with Agitprop Bora was appointed the local tax collector. He refused the job – how could he possibly collect tax from his neighbours? So he had to work in a mine instead. It took him a few years to dig himself out from the mine; he then started a travelling orchestra. Deda Bora played the clarinet at weddings, funerals and christenings. The money was good, but it was a hard life. 'Serbian parties tend to end in fights towards the morning. More than a few times the band had to run for cover to avoid getting involved,' he recalls. Deda Bora still has the scar on his leg from getting a wine bottle broken on it. 'Drunk Serbs are terrible people,' he says. But it wasn't the bottle throwing that turned him off the travelling roadshow. 'I started to lose my teeth about thirty years ago. You can't play the clarinet without teeth.'

After his stint as a musician Deda Bora set himself up as a tailor, all the while farming full time. He would sew until eleven o'clock at night, before it was time to go out and plough the fields.

The old sewing machine is still in the bedroom, and there are pieces of cloth, scissors and measuring tape on the table. Deda Bora was a tailor for twenty-five years, specialising in hats, aprons and skirts. His pleated skirts were renowned in the villages around here. 'I was the first one to add embroidery to everyday aprons. A lot of women in southern Serbia are still wearing my aprons and skirts,' he says proudly. At weekends he and Verica would travel around to various markets to sell his clothing. 'That's the best work I ever had in my life. There isn't a village in southern Serbia that I haven't been to, as a soldier, agitator, musician or salesman. When I was with the People's Front I walked everywhere. When I became a tailor I could afford a car.'

Deda Bora was invited to join the Yugoslav Communist Party, which was a great honour out in the countryside.

'But I gave up on communism when everyone else did,' he says. 'When Tito died.'

He inherited his faith in Tito from his parents, who supported the Partisan resistance during the Second World War. Borisav was just a little boy when the war started. 'The Germans behaved well here, they were polite and decent. Things got a lot worse when the Bulgarian fascists occupied us. They are like us; they killed and raped and destroyed everything they came across,' he explains. During the war all schooling was conducted in Bulgarian and Deda Bora still shudders when he remembers how all the kids were given Bulgarian names. 'Boris Georgijev Vojnov, they called me. But for me, my name was still Borisav Vojnovic.'

Deda Bora remembers well how the Partisans and the Chetniks demanded lodging in the village. You had to open your door, no matter who you supported. Once, more than forty Partisan fighters slept in their tiny house. 'The Partisans only took food from people who had enough. We didn't have anything but polenta and grease to offer them. They only ate once they saw that we kids had got some, too. The Chetniks, on the other hand, helped themselves to anything in our cellar.'

The Partisans took part in the resistance to the Nazi occupation, under the command of Tito, and served as the army of the Communist Party, which in turn won the Yugoslav civil war. The Chetniks were a monarchist resistance movement, led by Colonel Draza Mihailovic. In the beginning they were allied with the Partisans, but later fought against them, occasionally even with Italian and German forces.

After the midday feeding of the animals it's time for coffee at a neighbour's house. It seems half the village is here.

The theme today is the huge demonstration planned by Serbia's political opposition. 'They've been paid by the Americans to set it up, and if they gather a lot of people they get even more money,' explains Deda Bora. 'The Americans have bought a bunch of traitors who are willing to sell their own country. But we have a crafty intelligence agency, and they've uncovered their plans.'

'How do you know this?' I ask.

'They said so on TV. Luckily they've told us, so we all know what's going on.'

Deda Bora gets all his information from the state-controlled media. In this version Milosevic is the great saviour and anyone who is against him is a traitor. The USA is the main enemy. On TV there are repeated showings of footage of American KFOR (Kosovo Force) troops in Kosovo trying to calm down those whom the Serbs refer to as Albanian terrorists.

'The Americans have to get out of Serbia – look what they've done to Kosovo. They're stirring up the Albanians to make trouble. There are hardly any Serbs left in Kosovo, even if Kosovo is ours,' complains Deda Bora.

'They're really all Serbs,' says a neighbour. 'But some of them are Serbs that had to convert to Islam to avoid getting killed by the Turks.'

'Why is Kosovo so important?' I ask.

'Because it's Serbian. If the KFOR leave, the Serbs will return,' says Deda Bora, and explains that the American goal is to occupy all of Serbia. 'They want our wealth. But the Americans will never reach Belgrade. Just like Hitler was never able to take Moscow,' he says, and looks at the clock on the wall. It's time for the evening shift in the barn.

Once the work is done we sit down to watch a

documentary on TV. It's called *America and Kosovo* and explores the American conspiracy against Serbia. Deda Bora pays close attention and learns even more about the American scheme to conquer his country.

'The main problem now is that there are so many terrorists here,' Deda Bora sighs once the programme is over.

On my last day in Stanjinac we walk to the cemetery. Deda Bora lights a candle on Verica's grave. He stands there for a long time, looking at her headstone. Two serious faces look back at him. The names and images of both him and Verica have been carved into the stone, which reads: 'Verica Vojnovic 1930–1997' and 'Borisav Vojnovic 1931–'.

'She lies here and waits for me,' says the widower.

Next to the headstone stands a small cross of stone without any names. This is where their lost children lie.

'Some people say that hardship and loss make you stronger. That's not true – losing a child can't make you stronger, it only makes you weak. The mourning of the four children that never lived is something that is always with me. Whenever I visit the cemetery I can't do anything afterwards. I am all sorrow.'

But the animals need him. Deda Bora climbs the steep hills back to his house, a couple of kilometres from the cemetery. Halfway there we part. He is heading back for the midday feeding; I am going to Belgrade. Deda Bora presents me with an apron, brown with yellow and green flowers and along the bottom a string of black lace.

'You must give my regards to your parents. Take good care of them,' is the last thing he tells me before he continues to struggle up the steep hills.

*

It's almost Christmas before I see Deda Bora again. Serbia has lived through a presidential election and a revolution, Milosevic has fallen from power and in a few days, on 23 December 2000, parliamentary elections will be held. The Democratic opposition is expected to win a large majority. I'm excited to see Deda Bora again, and curious to hear his thoughts on everything that has happened over the last few months. Has he, like so many others, turned his back on Milosevic, now that he has fallen from power?

Danijela, Bora's grandniece, gives me a ride from Belgrade. We drive along the curvy dirt road, over the hillside, past the church, continuing uphill. We turn left by the grocer's and drive by fields and abandoned farms. There's the sister's house, there's Nikola's – and then – here, here's Deda Bora's house.

He stands there in his courtyard in the bleak December sun and stirs, steady and immovable, a large iron cauldron. As handsome as he was last spring – icy blue eyes, hair as white as snow and a gaze that won't let go of you. He kisses me three times on the cheeks, as is the custom.

'How are your parents?' is the first thing he wants to know. 'And how is your book going?'

I answer as Deda Bora calmly stirs the huge cauldron, which is filled with boiling bacon.

'I butchered my pig yesterday,' he explains. 'Came to 130 kilos; now I'll be making sausages, smoked hams and boiled *cvarak*.'

The bubbling grease in front of us will become *cvarak*. The bacon will be cut into cubes, then boiled first in water, later in its own grease. After four hours it's browned, the excess grease is pressed out of it and it's put out to dry and turn crispy. 'A delicacy,' grins Deda Bora. The grease that's left over, he uses for cooking.

Deda Bora adds more firewood, and allows himself a break in the stirring. Najden, who has come home to help his father with the butchering, takes over. Deda Bora invites me to join him for home-made plum brandy and Turkish coffee.

I sneak a look into the living room to see if the picture is still there. It is.

Deda Bora carves a few slices of his famous cheese and serves us. 'All's well with both Suba and Sredana, and Bonka the sheep,' he tells us. 'And we've got really nice plums this year. But other than that, it's been a miserable autumn – the sun burned off half our crops.'

To Deda Bora, the autumn of 2000 has been miserable in more ways than that.

'A coup,' he states. 'Paid for by the Americans.'

He's not alone in the village in believing this. In Stanjinac, Milosevic got by far the most votes in September's presidential elections. The final count showed that, out of 150 votes cast, Milosevic received 128. Twenty went to the candidate from Vojislav Seselj's Nationalist Party, while the Democratic candidate, Vojislav Kostunica, got all of two votes. Suffice it to say, the village was not at all in step with the rest of the country.

'In a while even more people will support the current government. In Serbia a lot of people always vote for the sitting president, just to be on the safe side,' Deda Bora explains. 'But the majority of us will still support Milosevic and his Socialist Party.

'And the picture I'll never take down,' he says, and points up at the young and energetic Slobodan Milosevic on the wall. 'He steered us through the toughest years Serbia has lived through since the occupation.'

Deda Bora has nothing but disgust for those in the

Socialist Party who now want to replace Milosevic as the head of the party. 'They were behind him when he was in power and stab him in the back now that he's down.'

But the old Titoist will now admit to more of Milosevic's flaws. 'He was too tough and refused to listen to anyone else. He should have been more flexible. His biggest mistake was removing himself from the people. He stopped travelling around and only made a few speeches from his palace. He wasn't among us. That was his fatal mistake.'

Deda Bora gets angry when I bring up the Hague Tribunal and the accusations of war crimes. 'All the Serbs that have been arrested for war crimes are innocent. They only did their duty, and defended us when we were attacked by Croats and Muslims. But the Americans are trying to get us. They want to have their bases here. And what the Americans want they usually get, unless someone fights back. I hope the new President understands this, but maybe he's already been bought by the Americans. I can't say for sure.'

There's a lot Grandpa Bora can't say for sure any more. The news broadcasts on TV no longer help prop up his opinions. He used to devour anything that was said on the state-controlled channel, but now he's not so sure about Radio-televizija Srbije. It doesn't quite fit with his view of the world.

'Maybe I shouldn't be saying this out loud,' says Deda Bora. 'But Serbia is not ready for democracy. I don't think it's good for us. Look at the prices – they've quadrupled since the coup, and my pension has gone up by just ten per cent. Serbia needs a new Tito,' he reckons. 'A firm hand. Only then will we get any order in this country. We can't manage ourselves. We're just not ready for it.'

Outside it's growing dark. Time to take care of the animals. We go to fetch water from the stone well that Deda Bora's father dug during the Second World War. 'This is the best water there is,' he says, manoeuvring the heavy bucket up from the well. 'Only the best is good enough for my animals. Suba and Sredana's milk is so fat my daughter-in-law has to cut it with water,' he brags, as he hauls up bucket after bucket of the best water in the world. Then we go down to the animals. Deda Bora takes his time, chats with the cows, pats them, gives them water and hay.

The courtyard is lit by the moon and a modest lamp. We can barely make out his son and daughter-in-law, draining the running fat off the bacon. They put the bacon between two wooden planks and salt it. We walk down to sample the first few bites. It tastes wonderful and melts on your tongue like a crispy Christmas rib.

Deda Bora says it needs more salt.

'You came here to get to know us,' he says. 'But to get to know a Serb you have to eat three hundred kilos of salt with him. Did you know that? It takes some time, eating three hundred kilos of salt.'

He fixes me with his eyes.

'Takes a lot of time,' he says.

Three winters go by, and another spring gets under way. Since I left Deda Bora by the greasy cauldron I've shared barely a gram of salt with a Serb. Nor have I spent much time pondering the mysteries of *Homo balcanicus*. I closed this door when I left here, a few days after the arrest of Milosevic, in April 2001, and didn't open it again until three years had passed, and it was April again. In the meantime other fates and other people's suffering had captured my attention. So the journey back to Deda Bora's is like travelling back in time; I brush the rust off the door, open it slowly; it squeaks as I step inside.

As a travelling companion I have brought Drago, a friend from my last visit. We're hurtling along at lethal speed on the road from Belgrade to Nis, until we turn off and head south-east. The road keeps getting smaller. It undulates over soft indentations and deep potholes. Eventually the white line in the middle of the road disappears, until all we're on is a one-lane country road again. The landscape is brown, the fields have not yet begun to sprout, but the cherry trees already have a soft, white veil. We pass picturesque villages, where the houses lean against one another in small groups and faded curtains wave from the windows. If you look a little closer you realise that the houses are dilapidated, that the fences have not been mended for generations. Some houses stand alone, sneaking a glance over at the other groups. Brown, poor, abandoned.

'They look angry,' says Drago.

'Who?'

'The houses.'

They *do* seem bitter.

'Look at them – they stand there with their windows boarded up, hating each other,' Drago goes on. 'And then people ask why there are wars . . .'

A couple of dogs fight over a bone beneath a stunning magnolia tree. Like a queen, the tree keeps itself way above the petty battle at its roots. The magnolia flowers are as large as champagne flutes; purple, then lightening out towards the petals, into the entirely white tips.

In gardens and fields women work in thick stockings, skirts that reach below their knees and flowery aprons.

They hoe, rake or weed. Their hair is pulled back, pinned up at the neck, and is grey, white or greying black.

The old men are wearing russet trousers and galoshes. Inside the galoshes they have home-knitted woollen socks. The trousers are shaped like jodhpurs: wide around the thighs, tighter from the knees downwards. The layers of shirts and sweaters are all in soft, fading colours. Their coats are open. It's like driving through a faded old movie from the fifties.

The young men belong in a different movie. They've adopted the fashion that invaded the countryside of Eastern Europe a decade ago: stonewashed jeans, sneakers and fake Adidas sweatshirts. Some are wearing leather jackets. These young men sit in the cafés, smoking, drinking coffee or *rakija*, and stare at the cars that drive by. There are hardly any young women in this movie. Sometimes you catch a glimpse of one, behind the counter of a small grocery store.

We continue on our bumpy way, leaving the open fields behind. We cross a small river and begin our approach to the hills below Deda Bora's village. A sign tells us Stanjinac is to our left. The metalled road comes to an end and we continue on an overgrown carriage road. The maples hang down like heavy curtains all around us, the branches slapping the car. Our eyes are drowning in the green of the buds and the newly sprung leaves.

We pass the cemetery, the first group of houses, then the next. And there – there's the five-hundred-year-old tree in the corner of Deda Bora's little garden. The tree that bears luck. It rears itself proudly – no, stiffly – towards the sky. The branches are bare, they have neither buds nor leaves, and the massive trunk is black. Since I've been gone the tree has died.

From the field behind Nikola's house across the road, an older man nods to us before he hunches over and goes back to work. The sun disappears behind a cloud. Our shiny, cobalt hire car turns into the courtyard. The wooden door to the red-brick outhouse is still not straight. The vegetable garden looks inviting, fresh and orderly.

A thin man in his socks comes out on the front doorstep. He steps into his galoshes and treads gingerly down the small stairs. Reaching the end, he straightens his back. Deda Bora has become a shadow of his old self.

He kisses me three times and welcomes us inside, but changes his mind when he sees the car. He wants to see the engine. Drago lifts up the hood of the Mitsubishi. Deda Bora inspects everything. Not saying a word, he nods, feels the wires, the pipes, turns a valve.

The furrows of his face have grown deeper. Even more teeth have abandoned him. The white hairs grow farther apart from each other. He looks up from the engine.

'So you're back,' he says, and pats me lightly on the back.

Then he invites us inside.

'How are your parents?' he asks at the bottom step of the stairs, and smiles wanly when I tell him.

A golden sugarloaf served straight out of the pan awaits us inside. Bora cuts thick chunks for all of us, fills the tiny *rakija* glasses to the brim, pours fresh coffee in three cups and takes his seat at the end of the table. We lift our glasses.

'A glass a day is medicine,' says Deda Bora. 'Two is poison.'

The searing shot is our first, his second. The first drink went down a few minutes after six o'clock this morning, as usual. 'Two glasses is fine once in a while, but never one after the other. One for breakfast and then one for lunch, that's fine,' he reasons.

The house is draughty, cool like a spring day before the sun comes up. Drago is wearing his thick winter coat, while I've put mine away, preferring instead to huddle over the warm cake and Deda Bora's firewater. The farmer is wearing a green army shirt with a purple padded waistcoat on top. Like any stylish tailor, he has his own taste, and doesn't have to follow local fashion.

The cake tastes of fresh eggs.

'They wanted change, and change is what they got,' Deda Bora exclaims all of a sudden, and knocks his spoon on the table. He looks at me, then at Drago, who is wolfing down his cake, and then back at me.

'I never wanted change. Zane the baker wanted change,' he says. 'Every time I went down to Kalna to get bread, he said he wanted change.'

Deda Bora has stopped eating. His arm lies shaking on the table, the spoon sticking straight up from his fist. There are yellow cake crumbs on the tablecloth.

'Baker Zane voted for the Democratic Party. I told him they'd sell Serbia to the Americans, but he said he wanted change.'

Drago drains his glass and makes a face.

'I never wanted change. Zane the baker wanted change,' says Deda Bora.

Once a week he walks nine kilometres to Kalna to buy bread. Each time he argues with baker Zane.

'There's no order any more. Under Tito there was order, and under Milosevic, too. What is happening?'

Deda Bora bites his lip, looks out through his kitchen window and answers his own question. 'Oh, they've taken over, all right,' he snorts. 'The *Democrats*.'

He spits out the word.

'Tito wouldn't have liked what's going on here now. Under Tito we had Goli Otok.'

Deda Bora's eyes are harder than they used to be, more bitter. Is it the changes of the past three years, or maybe just three more years of loneliness?

'We could use about five Goli Otoks now,' he says.

'Goli Otok' means 'the naked island'; it was Tito's island prison, where political prisoners were held.

In the background Deda Bora's black-and-white TV is on. There's a live broadcast from a debate in parliament. Politicians take their turn at the microphone, wave their fists, deliver harsh words and sit back down again.

'It's impossible to get what they're debating,' sighs Bora. 'They're all just saying, "I found it offensive when you said . . .", they're defaming each other, or just ridiculing someone. They don't care about doing something for the country, they just want to look good. Serbs have become lazy,' Bora concludes, and gets down to specifics. 'Maybe we always were, and that's why they whipped us to get us to work. Look at the kids today – they're not lifting a finger. Every time I go down to Kalna I see them, sitting in the cafés not doing a thing. Letting every hour of the day go by. They don't want to work in the fields. There's not enough money in it for them, so they just sit there. Maybe they have a little shop, selling things nobody needs.'

Then I notice. The picture has gone. Milosevic is no longer hanging on the wall of Bora's sewing room. He's been replaced by Tsar Lazar's secret meal or, if you like, Leonardo's *The Last Supper*.

'You took down Milosevic?'

'Yes.'

'You're not voting for him any more?'

'No.'

'Who are you voting for, then?'

'This last time I voted for Seselj.'

Vojislav Seselj is, like Slobodan Milosevic, in jail, charged with war crimes. He heads the only party that still rattles its sabres and speaks of a Greater Serbia. These Radicals argue that the Serbian part of Bosnia, as well as the Krajina region of Croatia, should be part of Serbia.

'We had a meeting at Nikola's. Everybody in the village was there, and we decided who to vote for. We decided on the Radicals.'

'Why them?'

'Because they're not corrupt.'

'And?'

'They're not dirty. The Democrats are criminals. They steal and gorge themselves, and sell the country to the Americans.'

This time the old people of Stanjinac are not as out of step with the rest of Serbia as they were at the first election after the 'coup', four years ago. The wave of euphoria that carried the Democratic Party – though not up to Stanjinac – eventually died down throughout the country. People were quickly disappointed when democracy didn't provide them with a better life.

'Next time the Radicals will win, for sure,' says Deda Bora. 'But there were a lot of people here who didn't vote – they couldn't manage the nine kilometres down to Kalna. Me, I do it in an hour and a half down and an hour and a half up – same time each way,' he says proudly. 'I bet I'd outwalk you any time,' he laughs and looks at Drago, well into yet another piece of cake. I have one more myself. The cake is soft, both moist and airy at the same time.

Grandpa Bora recalls the first election after the war,

while he was just a kid. Back then they had two voting urns; one was decorated with flowers, pretty ribbons and a majestic portrait, while the other was a bulky tin can. The first one was for Tito's votes, the second for anyone who dared oppose him. Everyone was given a little ball to drop in their chosen urn. Deda Bora laughs. He remembers the women who stopped to admire the lovely flowers and the fancy bow and dropped the ball there.

I want to get back to the man Deda Bora called Tito's successor.

'Why did you take him down?'

The old farmer studies the crumbs on his table.

'I was going to paint the walls.'

'But why didn't you hang him back up, once you'd finished painting?'

'When I had finished I realised that Tsar Lazar fitted better. Tsar Lazar is more important to us Serbs than Milosevic. Like Tsar Lazar, Milosevic was betrayed. But Tsar Lazar fought harder. Milosevic let himself get captured.'

'Where's his portrait now?'

'Come down to the cellar and we'll see if we can find him,' says Bora.

The cellar is filled with planks, old glass jars, buckets and tools. Deda Bora turns around a few times, stops to think. Then he walks over to a shelf, reaches up and takes down a picture frame. He turns it round and looks into Milosevic's fading gaze. A cat has danced on Slobo's face and left a jolly pattern of footsteps in the dust.

'I'll take it upstairs and clean it up,' Deda Bora says dutifully, but tosses it aside almost immediately. He straightens a door frame, picks up a link from a chain. Pushes a chair around, picks a few nails off the floor.

'One thing's for sure,' he says. 'There won't be any order around here until we have a dictatorship again.'

'Dictatorship' is pronounced as if it were something nice you once had in your house, something you'd lost and missed. Something righteous, like order, or peace and quiet.

Bora picks up the picture again. He turns it over and checks that the string is still good, before he puts it down again.

'The Serbs are a herd that needs a firm shepherd. We have no discipline. We're not cultured, like the rest of you.'

'Why is that?'

Bora falls silent, and taps a tin can against a table.

'That's what I'm wondering, too.'

We go back up. Milosevic remains on the shelf.

Snuggled against the cool foundation of the house are tins containing pale, fresh cheese, covered with white linen towels. On market days Deda Bora takes them to Kalna. He makes seven thousand dinars a month on his cheese, about a hundred Euros, as much as his pension.

'I get by. Prices keep going up, but I'm all right. I've already paid for the coffin.'

'The coffin?'

'I don't want to be anybody's expense but my own. It's ready for me, down at the carpenter's.'

'But you're in such great shape!' I protest. 'You've got another twenty years in you.'

'Oh no,' says Deda Bora and he looks at me, almost scared. 'Couldn't handle another twenty years. Maybe a couple more, then you'll see. Then you'll see it's enough.'

Deda Bora makes his way up to a lookout. I keep pace with him. He stops, and his shoulders shrink a little.

'Verica is calling for me. Living's become this sad thing. Everyone around me is dying. Since you were last here fifteen of us have passed. In this village alone.'

We go past the barn. I look in at the hay, where I used to let my thoughts wander, peering out through the boards, that spring I stayed at Deda Bora's. We drop in on the cows, say hi to the well with the best water in the world and stop by the ruins of the house Deda Bora grew up in. Where a ten-year-old Borisav stared in wide-eyed wonder at the Partisans who came to eat and sleep.

'I wanted to do the digging, too.'

'The digging?'

'Yeah. Wouldn't have taken me more than an hour or so. Dig a decent grave, just my size. But they wouldn't let me. My son put his foot down. "We'll take care of the diggers," he said. "Why waste money on diggers when I can do it myself," I asked him, but he just said, "Diggers I can afford."'

The cherry grove is bursting with white branches. Yellow wildflowers are intertwined with a few bluebells along the side of the carriage road. A hazy blanket covers the valley below; up here the sky is a pale blue. A thin layer of clouds covers the sun like a veil. Deda Bora smiles gently and looks out over the fields.

'Way over there, I own a bit of land,' he tells me. 'It's fallow. Nobody to farm it. But I'll tell you this: I could have done my own digging. Now they're going to have to pay both the digger and the priest. And I don't even believe in priests!'

He sits down on the stone well and makes room for me. The icy-blue eyes are firm. And there's still something of the obstinate boy in them.

'We'll see – I just may dig it yet. Nobody's here to stop

me. Could just stroll down there and start digging. When the time comes.'

We're silent.

'I mean, I know where I'm going to lie,' he says softly.

He turns his face away and lets his gaze run along the mountain ridge.

'Next to Verica.'

The First Lady of Treason

'Two things fill my mind with ever-growing wonder and awe: the starry firmament above me and the moral law within me.'

Immanuel Kant

'Terrible, terrible,' says Bojana Lekic, unable to look away from the screen. She's taking notes of the debate as if her life depends on it. '*Strasno*,' she repeats – 'Terrible. Now they're really tightening the noose.'

The debate is on the Milosevic-controlled network Radio-televizija Srbije, RTS. Although 'debate' is perhaps the wrong term, because on RTS everyone always agrees. There is only one point of view here – that of the regime. And tonight the discussion is about Serbia's independent media channels, dubbed the opposition media, or, in the government's parlance, the traitors. 'They are bought and paid for by the West. They're slaves to their American masters!'

Serbia's Minister of Information, Aleksandar Vucic, is barely thirty years old, and, like a young actor playing a wise old man, he has wrapped himself in affectations and portentous gestures intended to communicate that 'I'm here to tell you all what's really going on.' He'll stare straight into the camera, wag a threatening finger and promise to deal harshly with 'the agents and spies of the West'. Bojana, in her chair, is tense, all her attention on the screen, because she's part of what's being debated here. She is both the editor-in-chief and a high-profile reporter for the independent channel B2-92.

'They're lackeys of the West, wishing to destroy Serbia,' the Yugoslav Minister of Information, Goran Matic, agrees. The leader of Serbia's official journalists' guild, Milorad Komrakov, nods his assent. He is one of the heads of RTS and a member of the central board of the Serbian Socialist Party, which is run by Milosevic. The programme's chairman stokes the fires of consent and interjects questions that everyone has agreed on in advance.

'How do you know that the opposition media is paid for by the West?'

'Here's the evidence,' thunders Aleksandar Vucic, holding up a piece of paper. The camera zooms in on Vucic's face: 'B2-92 has received thousands of dollars in US aid — just look!'

He lifts the document as if it stinks. 'And here's their contract with the British Embassy, and their deal with the Soros Foundation. And all of these papers are signed by Sasa Mirkovic,' he points out with disgust. Sasa Mirkovic is repeatedly identified as a corrupt traitor out to sell his homeland to the West. He is head of the B2-92 network.

'They want us to be afraid,' says a clearly troubled Bojana afterwards. It's close to midnight and dead quiet on the

nineteenth floor of the Beogradjanka building. We've borrowed the office of the powerful news editor in Studio B to
watch a rerun of the debate; he is the only one in the building who has a VCR. After B2-92 was shut down the
editorial staff have been allowed to borrow offices and a
frequency from Studio B, which is owned by Belgrade's
municipal government and is run with an iron fist by the
opposition leader, Vuk Draskovic. Until the winter of 2000
Studio B served simply as Draskovic's very own propaganda outlet, but since that spring he has allowed access by
other opposition media outlets.

It's March 2000 and the issue of controlling the media is
becoming a crucial battle for the Serbian government.

'Of course I'm scared. I've received threats. But I can't
back down now. I have to fight for what I believe in – that
Serbia will become a free democracy. A lot of times I just
want to go to sleep, and wish that I lived in a normal country. But then I think, that's just what we're fighting for – to
create a society where people are free to live their own
lives. Instead of being paralysed by fear,' Bojana sighs. She
takes a sip of the coffee the news editor's secretary offered
us before she left. Bojana hadn't touched it until now, then
she realises she hasn't eaten all day. She looks at me sadly.
'It's just a matter of time before they shut us down again.
But we'll never give up.'

We go down a floor to the B2-92 offices. 'All these cabinets are empty. We can't keep anything here because the
police could show up at any moment and confiscate everything. Last year, when they shut us down, we lost our
cameras, our archives, everything. Now everything we have
left is in our flats,' she reveals. 'Well, not in mine, of
course. That's the first place they'd look.'

The office has two worn desks, a computer and a phone.

This has been B2-92's headquarters for a year now, since they were evicted from their own offices the night before the first NATO bombs fell. That's when Belgrade's Youth Alliance, an arm of the regime, appropriated B2-92's offices, equipment and frequency, and turned the then B92 into a propaganda machine. The original B92 changed its name to B2-92 and a few months later the editors were able to broadcast a shortened version of their old programming. At this point the Serbian government pulled out all the stops to silence opposition voices: killings, jail, fines, closure of both print and broadcast outlets.

In October 1998 the Serbian parliament passed the most restrictive media law in Europe. It went through without debate, given that Milosevic controlled about 200 of the 250 seats in parliament. The law made it easy to fine and close newspapers and silence broadcasters. The media could be summarily sentenced, without due process or a chance to defend themselves in a court of law. During the spring of 2000 several dozen newspapers, radio and TV channels were shut down and others forced to pay massive fines. Unless these fines were paid within twenty-four hours, the government could confiscate their assets and equipment. Several editors and journalists were jailed. The editor of *Dnevni Telegraf*, Slavko Curuvija, had already been punished numerous times by the new law when he was killed outside his house in Belgrade on 11 April 1999.

The Serbian Vice-Prime Minister and ultranationalist Vojislav Seselj made clear and obvious threats against independent journalists. 'We won't be treating you with kid gloves any more,' he said at a press conference where he blamed the journalists for the murders of both Arkan – Zeljko Raznatovic, who led the Serbian Volunteer Guard during the war in Bosnia and was a widely feared and brutal warlord until he was assassinated in January 2000 – and Pavle Bulatovic, the Minister of Defence. 'We'll use the same methods on you if it becomes necessary,' he promised.

Bojana Lekic is highly respected, even among her opponents, for her sharp questioning and well-prepared interviews. Vojislav Seselj called her before making his threats publicly. 'When I confronted him, he said I was abnormal. But at the same time he told me not to worry. For some reason he seems to like me,' Bojana believes. Seselj is a notorious debater, known for his bullying, boorish tactics, but in an interview with Bojana, his case was picked apart, argument by argument. 'Bojana Tames the Tiger', read the headline of the government paper *Politika* the next morning.

Bojana can't shake the feeling that she's operating at the mercy of the mercurial politician, and recounts how a furious Aleksandar Vucic, the Minister of Information, approached her as she was getting ready to deliver a report from the parliament. 'We've just spent half a day discussing you and your shows,' he snarled. 'I don't know why he protects you.' 'He' was Seselj.

Bojana's parents are far more terrified than she is. 'My father said just the other day, "If you get killed, no one's going to name a street after you. But we'll have lost our only daughter."'

It's way past midnight. The phone rings, and Bojana's voice goes soft.

'Are you at home?' she asks into the phone.

'Late,' she says next. 'Don't wait up for me.'

'That was my husband,' she explains, lighting a cigarette. 'He called to see if he'll see me tonight.' Tonight is the night before several opposition media outlets will collaborate on a large-scale evening broadcast to protest at the government's threats. The broadcast has been named 'Stop the Suppression, Stop the Fear', and Bojana heads the entire project. Her workday frequently runs to fourteen or sixteen hours. 'I'm not a great delegator – it often takes just as long to explain something to someone as it does to do it yourself.'

Bojana finds stories, assigns them to reporters, does research, orders and supervises jingles, edits, and assists the other anchors.

I spend the night listening to her stories, about the husband she hardly sees, the parents who worry so, her insomnia, how tired she is. She seems to enjoy having me around – even if it's only to distract her from the task of putting together the next night's broadcast. It seems few bother to ask Bojana how she's really feeling. On the surface she is hard, unattainable, beautiful, successful, efficient, sharp, tough as nails; a super-reporter.

The next evening I watch the broadcast with Bojana. I realise that I'm watching a mirror image of the RTS debate from last night. Even on the independent channels, everyone agrees. Again the recriminations and accusations are directed at absentees. Bojana explains: 'We're boycotting each other. The regime and the opposition are two different worlds. Milosevic's party and the government refuse to speak with us, and we in turn are boycotting the Radical Party following Vojislav Seselj's threats. The opposition is never invited on RTS. This country is divided in two,' she says. 'I used to know several members of the government back when things weren't so tense. They'll still kiss me on the cheek and make small talk, but they're not going to give me a quote. I recently ran into the general secretary of the SPS, Gorica Gajevic, at the hairdresser's. "Hi, Boka – how are you doing?" she asked, and we talked about life and death right there, in the salon. I'd just come from the hospital, where my godmother was seriously ill, and had been crying. After I left, Gajevic said to my hairdresser, Duska: "How vulnerable and human she is . . ." I mean – did she think I was some sort of monster?'

We're sitting in a room next to the studio. A colleague of Bojana chairs the programme. Bojana receives questions from the phone-in audience, and passes them along, as notes, to the chairman. 'It's not usually part of the editor's job to answer the phones, is it?' I ask. 'Who else is going to do it?' she responds. 'My colleagues are as worn out as I am.'

The next day we're at Duska's, on Terazije, in the centre of Belgrade. Bojana is getting her hair done, her face made up. Tonight is the taping of her weekly show, and her guest is Zivorad Jovanovic, one of Serbia's student leaders. Colleagues pop in with manuscripts, reports and schedules. The office, the editing room and the studio are all in different parts of the city, so Bojana has no fewer than three meetings scheduled at her hairdresser's. As B2-92 doesn't have its own studios, interviews are conducted wherever they can get done – from flats to nightclubs. After Duska's, Bojana heads straight to the 'studio', which in this case is a club in a basement. The walls are covered with rock posters and flyers for parties. The guest is already here, the interview can start. I watch on the monitor. The taping appears professional; the viewers can't tell that Bojana's been running around all day.

'There are far too few of us, and we have just a couple of cameras. I'd love to have more reporters, but we just can't afford to. Those who accuse us of being bought and paid for are the ones driving around in Mercedes. I don't even have a decent car – just an ancient Yugo that barely runs!'

However, the government is correct in its assertion that B2-92 is funded by the West. Around three quarters of its operating budget comes from foreign donors; the rest is from advertising. But it's always a challenge to find advertisers – they risk losing their contracts with the state media if they advertise on B2-92 as well. In addition, the independent media need help paying the fines the government continually hits them with. Because the banking system doesn't work, there's no way to transfer money from abroad. The money must be deposited in an account in Hungary, then the bills need to be physically transported into Serbia. 'It's a grey economy,' explains the head of B2-92, Sasa Mirkovic. 'Ninety per cent of our budgets are not in the books, and everyone is paid in cash. Of course it's illegal. But you can't not break the law in Serbia today.'

The interview with the student leader needs to be edited, and once again I follow Bojana across town. I'm starving. I'm always starving around Bojana, who never takes time to eat. She's got the tapes in her pocket and takes one of them out. A fading flower falls out. It's 8 March, International Women's Day, and a colleague had given her the flower this morning. She put it in the pocket of her coat as she ran out; now the flower lies limp and dead in the palm of her hand. 'I'm not a woman,' she sighs. 'I'm a machine.'

After a fourteen-hour workday, Bojana disappears into the editing room. An hour later my head starts spinning, and I head home. Sitting in the cab, I feel guilty about leaving Bojana alone in the dark editing room. I was supposed to spend a day with her. I'm embarrassed to compare my own life as a journalist with hers.

The next time I see her is on another noteworthy date – 24 March, a year after the night that the first bombs fell on Belgrade. 'I'd forgotten what day it was when you called,' she says. 'Not that it's cause for celebration or anything.' The Milosevic regime disagrees with Bojana and arranges mass demonstrations and free concerts, while the opposition ignores them all. 'The bombing was the worst thing the West could do to us – it only validated Milosevic's rhetoric about the West hating the Serbs. The West has committed a series of blunders in its dealings with Milosevic,' Bojana explains.

'If you're trying to accomplish something, you need a carrot and a stick. So far the West has only applied the stick. Now that Milosevic is accused of war crimes, he has nowhere to go. He has nothing left to lose. If the regime does what it has hinted at – tightens the reins and kills off more journalists – what can the West do about it? It has run out of options, it has nothing to bargain with. Milosevic is cornered, his back against the wall – he's a wild animal, and when wild animals are cornered and threatened, they become truly dangerous.'

We're meeting for lunch at Bojana's regular haunt, the New York. Bojana drinks a small white coffee with her food. She looks more run-down than when I last saw her, thin and pale. She goes through several packs of cigarettes a day.

'"You look older than your mother," my father said yesterday. I'm thirty-three! I've been married for fifteen years, but I never felt that I could have kids yet. How can I bring a child into this society? Besides, my job's not just a job; it's a mission, and I can't do it halfway – no more than I could be a halfway mum.

'I hope I'm still alive when your book comes out,' she suddenly blurts out. The night before, she'd got another scolding from the Minister of Information, Aleksandar Vucic.

'But who believes in his accusations?' I ask.

'A lot of people believe him: farmers, the elderly, everyone who is used to believing everything the government tells them. If you repeat a lie often enough, it becomes the truth. This country is very tense after the bombings, the war in Kosovo, all these deaths, the miserable lives we all live, the killings – it makes people believe anything at this point, just so they have something to hold on to. Me, I simply don't have the time to consider the threats I get or my miserable life. When I can't sleep at night it's not because I ponder and brood over existential matters, but because I'm worried about where I'll get an editing room the next day, where I can borrow a car, find a cameraman, who I can ask for a favour, how we can best get through to people. I don't have a life outside my work.'

Only once in a while does Bojana take a bite of the steak she ordered. Instead it grows cold as she talks. 'I went to Montenegro last week and I had an hour to watch the ocean. One hour. I spent that hour thinking about how rarely I feel happy. I wake up in the morning with a headache and sore muscles and feel like an angry old hag. Then I go to work, and I wonder, Why am I acting like a jerk when I'm really a nice person? This system has ruined so much; so many relationships go to pieces because there's just nothing pleasant to do together. People can't afford to go and see a movie, or take a holiday – things that used to be completely normal. I barely have any energy left at this point, but I want to stay in the ring for these last few rounds. I think this is it now. Last year I swore it was Milosevic's final year. I say the same thing now. Eventually I'll be proven right, no? I can't relax until Milosevic is gone. Only then will I start living.'

*

Things do not quieten down for Bojana Lekic. Through the spring of 2000 the independent channels are shut down one by one. On the morning of 17 May, I turn on B2-92, as I do every day. I get classical music. I assume I've set the dial wrong and try again. But no – where there used to be news there is only classical music. I switch to the BBC: 'Last night Serbian authorities closed the independent TV network Studio B, accusing it of fostering rebellion and sedition. B2-92, Radio Index and the newspaper *Blic* suffered the same fate,' the voice says. I jump on my bike and I'm outside the Beogradjanka building in a quarter of an hour. The journalists from the banned outlets are denied access to the building. I call Bojana. 'We've moved the editorial meeting to the café at the media centre – come here.'

The journalists are figuring out how to cover their own shutdown. Bojana coordinates the camera teams and tries to grasp their situation. The heads of the banned news organisations are discussing their next move. 'We should be getting used to this by now,' Bojana says sarcastically. 'What'll it be now – B3-92?'

The café is buzzing. The sound system is tuned to Radio Pancevo, the only remaining independent radio station that can be heard in Belgrade. Later in the day their frequency is also distorted. From now on the only news the citizens of Belgrade can get is what the regime tells them through its outlets. There are still a few independent stations left in other parts of the country – Bojana's staff are hoping to report for these channels. So far they've used Studio B's transmitters, but a new plan is hatched over the café's tables. The tapes will be couriered to Montenegro on the six o'clock flight and sent back to the Serbian stations from there – via satellite. The timeframe is tight. Bojana is getting stressed out, and doesn't seem to exhale until the tapes are on their way to the airport.

Just in time for the demonstration. At seven a huge protest march is set to start in the square in front of the city hall, where news will be read over the speaker system. This turns into a tradition. Every evening through the spring and summer of 2000 the news is read aloud from this spot. When I get home I watch the news on RTS. They tell me that Bojana's station has been shut down because they're all agents, quislings and spies working for foreign interests trying to destabilise the country. I switch over to Studio B. At some point during the day it has become a channel for old movies.

'I've become a guerrilla soldier,' says Bojana when I see her a month later. 'We've gone underground. We'll out-smart this regime.' A small flat is now the new headquarters of B2-92. After this move from a landmark building like the Beogradjanka, directions are more com-plicated now. 'Behind the Tasmajdan park, second street on your right, third house on the right, up two stairs, first door to your left, just knock, there's no name on it,' were Bojana's instructions. 'They know where we are, but you don't want to help them find us.'

At this point the office consists mainly of boxes and bags – it's as if nobody dares to unpack, having been made to move so many times already. Bojana asks me to turn off my mobile. Because the government controls the mobile network, it functions as something of a surveillance system, she explains.

'Bijeljina,' she says. 'Two hours' drive from Belgrade, right across the border into Bosnia, in the Serbian zone. We've made a deal with Radio Drina, where we'll build our transmitter, so it will reach large areas of Serbia. Tapes and equipment will be smuggled back and forth across the border, but the anchors will have to remain in Bijeljina. The reporters don't have to cross the border – they'll report from Belgrade. And the transmitter will be powerful enough to resist any attempt at distorting or blocking it. In a few months it'll all be up and running – plan A, plan B and plan C. But until then you'll have to keep this to yourself.'

Just before I leave for my summer holiday I call Bojana and am listening to a despondent woman at the other end. 'I don't know how much more of this I can take – I'm just confused,' she says. 'I'm just banging my head against the wall. And all I really want to do is to escape – from my job, from the responsibility, from this notion of freedom. I'm running on empty. Last night I had this awful nightmare – I dreamed I was dead. And all I could think was, Now I'm dead – now I can get some rest.'

She falls silent. And then breaks the silence herself: 'I can't give up now. This summer and autumn will be a scorcher – we might even have a civil war. We're at the endgame now,' she mumbles.

'But write and tell me about your life in Norway,' she says by way of goodbye. 'Tell me about something beautiful; I need air . . .'

The summer and autumn of 2000 are indeed a scorcher for Bojana, but there is no civil war. Only a final day of battling tear gas and policemen on 5 October, when the opposition reclaim the victory Milosevic stole from them in the election. On this day B2-92 erects a transmitter from a high-rise in Belgrade, and for the first time in months the people of Belgrade can get reception. The next day B2-92 reclaims its old name, its offices and its timeslots, and

Bojana can finally restart her old show, *Face to Face*. My neighbour, Peca, tells me how he watched, with tears streaming down his face, as Bojana demolished multimillionaire and Milosevic ally Bogoljub Karic in her first programme. 'First she crushed him,' Peca explains. 'Then she picked up the pieces, one by one, and showed him — and us.'

On Sundays at eight o'clock people gather around their TV sets to see Bojana take someone apart. 'When the lights go on I know that everyone is sitting at home, rooting and cheering for me to "score",' Bojana says. 'I can't let them down. I'm their voice, and I have to go after those in power, the new and the old.'

After the fall of Milosevic, Bojana could write her own ticket. She was politically untouchable and was offered her own show on RTS. The state channel was as committed to the regime as ever; it was simply a different regime now — that of Vojislav Kostunica.

'In less than an hour, thousands of people just crossed from one side to the other — to the winning side. It actually made me sick to watch,' says Bojana. 'But I kept telling myself that getting rid of Slobodan Milosevic and not living in a police state any more was the most important thing. I turned the RTS job down, because I knew they'd revoke the freedom they promised me. I'd rather stay with B92; we've always been critical of the government, and will always be.'

According to Bojana, there's much to be done before Serbia can deem itself an actual democracy: 'A lot of people seem to think that democracy just descended on us once Milosevic fell. But democracy doesn't come all neatly wrapped up in ribbons. You have to fight for it, every single day. I'm not going to stand by and let these new politicians behave just like the old ones, like they did when they tried to overtake the central bank with their own paramilitary troops. But I'm fine with Kostunica in charge of everything; he's a law professor, a legal mind. He should be able to get things in order,' says Bojana, who then looks at her watch. She's due in the studio in an hour. Her schedule doesn't seem any lighter.

'The media is another problem – journalists here have been taught to repeat what they've been told and have grown up in a culture of self-censorship. Most of them do what they've always done – they just have different bosses. And the new power base is happy to exploit the situation. Already we've been denied space on Kostunica's plane four times. This regime isn't a big fan of B92 either. Even if we're not at all as critical as we could have been. We've observed a sort of honeymoon; they've only governed for two months, after all.'

Bojana calls the period until the 23 December election, when the Serbian government will be consolidated, an 'interregnum'. The old guard has not gone yet.

To Bojana it's crucial that Serbia confronts its own past. 'The only way for a reconciliation to occur is by knowing the truth about what has happened here. So many atrocities have taken place, but in order to forgive I need to know who I am to forgive, and why. It will be a difficult and painful process, but we have to go through it in order to proceed. We need a truth commission, like in South Africa. If we don't determine who is guilty of what, the entire nation will be guilty – just of being Serbs.'

The Serbian media is still silent about Serbia's conduct in the wars of the 1990s. 'People are worn out, bitter and poor. They want to know who stole their money, who lives in the fancy villas and has gold deposits in the bank, while they can't feed their own children. But, as the openness increases, there's more room for discussion of war crimes as well,' Bojana believes.

At the studio the make-up girl is waiting for her. As the dark rings under her eyes are gradually concealed, Bojana keeps talking and smoking.

She has no reason to feel that she herself is out of the woods. 'The morning after Milosevic's fall, my car was sprayed with some white, nasty foam. Since then I always park in different spots, and never near my house. But it happened again, even when the car was parked several blocks away. I told the police, but they said they couldn't do anything.'

Bojana looks just as tired as she did in her 'underground guerrilla' days. She used to say that she'd relax once Milosevic was gone. 'In this country something extraordinary happens every day. It might be a coup, a revolution, another election. Today there's trouble on the Kosovo border.'

The super-reporter falls silent. 'I'm not any happier than before,' she says as the make-up girl puts the finishing touches to her face. 'My time is never my own.'

Her guest has arrived. Bojana runs into the studio just in time for another hard-hitting interview for people to cheer.

Every time I talk to Bojana during the spring of 2001 she has a thousand things to deal with: broadcasts, offices, equipment, lawyers, reporters. 'It's hysteria here – the world press has flown in to watch Milosevic get arrested. And on top of that,' she adds, 'my car got sprayed again last night, with that same nasty stuff. Give me a call sometime next week.'

When I finally meet her again, in her tiny, messy office,

where the walls are covered with posters from rock concerts and movie premieres, Bojana is as pale as a ghost. Her
hair is stringy and her gaze is flat.

'Someone threw a big rock through my window last
night.'

Her hands make the shape of a rock the size of a child's
head. 'It crashed through my kitchen window and landed
several metres inside. Ten minutes earlier I was in the
kitchen, right where it must have shot by. If it had hit me I
wouldn't be here now.'

Her husband had called the police. They said they had
neither the time nor the resources to come out, and asked
the couple to come to the police station the next day to
make a report. '"Fuck your report," I told them this morning,' remembers Bojana. 'They know who I am – I've
reported the incidents with my car three times already.'

I ask her if she thinks she knows who's behind this. She
shakes her head in a gesture of hopelessness. 'I was never
physically threatened under Milosevic. They had me under
surveillance, they knew who I talked to, what I said on the
phone. Ironically, their surveillance served as a protection
of some kind; nobody could do anything to me without the
regime knowing about it. God knows what their plans
were, but nothing happened.'

Bojana tries to mask her fear behind her trademark
tough-girl stance. She talks about her parents, who've
asked her any number of times to slow down, take a break,
be less strident in her criticism. As she says this her phone
rings and she recognises her father's number. After talking
to him she says, 'He wanted to come over to my flat with
some food. If he sees the rock and the broken window . . .
I haven't told them what happened last night; I just don't
want to worry them. What am I going to do now?'

I can't think of anything to say, so I reach out to pat her on the cheek. That's when the tears come. I walk around her desk and hold her as she cries, her elfin body trembling.

Once she has dried her tears she says, 'I remember this character in Stendhal's *Scarlet and Black* that I just couldn't stand – he was all about duty. Now I feel that same sense of duty myself, as if I'm responsible for getting this country up and running. I've become worse than he ever was. But I don't know who I'm fighting for any more. Under Milosevic we had an enemy. Now we've got rid of the dictatorship – but what do we have instead? I fought for a different Serbia, not just a Serbia without Milosevic.'

One of the reporters enters, on his way to the Presevo Valley, where Albanian rebels are holding several villages. Bojana becomes the editor-in-chief again. 'Remember, you always have to know why you're doing a story,' she instructs. 'Your last piece had neither an intent nor a focus. The footage of the military action was great – but what was the story about? We've had this conversation before. Have a good trip,' she ends by saying, and the kid backs out of her office. Another reporter wants to show her a story he's just done. Bojana promises she'll be there shortly. Her mobile rings again. It's the Federal Minister of the Interior, Zoran Zivkovic. Bojana tells him about the rock. Zivkovic promises to take the matter to the Serbian Minister of the Interior, Dusan Mihajlovic, the next day. 'Zivkovic was angry,' Bojana reports. 'At the police, who wouldn't take this seriously.'

I call Bojana several times over the following days, just to ask how she's doing. Each time she responds the same way: 'To be honest, not so good.'

On Sunday evening I watch her show again. Bojana is as feisty as ever. The TV lights make her sparkle. She once said that it's like hitting a switch when she's on the air. This time it's the parliamentary leader of the Socialist Party, Branislav Ivkovic, who gets his turn in the hot seat. Bojana questions him relentlessly about Milosevic's crimes, the way the party has been run this last decade and the fortunes they've hidden. There's nothing to indicate that she's living through her own personal hell.

A few days later a weak, soft voice answers the phone. 'The doctor ordered me to stay in bed for a few days,' she wheezes. 'Something about my lungs, I think. I'm not sure I know what's wrong with me, but I've been told to cut down on the cigarettes and to get some kind of therapy. The doctor said my immune system is shot.'

As we talk her doorbell rings. 'Ah, someone's here with these documents I have to look through,' she interrupts. 'I've got to go – talk to you later.'

I make a house call. The flat is darkened, full of cigarette smoke. Bojana is sitting at her computer when I arrive. Her phone is ringing off the hook; editors want her advice, reporters need help, friends want to know how she's doing. As she talks on the phone I go to the kitchen. The double-glazed window is smashed. Bojana hasn't changed the glass or done anything to cover up the window. Luckily it's warm outside.

A week later, on Friday 30 March, she gets the first news. She cancels the therapy ordered by her doctor and goes to work. In parliament Branislav Ivkovic announces that the police plan to arrest Milosevic. At eight o'clock that evening a massive police force surrounds the former President's villa in Uzicka Street. Bojana directs her teams of photographers and reporters as the events unfold. Later that night she gets a call from Ivkovic. 'I'm here having a cup of coffee with Milosevic – care to join us?'

It's 1.30 a.m. Bojana heads for the villa with a camera-man in tow. Ivkovic comes to get her by the back door, but at the same instant the Special Forces enter through the front door and Bojana isn't allowed any further.

Rumour has it that Milosevic has barricaded himself in with his closest associates, bodyguards and a huge cache of weapons. 'I'll never leave my house alive. I've got a gun with twenty-five rounds – twenty to defend myself with and five for myself,' the reports have him promising. Two policemen are wounded when Milosevic's bodyguards open fire, adding the charge of resisting arrest to the list.

The next day Bojana sleeps in. Up along Uzicka Street, everything is quiet. A handful of Milosevic supporters are joined by hundreds of waiting reporters and photographers. Once it gets dark Bojana is back at the office. She has five teams in place around Milosevic's villa. Cars come and go, in and out of his residence; as the calendar turns to 1 April the negotiations are in full swing. The once-mighty leader wants a guarantee that he won't be handed over to The Hague. He demands the right to daily visits by his family, and that he is to be charged as an ordinary citizen and not in a political court.

B92 broadcasts all night long. Bojana smokes and makes calls. She is the conduit of all information, and the general in charge of it all. The reporters call her about what they see and she passes the information along on the air. The directors are told what footage to use with which stories. Throughout the night B92's coverage surpasses any competition, and Bojana beams whenever other channels and bureaux refer to its reports. 'We're the only outlet with people at the inner police barricade. Our reporters always know who's inside the cars that pass by. When everyone reported that Milosevic was arrested last night, we didn't – I knew he was still inside, negotiating.'

But Bojana won't predict what the outcome might be. 'Anything can happen. He's insane enough to shoot himself and his family to avoid a trial,' she reckons. 'By the way, now we can say anything we want on the air – it's April Fool's Day!'

Bojana laughs. The mood in her office is tense but light.

She gets another call: the next phase will begin two hours after midnight. She updates her teams. One of them is following the police forces, who calmly take up their new positions. Sixty Special Forces personnel from the anti-terror squads enter the building. Everything is still very quiet.

'Maybe this will be the last night I don't sleep because of Milosevic,' Bojana says optimistically, stifling a yawn. The nightwatchman brings her coffee and chocolate, while B92's coverage fills the screen. At four in the morning a spokesman for Milosevic calls and announces that a solution has been reached, a peaceful solution. 'Serbian blood will not flow by Serbian hands,' he says. B92 broadcasts his interview. Suddenly shots can be heard from the villa. Everything goes quiet. Then Bojana's source calls back and says that they really have arrived at a peaceful solution now. At 4.30 a.m. Bojana goes out live, on both TV and radio, to announce that Milosevic is in custody.

'We were first! Sometimes I love being a journalist,' she exclaims, almost ecstatic.

One of her teams reports that Milosevic is leaving his compound in a police car. Milosevic is going to jail.

'It's over,' Bojana smiles at me between phone calls. 'It's finally over.'

But the mood is hardly festive in the editorial offices,

even though the vanquished dictator is being taken to a two-by-three-metre cell in Belgrade's central jail.

'Most of all, I just feel empty,' says Bojana. 'I feel like I've been run over by a truck. But one thing is certain: Milosevic no longer has anything to do with my life. He's finished.'

Two months later, after massive international pressure, Milosevic is put on a flight to The Hague. At the same time Bojana's career takes a hit – a first. Her integrity is questioned, she's the subject of rumours, a vicious campaign, and in the end she can't do anything but resign from B92, the network that at times has been her entire life.

It began with an award. In the summer of 2001 the wealthy and controversial businessman Bogoljub Karic handed out some one hundred awards to individuals who had made a worthwhile contribution to society in areas such as culture, media and science. One of these prizes, and 30,000 Deutschmarks, went to Bojana Lekic. She discussed with her boss whether she should accept it. He hesitated. Karic was known for his close personal ties to Milosevic, not to mention Milosevic's financial transactions. When the dictator was still in power Karic said in an interview that he had breakfast with Slobo every day. After Milosevic's fall he denied ever having met him. A meeting wouldn't have involved more than crossing an alley; Karic and Milosevic were neighbours in the notorious Uzicka Street, where they both lived behind high walls, protected by armed guards. The gate to the Milosevic residence was made out of broad, black metal doors. Only the roof of the huge villa, and the tips of the white columns that enveloped it, could be seen from the street. Karic's house looked like a pink wedding cake made of marble, complete with gold ornaments, perched at the end of a flowery driveway. The wrought-iron fence around his property allowed everyone to see just how wealthy he was.

The big question was: could a journalist accept a monetary award from a businessman — and a businessman who owned his own television station, BKTV? A man Bojana had interviewed on her show and torn to pieces in the process?

It was a considerable sum. Others accepted their prizes. Nobody seemed to mind. So in the end Bojana accepted the award.

The outcry came immediately. Bojana was front-page news for weeks, accused of being bought and paid for by Milosevic's former crony. What hurt even more was that several of her colleagues turned their backs on her. She was attacked relentlessly and there were demands for her resignation. Overnight she became a liability for B92. So she handed in her resignation.

'You know, the hardest part of leaving B92 was the loss of any illusions; the realisation that we no longer had the same goal,' Bojana told me on the phone once she had made her decision. 'There's so much about all this that I'll never go on record with, but understanding that we weren't the same people any more hurt more than anything. Once we were rid of the dictatorship we didn't have anything in common any more,' she whispered in a low, hoarse voice.

'The corruption began to make me sick — watching some grow fat on other people's labours. I had closed my eyes to it for a very long time, refusing to acknowledge it while we still fought for the same goal. But to many of the bosses in B92 the only thing that mattered was carving out the biggest pieces of the corporation. To me B92 was always an idea, not a cake I earned percentages from. They tried to pay me off with stocks to be rid of me. This, on top of the disdain and slander my colleagues served up, made me walk away.'

After this conversation I couldn't get hold of Bojana for a long time. She didn't answer her phone or her mail. It turned out she'd finally taken a holiday. For several months she stayed with friends in the US, ate well and watched the waves on the beach. 'Finally I could breathe. Nobody needed anything from me. I received a flood of offers from other stations, but didn't respond to any of them. They were left in a pile at home, unopened, or as chattering voices on my answering machine,' she told me later.

At the end of 2001 she returned home and accepted the position of editor-in-chief for the news division of RTS, her old nemesis. Again there was an outcry and screaming headlines. Bojana went back to work with her high-minded ideals. 'I wanted to try to build up a decent, national broadcasting company – a Serbian BBC, if you like. Put the past behind me and move on. I endeavoured constantly to remain independent, to lean neither left nor right. I tried to build a staff without relying on those who had sold their names and faces to Milosevic. But given our limited resources, we couldn't hire many new people. Not a whole lot had changed at RTS and, to be honest, I basically swallowed a rusty hook when I took the job. It was like swimming in leg irons and handcuffs. So the fact that I kept myself afloat must mean I'm a good swimmer! Still, I couldn't get done anything that I wanted to do. The institutionalised power structure and subservience to the authorities were too deeply ingrained. If you want to be a slave you'll always be a slave, even if your owners change.

I finally realised that rebuilding an entire institution required more than one person to fight.'

Bojana looks out of the window, where the rain is pouring down. It's been three years since I last saw her.

'As far as my own part in all this is concerned, I'm proud of what I did. Even those individuals who criticised me at every turn, as I did them, during the Milosevic years, are now complimenting me. Aleksandar Vucic admitted recently, at a press conference, that when I ran RTS the coverage was impartial, as opposed to now, when it's once again a tool for the government and the powers that be.'

She clears her throat.

'Last year was the toughest year of my life, both professionally and emotionally. I had to swallow not just the rusty hook but my own feelings as well. In the end I just couldn't take any more,' she sighs. 'It's always like that, isn't it — in the end God shows you the way. You grow tired, then sick, and then you ask yourself, "Where am I?"'

She looks at me, questioning, as if wanting confirmation.

'I never think of myself until I'm standing at the edge of the cliff,' she continues. 'Only then do I wonder, Wow — how did I end up here? When I fell ill again I had an epiphany: I realised I'd done enough. That someone else would have to go on from here.'

Bojana inhales deeply on her cigarette. At this point RTS is history as well. In the winter of 2004 Bojana changed employers once again. That she went to work for BKTV — Bogoljub Karic's network — caused another stir.

We're in Bojana's new office. The building is covered by mirror glass set in steel, and oozes money. It's the first day of the Easter break, and Bojana is the only one here, except for a sturdy young man who works as her secretary and driver.

When I asked for her in reception, the guard said, 'There's nobody here.'

'Call up anyway,' I insisted.

'OK, so she is here,' he said after hanging up. In other words, business as usual. Can't she just take a break, like us mortals? I thought as the secretary came down to get me. His steps echoed through the darkened lobby, to the accompaniment of a sad fountain.

Bojana lit up when she saw me.

'Look! I finally got a real office! What do you think?'

Bojana is particularly fond of the large, tiled, covered terrace outside her glass doors. She's had crates and large pots for flowers installed. Improving the less immediate view would be a taller order: the terrace is facing a shabby brick building, an ordinary Yugoslav block of flats, with laundry drying, balconies filled with rubbish, flaking paint and creaking doors. Not even Bogoljub Karic can wall himself off from the reality of Serbia, no matter how many panes of mirror glass and fancy office furniture he buys.

'I'm in charge here,' says Bojana with a sweep of her arm. 'I'm the editor-in-chief of all of BK's programming.'

'This one too?' I ask, and point to an entertainment show that's on the screen – complete with scantily clad girls, dancers, a studio audience and a saccharine-sweet, bleach-blonde hostess.

'Everything,' Bojana replies with pride. 'News, features, debates, entertainment, movies.'

It's pouring down outside the glass doors and the flowers closest to the edge are struggling not to get washed away by the deluge, while those along the wall seem to lean into the humid air. I've brought Bojana a copy of the first draft of my book, and Bojana wants to know what I've written about her. She sends smoke rings towards the ceiling and listens in silence as I read.

'It's sad to see that we haven't really got very far, isn't it? Makes you wonder why we're still so far away from Europe . . .'

Bojana looks pensively at the grey fog outside.

'It's as if we just stopped somewhere.'

She leans back in her chair, her gaze still fixed on the grey wall on the other side of the glass. Someone has hung some faded underwear on the balcony directly opposite. Others use theirs to store potatoes and grain. The building is overcome by an increasingly thick mist that dulls the colours.

'Serbs will drag up their past beyond the point of embarrassment,' Bojana sighs. 'How many times has someone, whether it's Serbian leaders or regular people, reminded us that in the twelfth century we used utensils of gold, while the Brits ate with their hands? To which I can only respond, "Yes – that was nine hundred years ago."'

Bojana crosses her arms over her chest. 'It's interesting to hear what I was thinking just a few years ago – it brings back all these memories. You start my story with Aleksandar Vucic . . .'

Her mouth erupts into a smile of recognition, of memories of a time gone by. 'He was so powerful back then, and did all the dirty work for the party. Now he's the opposition, while his old boss, Vojislav Seselj, is sitting in The Hague with Milosevic. But even so, the Radical Party has more support than ever. Makes you wonder why it's so. Why do more people than ever long for our nationalist leaders?'

She answers her own question: 'People are more depressed these days. We've had several bouts of depression, starting with the horrifying wars that broke up

Yugoslavia. Everyone was devastated, and I remember how it felt in 1996, when the war in Bosnia finally ended. People wanted something new, but nothing happened, except for another wave of depression. People lost faith. But then we suddenly had these mass demonstrations, with whistles and drums and resistance, and Slobo had to relent. Then he pulled the reins back in; you remember how he punished us. People took to the streets again, and eventually the dictator fell. I know that energy is still here somewhere; it may be hiding, but maybe it could be teased back out again.'

'But people don't even show up to vote now.'

'It's not their fault. If people won't vote it's because the candidates aren't compelling enough. It's never the fault of the voters. Ordinary people don't like political intrigues; they think politicians are only out to further their own agendas, not to improve anyone else's lot. So they fall back on the tried and true: the myths, the epics, the heroic poetry, the greatness of Serbia – and, yes, the gold utensils.'

Bojana laughs, but then quickly becomes serious again.

'I'm still not happy with the Serbian media, even if it's better than it used to be. We're now far too sensationalistic. You can read any amount of exorbitant lies in the papers every day, and you can read headlines that have nothing to do with the articles. And because we don't have a proper judicial system you can't sue the newspapers for their slander. Facts are irrelevant. I tell all my reporters, "At the least you should be like waiters. Waiters serve you what you order, not what they think you should eat. And so you need to tell people what is actually happening, not what you think should be happening." Bojana sighs. 'Here journalists seem to think that their opinions matter more than what's actually taking place.'

Bojana's cheeks have hollowed even further and her cheekbones are more prominent. Her eyes are as haunted and sleep-deprived as before. It adds to a look of hunger – but also of weariness. She still works more than twelve hours a day. Maybe she needs it to be that way; maybe she has to live on the edge of exhaustion. Whenever she solves a problem she finds another one.

Soon she'll get her own show back on the air. 'The audience expects it, even the politicians,' she says. The most popular political talk show in Serbia has by this time lived through three networks, and was last seen on RTS the previous January. Now it'll kick off on BK. 'You have included how I tore Bogoljub Karic to pieces. It's quite a paradox: he liked the interview and said that was exactly the sort of programme he wanted on his network. That's why he gave me the award. Now he's my boss. Anyhow, he wants good, professional coverage,' she concludes firmly, before explaining her own success.

'I always try to reveal as much as possible about the person in front of me. And then let the audience draw their own conclusions. People ask me how long I prepare for each interview, and I always reply, "Twenty years." In addition I prepare for each interview as if it were a finals exam. But, honestly, I'm getting a bit tired of all this. It's always the same faces, all these years; they change sides, they change their positions, they gain power or lose it, but it's the same faces. Now people deserve to know who enrich themselves at society's expense and how. Who runs this Mafia. And, not least, who killed Djindjic.'

On the second day of Easter the sky finally clears. The rain that has hammered Belgrade throughout Easter week finally gives way this morning. A brilliant sparkle one had almost forgotten existed suddenly reflects off everything – sunlight. Now it shines mercilessly down on this weary city with its brown brick tenements and dirty neon signs. Passing cars send explosions of muddy water out of the crater-like potholes.

Bojana is waiting for me outside a café along Revolution Boulevard. The spring breeze plays with her bleached hair. Black trousers, black coat, high black boots. Her appearance is more exclusive than before. Her skin is covered by layers of concealing creams and powder, her eyes are meticulously made up. She's pale – almost deathly pale. Like an ice queen in springtime.

It's not noon yet and the café is empty. We order coffee. The waiter takes it upon himself to add two gigantic pieces of cake, with chocolate and nuts, and a basket of Easter eggs, which he serves us with a wink.

'Did you notice that the waiters address me with the informal "you"? And call me by a nickname?' grins Bojana. 'Normally we use the more formal version in Serbia. But they feel that they know me, even though we've never met before. Under Milosevic people also behaved this way – as if we were all on the same team, as if we were hiding something in common and had to remain underground. These waiters would never have addressed a politician like that, but they treat me as if I were their neighbour. It means I'm headed in the right direction,' she says, almost dreamily.

We sip our coffee in silence. This is when we will talk about the hardest part. The terrible thing we never got around to, or didn't have the energy to talk about in her office. The worst aspect of Bojana's worst year.

'I'd sent a couple of reporters to the government building to cover a press conference and was sitting in my office when I got the call. "Something's happened," they said. A couple of minutes later they called again. "They say it could even be number one."' He lost consciousness on the way to the hospital, and even though it was hopeless, the doctors operated. As if they couldn't bear the thought of losing him.

Bojana stares straight ahead as the coffee grows cold in front of her. She hasn't touched the cake. She pushes it aside and looks straight at me.

'We were very close – kindred spirits,' she confesses. 'He called me several times a day. There were all kinds of rumours about us, but we were just friends – a close friendship that his wife knew all about. There was never anything else between us. I was always professional. Whenever I interviewed him some people thought we were friends, others that we hated each other with a passion. He was a great guest, I was a good host. We had a relationship based on complete honesty. I really lost a dear friend, not just a Prime Minister. Did you catch that? I said, "just a Prime Minister", as if a Prime Minister is something you can apply the word "just" to . . . But a friend is something that's more important than any position, even Prime Minister. For Serbia, for this country, this loss was insurmountable. The whole nation lost its energy, its sense of direction.'

Now Bojana regularly meets Zoran Djindjic's widow. They are trying to get to the bottom of who was behind his assassination. Djindjic's successor, Zoran Zivkovic, launched a massive campaign against the Mafia after the murder, and arrested the gunman. But whoever hired him was never caught, and when the more conservative Vojislav Kostunica took over as Serbia's Prime Minister, nothing much happened until the suspected mastermind of the assassination allowed himself to be arrested on 2 May. A former colonel of Serbia's Special Forces, Milorad Lukovic – better known as 'Legija', owing to his having served in the French Foreign Legion – had deep ties to both the Mafia and the security forces and was taken into custody without incident outside his luxurious house in Belgrade.

'Zoran fought too many battles at once. Made too many enemies. In the end a lot of people were gunning for him and we don't know who gave the ultimate order. Only three days earlier he had outlined a plan for an extensive cleansing – several notable members of the Mafia and the old regime were to be arrested, and some even sent to The Hague. He said he had something important to tell me, something he couldn't say on the phone. We could discuss it on my terrace, he said. I couldn't meet him that evening and we decided to meet that coming Saturday.'

Bojana looks right through me and her lips twist into a bitter grimace.

'I'll never know what he wanted to tell me.'

She keeps going.

'The night before he was killed he told me he had changed his plans for the next day. He wasn't going to attend a conference as originally planned. Instead he was heading straight to the government building to meet the Swedish Foreign Minister, Anna Lindh. He always tried to evade potential attacks. He was always on guard.'

A month earlier Zoran Djindjic had survived an attempt on his life. A truck by the side of the road had suddenly jumped into the path of the Prime Minister's vehicle. If not for the alert reaction of his driver, Djindjic's car would have been destroyed. The truck and its driver got away, and Djindjic uttered the words people would quote later: 'You may kill me, you may take my life away – but you will never be able to stop the process of reform that I've started.'

'There was a lot that he never told me. He never lied to me, but there were things he just didn't talk about. That's why I was always a step behind. I lost time and wasn't able to warn him. Towards the end, when he took on just about everybody, he made increasingly saintly pronouncements. It was as if he was trying to cleanse himself, come clean and die without any sins on his conscience.'

Bojana falls silent for a minute.

'They declared a state of emergency. Kept a lid on all information. We tried to do the best we could. Then I fainted. They put me in a hospital. And I just stayed there.'

She emits a small, dry laugh. 'I always collapse in the end.'

Bojana looks at her watch – she should be on her way to have Sunday lunch with her parents.

'Let me say *something* positive,' she says. 'We're no longer afraid. Our leader made us trust in ourselves. He brought us into a new era. Even if he ended up paying with his life, we are not afraid any more.'

'What about the threats on your own life?'

'They never discovered anything. They increased for a while, and then they suddenly stopped, completely. At that point I was almost used to them. I never knew if they were politically motivated, or simply the ravings of some lunatic. I almost hoped they were political; if I were to be killed it would be too stupid to be killed by some lunatic – not after all the battles I'd fought!'

A waiter flutters near by. For twelve years Bojana has been telling people what's been going on. Now many are merely attracted to her aura of power, money and beauty.

She's profiled in the big women's magazines, smiles back from glossy covers and is held up as a role model for young women.

'Maybe it's time to give something to Bojana now. Fill my head with good feelings.'

She weighs her own words and looks right at me.

'I think I want to have children. I'm thirty-seven and time is running out. When I see friends who have kids, I envy them. No matter how bad your day has been, when they get home and see their child smile back at them, they can leave everything else behind. Other things become more important – and I can't be all that different from most other women in the world?'

Bojana laughs. Her laughter turns into a dry smoker's cough.

La Vie en Rose

'It is spring – and I'm still in Belgrade.'

Graffiti on a wall in Belgrade

'*Na stanitsu*,' barks the policeman. 'To the station,' he repeats when Miroslav Nikolic, aka Michel, doesn't seem to react. Three officers are ransacking his store. But Michel's stall in the Kalenic market is empty. Michel is wearing his 'goods' on himself; his pockets are bursting with wads of Deutschmarks and US dollars, not to mention worn-out dinar notes. Michel buys and sells currency; he's what in Serbia is known as a dealer. I'm being searched as well and the officers are emptying my bag. Sunglasses, my swimsuit, goggles, a towel and a Serbo-Croatian–Norwegian dictionary. Nothing to get me into trouble, but they examine my passport and I tell them I'm a student. They're after the dealers anyway and seldom bother with their customers. 'You can leave,' they tell me. 'You are coming with us, Michel.'

'*U picku materinu*,' Michel responds. It is his favourite expression and means something like 'your mother's cunt'. A long time goes by before I get hold of Michel again. His mobile is out of service, probably confiscated. But then he calls, after what sounds like a long night of celebrating. 'I've been released!' he roars. 'But they took everything I had on me, those devils; several thousand German marks. Those bastards! Sons of whores! *U picku materinu!*' Michel screams himself hoarse into the phone, before he finally calms down enough to explain his predicament to me.

'They were trying to get me to cut them a deal for weeks, for a share of the profits – but I refused. I don't want to work for anyone, least of all some police Mafia. I offered them a favourable exchange rate, and whatever loose change I might have had on me, but that wasn't good enough for them. So they arrested me just out of spitefulness. They'll live to regret it, though – I have friends in higher places than they do. I'll let it go this time, but if they ever arrest me again they will rue the day they were born,' sputters Michel. 'No one can buy me off; I built my own business from scratch and I'm keeping it that way.' Michel continues and denies any association with Belgrade's various Mafia groups. He merely has 'friends' who look out for him. 'We all help each other out. I don't want anything to do with the Mob – then you end up getting involved in their internal battles.' There are gang wars and brutal murders every week in Belgrade's underworld.

Under Milosevic the buying and selling of currency was illegal. The police would occasionally crack down on the dealers, but as soon as they were released or fined they were back on the street again. Given that the banking

system barely functioned, currency exchange was a lucra-
tive enterprise. While the official exchange rate for
German marks was at six dinars, the black market paid
you twenty-two. The dealers did their business in broad
daylight, loitering on street corners and getting your attention with whispers of 'Zzz!' This derives from the word
devize, meaning currency, and when said fast it sounds like
a low buzzing.

The day after his release Michel is back at his stall. He
had just bought it when he was arrested – before that he
used to work from a regular table at Restaurant Kalenic
around the corner. But now he is the proud proprietor of
a whopping ten square metres of business space. Were he
to open his arms wide he could touch both walls of the
narrow intestine of the stall. The shelves are empty, but
will soon be filled with ladies' stockings. 'Only the very
best – from Paris, Rome and London,' Michel assures me.
'And I really should do something about the décor here –
perhaps hire an interior designer? What do you think –
Italian or French?'

Michel hardly epitomises a lingerie salesman. He must
weigh at least a hundred kilos, his head is shaven and he's
got a gold-studded diamond in his ear. Around his neck is
a bundle of chains and amulets, an Orthodox cross, his
astrological sign and a chain with the four 'S's – the nationalist slogan '*Samo sloga Srbina spasava*', 'Only unity saves the
Serbs'. Sometimes he'll accessorise his appearance with a
red silk scarf. But whether or not he sells a single pair of
stockings is irrelevant; this is only a matter of keeping up
appearances. The store is merely a cover for all of Michel's
other enterprises. Currency trading, of course, but he sells
other things as well: gold, jewellery, glasses, watches, cars.
'Now that I have a proper shop it'll be harder for them to

arrest me. Now I can register part of my income. When the police ask what I do for a living I can point to my stockings,' he reckons. Until now he's had no official income. Nothing is recorded and he pays no tax. And even if they are just a smokescreen, 'My stockings will be the finest in all of Kalenic.

'I'll have business cards made up, too,' he brags. 'What do you think I should name the store – Michelle?'

Michel has lived all over the world, in Italy, Kenya and Sweden, but he liked Jamaica the best. His brother lives in Gothenburg, where he imports mineral water from Serbia. Michel speaks fluent French after six years in Switzerland, which is also where he found his French moniker. While there he ran a disco with an Italian, but is happy to recount that he left in the nick of time – the Italian put a bomb in the basement of the disco, hoping to collect two million Swiss francs from the insurance company. Collect he did, but he kept the money only until he went to jail for five years for fraud. And at that point Michel was safely back in Belgrade.

'I'm finally back in the motherland,' he laughs. 'It is possible to earn a living, even here, even as the country goes to hell. Nobody respects the law, so we make our own, and try to stay a step ahead of the cops.'

Michel suffers no pangs of guilt for his shady dealings. 'When the government itself is criminal, it's merely a free-for-all,' he concludes. 'The banks don't function, so we have to do their job for them.' According to economists, the grey economy makes up about a third of Serbia's GNP. This is only a best guess, as nobody can determine the GNP's exact size. Dealers like Michel are only a minuscule fraction of the black market – the biggest player on the market, and the entity that controls the isolated Serbian market place, is the government itself.

The dealer is full of admiration for Switzerland, which he says 'runs like clockwork'. But not everything there is preferable to Serbia: 'The Swiss are a depressed bunch,' he says. 'Everything is so streamlined. There are no practical challenges left. Here people are worn out, but have no time to brood on the dark corners of their souls,' he laughs. He has found his own private solution to the overall malaise on the Serbian street – he's wearing sunglasses with pink lenses. 'Try them,' he urges me. And life does look a bit brighter through rose-tinted glasses. 'It looks like the sun is always shining, doesn't it?' he giggles. '*La vie en rose* – even in Serbia!'

Michel is proud of his mastery of the French language. '*Trois cents, quatre cents, cinq cents,*' he counts in a rapid tempo. The back of his business card bears the imprint of the ideals of the French Revolution: '*Liberté, Fraternité, Egalité*'. The front of the card reads: 'Michel – Perfection. Suisse Méthode' and underneath is his mobile number against a backdrop of dollars and Deutschmark notes. A steady stream of visitors stops by to congratulate him on his release, his new stall, or to exchange currency. Most of them are on a first-name basis with Michel, who serves his very best customers coffee and *sljivovica*. Most of the transactions involve minor sums: forty marks, sixty marks, a hundred marks. Many include a story with the deal: one lady is paying for her husband's operation; an old doctor is saving up for his son's education. Michel licks his fingers and counts out the worn dinar notes. If there are larger sums he wets his fingers on a sponge in order to count faster. Apart from a radio and an ashtray, the sponge is the only item on Michel's counter, except of course for the shot glasses that are in constant use. He keeps changing the station – each time they play a sad tune he groans and searches for something more cheerful: 'I can't stand sad songs!' Michel has been married and divorced three times. He has two daughters. Fourteen-year-old Kosara lives in Belgrade with Michel's second wife, but he hasn't seen her in years and says he wouldn't recognise her if they passed on the street now. His ex-wife won't let him see her.

Eight-year-old Aleksandra lives in Switzerland with Michel's third wife, but he has no contact with them either. He won't tell me why, so we let the past be. To Michel, it is the future that matters. His mobile is constantly ringing, rates negotiated. If buying, 22.2, 22.3, 22.4 dinars for a German mark; if selling, 23. If larger sums are in play, Michel's eyes narrow and he squints as he calculates his profit. 'Six thousand dollars in marks?' he asks and pulls from his pocket a calculator half the size of a business card. 'Can I call you back in ten minutes?' he pants. Over the next few minutes he makes a feverish round of calls to friends and other dealers to get such an amount in marks. 'What's your exchange rate now?' he asks, and presents the deal. Soon he has collected the money and determined his own rate. He calls the customer back and they seal the deal. They agree to meet at six o'clock outside the National Theatre.

For larger transactions Michel generally makes a house call or agrees to meet the customer in a restaurant or a car at an appointed place on the outskirts of Belgrade. A few words and greetings are exchanged. Michel and his counterpart count the bills meticulously. The German mark is the reigning currency in Serbia these days, but you do get people who have dollars from dealings in Russia and Iraq. Because of the sanctions there is little trade with Western nations.

One evening I join Michel for one of his house calls. He is going to sell dinars to a guy in a bar on Revolution Boulevard. Once the deal is completed over a glass of *sljivovica*, Michel runs into a colleague outside. He asks Michel if he can exchange a thousand German marks.

'Who said, "One thousand German marks"?'

Two large men come up to Michel and the other man. They're in civilian clothing but show their police badges. I pretend to study the supply of nail polish that a man has displayed, most delicately, on a stool on the pavement. Michel's acquaintance admits that it was he who spoke about the German marks. The policemen search him and pull wad after wad of cash from his pockets. 'Give it up,' they yell, holding him tightly.

'And you, who are you?' they demand of Michel.

'I've just been to this restaurant with my Norwegian friend,' he offers, as if I could guarantee his innocence of anything. 'We just went to have a glass.' I can tell that he's nervous – it's only a few days since he got out of jail.

'Are you a dealer as well?' the policemen ask suspiciously. Michel looks like a poster child for black marketeers.

'No, no, how could you suggest such a thing?' whimpers Miroslav Nikolic. 'I have a stall at the Kalenic market, where I sell stockings – you should stop by some time!'

He's asked to empty his pockets, but they do not search him. Michel is able to pull a few paltry dinars out of his pockets. The policemen let us leave, and remain with the other dealer. Michel is about to erupt as soon as he's safe in the car and can drive off.

'*U picku materinu!* That's just about enough! That's twice in one week. I was lucky they didn't catch me! I'm carrying several thousand German marks – thank goodness they never searched me. Sure, I can afford to lose them, but enough is enough!'

Michel's face is bright red, his eyes are bulging and he can't stop ranting, cursing the police, the Serbs, the system.

'*Ça suffit!* That's enough – I won't stand for this any longer. I'm going to stop trading currency and become a legitimate businessman. Twice in one week. *Ooh la la, merde, fils de putes! U picku materinu!* Sheer luck that they didn't recognise me, really. A lot of cops know who I am; I could have been hauled back inside again. Which would have made it five times this year. I can't afford to keep going like this!'

I ask what will happen to his friend. 'It all depends. Either they cut a deal and he gives them ten or twenty per cent of the money he had on him, in which case the money goes straight into the cops' pocket. Or they'll take him to the station, then he'll lose everything and have to do time on top of it, like I did. Poor sucker, he's a refugee from Croatia, he left everything he owned – his house, his farm. Now he trades on the black market to feed his family. *Quelle horreur de vie!*' Michel assures me that he is leaving the currency business. 'Four arrests already, this year alone, *c'est trop*, it's too much! I want to be a proper businessman,' he says with finality before he heads back to the empty shelves of his stall at Kalenic.

A few days later he calls and says he's going into the restaurant business. 'Come along and meet the estate agent!'

I meet him at his stall and Michel says I cannot be considered a buddy until I've had a glass of *sljivovica*. Apparently he's had quite a few himself. He is in a brilliant mood. And, as usual, he has several deals going on at once.

We'll stop by a few customers on the way, so obviously he's still in the currency business. A shopping bag of woven plastic, of the sort that old ladies still carry their groceries in, is getting stuffed with twenties – dinars. He douses himself in Hugo Boss and sings a Yugoslav pop standard as he walks to the car. 'My other car is a Mercedes,' he assures me. 'But the plates are from Montenegro, so I can't use it here.' He cranks up the volume of Goran Bregovic's famous 'Kalashnikov' from Emir Kusturica's film *Underground*. 'Sheer genius,' he shrieks over the music.

Michel is back to his old, irrepressible self after the arrest scare. He does brisk business. A customer is waiting for him on a street corner, a paint seller gets a visit in his shop, another man in a restaurant.

The last piece of business takes place in the office of the estate agent. Even he uses the opportunity to exchange some money, since Michel's rates are so good. Once the dinars and marks have changed hands, we're offered a choice of vodka, *sljivovica*, apricot liquor or cognac. Michel wants vodka. I'm given some sweet concoction and Michel introduces me as his Norwegian girlfriend. Then it's down to business. 'Do you have any restaurants?' asks Michel. 'I want my own restaurant, with a disco in the basement and a hotel on top. Wouldn't mind a motel somewhere on the outskirts of Belgrade.'

The estate agent does a search on his computer and offers a few choices. More and more employees from Grand Properties stop by. They join us around the table and discuss Michel's disco–restaurant–hotel plans. His whim quickly turns into the most exclusive, luxurious restaurant complex in the Balkans. In short order I am offered positions as a croupier, a bar hostess and part owner. Numerous toasts are proposed for this lavish plan.

The afternoon gave way to evening a long time ago, and the property deal has turned into a drunken bash. Equally sick of apricot liquor and being Michel's girlfriend, I slip away.

A few weeks later I see Michel again. This time he's in a foul mood. 'The dinar market is dying. First, Bosnia stopped using dinars, then Kosovo, and now Montenegro, too. Every day it gets worse,' Michel says. His shelves are as empty as ever, except for the gathering dust. Nobody has washed the floors since he bought the shop, and it has rained through the ceiling. The radio, the sponge, the ashtray and the glasses are still the only items around.

But Michel has had business cards made up, and the shop has indeed been dubbed Michelle. In place of dollar signs they now carry an image of a woman in stockings, from the hips down. On the back, it reads:

Michelle Perfection – Pariz, London, Rim.
The best in women's stockings from 2 DM to 150.
Three months' payment plans.
Quantum rebates. Rebates for gentlemen.
The best exchange rates in the market.
 Suisse Méthode.
 Liberté, Fraternité, Egalité.

Despite the extravagant business card, Michel has postponed his future as a shopkeeper until the autumn. 'The market isn't ready for my stockings; people just don't have the money,' he says. 'I want to see how this Milosevic business turns out first. Right now the entire country is isolated, we hardly produce anything at all, and this just isn't the right time to start a business,' he says, visibly disappointed. It's as if some part of Michel has gone missing. The rose-coloured sunglasses have disappeared and much of his once so significant gut has followed suit. 'I've gone from a hundred and four to ninety-five kilos,' he mumbles, and looks depressed and worn out. 'A lot of people are going abroad. Everyone who wants to make something of themselves has left. And if nothing changes soon, I'll move too. Maybe I'll go to Cuba. I could start a little inn, get married, live the good life. Or maybe Sweden or Paris. I could rent out this place and my flat here in Belgrade, and buy a little hideaway in Paris. I wouldn't at all mind living in Paris. It's just impossible to earn a decent living here in Serbia unless you're connected to the authorities or the big criminals. Drugs, cigarettes, oil – that's where there's money to be made.'

'What about your plans for a restaurant?' I ask. Michel doesn't respond. I repeat the question.

'This is not a good time to start a business, I said! People come by and ask me to change ten or twenty marks. How am I to make a living from that? And who will be able to afford to eat at my restaurant? The economy in this country is a disaster, factories are closing every day and nobody dares to invest in anything.'

I offer a sympathetic ear and it seems to put him in a better mood. Suddenly he gets an idea. 'Perhaps I should buy a bus – transport is a good business. People can't afford to drive themselves these days, and have you seen how full the buses are? I just have to wait for them to increase their ticket prices. Right now it's three dinars – there's just no way I can make a living from that,' he says, and falls into a reverie of better days. 'You should have been here during the bombings – those were the days. I sold petrol on the black market and the exchange business was booming. Back then a man could make good money. Maybe we need another war?'

There isn't another war, but the next time I catch a glimpse of Michel, he's in the throng of people outside the federal parliament on the day of the October revolution. I try to go over to him but lose sight of him in the chaos that ensues when the police fire tear gas into the crowd. Some ladies in front of me fall and the pressure from behind makes me lose my footing and I fall over them. On the ground, I have a panicky image of exactly how the stampeding crowd will trample me down as they flee the tear gas. I grab hold of the bottom of the lining of a large man's leather jacket, knowing instinctively that he won't fall, then pull myself up by his jacket and follow him out of the crowd – heaving, gasping for air, with red, running eyes.

Michel was of course in the thick of things. He took part in the storming of the parliament, he was there when they set fire to the notorious RTS station and he helped beat up the bosses who didn't get out in time.

A few days after the revolution Michel is still black and blue and his face is still swollen from his battles against the station's security guards. I happen upon him by chance, outside the parliament, where he has been volunteered to stand guard. 'I am defending the revolution, Kostunica and Serbia,' he announces with great pride.

I am in town to report for NRK's evening news and Michel is more than willing to go on camera. He recounts in great detail his heroic fight to liberate the motherland, claims to be a member of the Democratic opposition and says he will defend Kostunica with his own life. I never use any of the footage.

Later, at a photography exhibit about the October revolution, I see a large photo of Michel. From a cut on his forehead, blood runs down his face like a fan. It looks remarkably dramatic and his eyes are wide open. But even with the contextual aid of genuine revolutionary drama, there's still something about him that makes him look like a crook.

Michel has given his little shop a facelift. He's repaired the leaking roof, painted the walls white and will soon install mirrors. 'I found a girl to take care of the customers, so I can attend to my business,' he roars into the phone one day. 'Before, she used to work in a very exclusive store for baby clothing at the SavaCentre. Arkan and his wife always went there when they were shopping for their kids,' he brags. Michel's shop girl is clearly intended to complement his stockings, rather than the shop and the market, where Michel's closest neighbours sell kebabs, bathing suits and goldfish in plastic bags.

After spending a few weeks as a news reporter I want to see how Michel fares in the newly liberated Serbia. I fear the worst as the dealers are almost never to be seen on the street any more. Once the exchange rate in the banks matched the reality of the street dealers, people chose to take their business to the banks.

Michel is in the middle of a fierce and excellent row just outside his shop. He swears and curses a blue streak, and waves his arms around, wearing a brand-new leather coat and fluttering silk scarves. The gold chains around his neck are the same, but the dancing belly seems larger. Despite appearances, he tells me his profits are slim. 'I might make a few German marks on any given day if someone happens to want to change some money, but I need a new line of work. I've bought some run-down flats that I'll fix up and sell. Maybe I'll open a restaurant or a disco, but the prices in the centre of town are just insane, so I have to go into partnership with someone and I can't find anyone I trust,' says Michel, and outlines a dream of a floating restaurant on the Danube.

His stall is now full of children's clothing, and the girl he bragged about is here. The selection is rather random, and not that exclusive. There's usually just one of each item, and some of it is second-hand. Although for some, like grandly coloured socks, the supply seems unlimited.

Michel still uses the stall as his main base of operations, and since I haven't stopped by for a while we have to make a round of greetings in the immediate neighbourhood: the goldfish seller around the corner, the gypsy who sells garlic and dried peppers, the bar owner across the street, the ladies in the bathing-suit shop next door. We stop by Michel's regular bar and Michel downs two fast beers as he brags about me writing a book about him. With great pride he counts himself in the company of the TV celebrity Bojana Lekic, the rock star Rambo Amadeus and a girl from the student resistance organisation Otpor. But he's most proud of being in the same book as the former mayor of Nis, who has since risen in the corridors of power and is Minister of the Interior. 'A cross-section of Serbia,' he explains, and everybody nods.

As per usual, we drop in for a cup of coffee with Zoran the hairdresser, who owns a small, pastel-coloured shop. As usual, Zoran thinks my hairdo is terrifically boring. 'Sit down,' he says and points at the chair. 'Your hair is much too dry,' he thinks. Soon my hair is full of grease. 'Look,' he says after a thirty-second treatment. Indeed, my hair is no longer too dry. However, it does look as if I haven't washed it for weeks. As usual, he invites me to go to a bar with him. As usual, I decline. 'It's too bad,' he says, as he always does. 'We have so much in common.'

After this round Michel invites me to lunch, so that even

the waiters and customers at Restaurant Kalenic can learn about this book. Spurred on by a few glasses of *rakija*, Michel outlines his plans for an import–export firm. 'Serbia barely makes anything any more, so there's a fortune to be made in imports. Or perhaps I'll emigrate to the Dominican Republic and start a restaurant there.

'Nails!' he suddenly yells. 'Nails!' He explains when he sees my startled face. He points at a nail in the wall. 'In Macedonia they make the best nails. I could import nails – and tons of raw ore. That's a great business.'

He's on his third glass. His skin is shiny with sweat.

'*Saumon fumé!* Smoked salmon!' he exclaims. 'I could import smoked salmon from Norway; yours is the best in the world. You could help me,' he suggests, and proposes a partnership, only to abandon the whole idea a few seconds later. 'Who can afford to buy smoked salmon here? People have no money. Look around – this place used to be packed and now there are more waiters than customers.'

Lunch is finally served and should suit Michel's metabolism: hearts, kidneys and liver marinated in garlic and parsley, sow's ears in aspic, beans, stewed peppers and pickles to start with, then calf soup and various grilled meats with potatoes and mushrooms, and finally a Serbian Napoleon cake and coffee.

Michel complains about having added a few kilos. 'It's the lifestyle. And the stress. It's just wearing me out always to have to think about whether a deal is worth it or not, and how much I make or lose when the rates change. A friend of mine, another dealer, died from a heart attack recently. He just fell over. Makes you think.'

He reveals to me how he plans to lose the extra kilos: 'I'll work out three times a day, swim, take saunas and cycle. And then I'll only eat vegetables and drink juice.' I am listening to his ambitious schemes with one ear and suspect that Michel's impressive diet will most likely suffer the same fate as the imported nails from Macedonia and the floating restaurant on the Danube. I expect Michel to be just as charmingly fat and slightly worse for wear the next time I see him. But over the course of the meal his plans become increasingly weightless. He'll fix up two flats and sell them and buy a houseboat and a restaurant. Or was it a disco? Or a bar?

Michel — Perfection. Suisse Méthode.

Three years later, in the spring of 2004, back in Restaurant Kalenic. I'm looking around the room. I search the tables but there's no sight of the one I'm seeking, so I ask one of the waiters.

'I'm looking for Michel.'

'Ah yes, Michel. It's quite a while since I've seen him.'

'Do you know where I can find him? The mobile number I have no longer works.'

'No, I don't know him that well.'

'Could you give him a message from me if he does show up?'

I leave the waiter a note asking Michel to call me. The waiter promises to pass it to Michel if he comes in.

A week later I go back to the restaurant. The waiter heads towards me and looks for some place to put his tray down. He comes right over when he has served his table.

'Have you heard from Michel?'

'Yes,' the waiter says, avoiding my eye.

'Where is he?'

'He's not in a good place.'

'Well, where is he?'

'In CZ.'

'Where?'

'In CZ. Centralni zatvor.'

'Ouch . . .'

The waiter lets the information sink in.

'What is he in for?'

'Don't know – it was some friends of his who told me. He's been in and out these last few years. I think he's a little cracked, if you get my drift,' the waiter explains. 'He'd get more and more rambunctious, would always end up in fights. He got beaten up by the police a lot. And then he started drinking a lot.'

The waiter shrugs. He hasn't got more to tell me and wants to get back to work. I leave. *Cracked?*

Centralni zatvor is Belgrade's top-security jail. This is where Milosevic sat while waiting to be extradited to The Hague. I never got permission to see it from the inside. And once the summer heat kicked in I left town.

Back in Oslo, a few months later, my phone rings. 'Unknown caller' reads the display. I answer it and hear heavy breathing at the other end.

'*Allo? Allo? C'est Michel!*'

'Wow, you've been released!'

'I've been to Kiev. For months now. Kiev, in the Ukraine. I have a business there. I was so happy to get your note. Are you coming?'

'Well, I'm back in Oslo now. I'm really busy. Have you . . .?'

'Come to Budva this summer. Budva, in Montenegro. Come in July, that's the best time. I have a house there. You could be my guest. I have a boat and we could go swimming.'

'I'm not sure . . .'

'August, then?'

'I . . .'

'You can swim through September, really. Yes, even in October – although in October it does get a bit windy. So when are you coming?'

'Well, listen, I . . .'

'OK, I'm counting on you. I'll call . . . *Au revoir, mademoiselle. Je t'appelle! Au revoir!*'

On a Mission from God

'I am the way, the truth, and the life.'

The Gospel according to St John 14:6

Sveta ponders the shoes in the window for a long time. 'What do you think of those?' he asks, and points to a pair of elegant black leather shoes from Italy. Before I can reply he dismisses the extravagance from his mind. He points to a pair of sneakers instead. 'They're cool, but someone could take offence,' he thinks. 'They don't match the style.' Then Sveta spots another pair – with narrow points and thin, flat soles. 'They look nice – perhaps I'll try those,' he says.

'They don't look too comfortable – with those thin soles,' I object.

Sveta just snorts. 'I can worry about being comfortable in twenty years. Now I want to look cool.'

'But nobody's going to see your shoes under the *mantija*, right?' I wonder.

'Oh yes – when I walk, or sit down,' a deadly serious Sveta responds.

Sveta is shopping for shoes for a very special occasion. In a few weeks he will become a deacon. The *mantija* – his cassock – already hangs in his closet; the trousers and his shirt are almost ready to be picked up from the tailor. Only the issue of black shoes remains unresolved. But it's late, the shops closed a long time ago and we've done all the window-shopping that Sveta's hometown of Nis, in southern Serbia, can provide. So we go for a beer instead. But Sveta can't get his mind off the shoes. 'It's important to look good in order to attract young people to the Church,' he assures me. 'As a young priest my job is to convert young people, and I should look youthful and hip. You know, Jesus is forever young.'

Sveta needn't worry so much about making a fashion statement. It's already hip to go to church in Serbia, especially in the larger cities. Each Sunday the house of God is filled by urban, often highly educated, people. Getting baptised is 'in' and atheism is old fashioned. Young, educated people are even flocking to monasteries, looking for something to believe in. Quite a few have elected to turn their backs on whatever life their critically damaged society can offer, in favour of the habits of monks and nuns – sometimes to the great dismay of their parents. Because their parents' generation has not returned to the Church. The population of Serbia was more or less secularised during communism.

Sceptics dismiss this attraction to religion as a mere fad, while the Orthodox describe it as a spiritual awakening. A poll from 1982 revealed that a mere 3 per cent of the youth in the traditionally Serbian Orthodox areas described themselves as religious, while the figure in

Catholic areas was 30 per cent. By 1999 the situation was almost completely reversed, when a whopping 58 per cent of the entire population regarded themselves as believers. One might want to take into consideration the reliability, or lack thereof, of religious polls undertaken in communist Yugoslavia. The 1982 poll was conducted by *Ilustrovana Politika*, while the numbers from 1999 are taken from the Institute for Social Research in Belgrade.

'The youth of Serbia hunger for something to believe in, something eternal. In the Orthodox faith they find both eternal love and the mystic,' Sveta explains, once we've found a table in the noisy bar. 'We've been fed so many lies, and have lived under false ideologues, heard so many utopian fantasies. Now Serbia is in a crisis and there is only one way out of it. We have to find our way back to our original faith and build a society on Orthodox values, where the Church is the primary institution. These days this country is built on a pseudo-culture, where we can no longer tell what's ours – what is Serbian and Orthodox. We're squeezed in between Europe and Asia, and over the centuries we've become mixed up. So we need to recover our spiritual core and become a healthy society. Our true heritage is Orthodoxy and we can only achieve this through religious purification.'

It's not just the culture that needs cleansing, but the individual human being as well. If one were to follow the tenets of the Orthodox Church to the letter, one would fast for about six months of each year. Sveta does. Right now he's in the midst of the longest period of cleansing of the year, from Lent to Easter. Meat, eggs and dairy products are forbidden.

'I stopped smoking when the fast began,' Sveta says,

casting a longing glance at the table next to us, where they're smoking up a storm. 'I've given it up for good now. If you are addicted to something it means that your faith isn't strong enough. When I am a priest I will have to provide an example for others. I will have to be more serious and consider my every word, because people will watch me and judge me.' Sveta, whose name means 'the holy one', seems to be looking forward to this responsibility. As soon as he is ordained he is supposed to wear his cassock wherever he goes. 'I won't be able to have too many beers when I'm out on the town,' he laughs, well into his second pint.

The twenty-eight-year-old will have to make other changes as well. He is growing a beard and is still unaccustomed to seeing this new countenance in the mirror. 'I suppose I could have kept smoking – there's nothing that specifically forbids it – but the beard is obligatory. Jesus had a beard.'

In contrast to Catholic priests, who can never marry, you have to be married in order to be ordained as a priest in the Orthodox Church. Sveta's father, Rasa, a priest himself, suggested that Sveta get to know Jelena, a member of his congregation, and they made a visit to her parents' house.

'If you like her you will accept when she offers you coffee. If you don't like her you politely decline,' Rasa instructed Sveta. The son accepted, the romance was on and a few months later they wed. Sveta thinks it is right that parents have a say in who you are to marry. 'They know you and know what you need. It's much better than looking for someone out on the town.' As soon as she has put their baby to bed, Jelena joins us in the bar. It's getting crowded around the table. Dejan, the deacon, has arrived with his wife in tow for a round of beers. He's not wearing his *mantija* and smokes a lot. 'When I go out I'd rather not attract too much attention,' he explains. Sveta can't take it any more and sneaks a smoke. 'OK, this is my last one,' he swears, laughing. But when the conversation returns to religion and Serbian culture he grows serious again. It's his friend Bane who brings the subject up again. 'We're poisoned by Western culture, by America,' he offers. 'If you put a heart or a liver in Coca-Cola overnight it's all gone the next morning – did you know that?' he asks. 'This is how America tries to exterminate all genuine culture in Serbia. They want to rule the world, and attacked us because we refused to submit.' The whole table nods in agreement. 'I can't say anything positive about Western culture today,' says Sveta. 'There's nothing genuine there. It's an empty culture – soap operas, McDonald's, Coca-Cola; throwaway consumerism,' he says, and adds infidelity, crime, commercialism and stress to the list of charges. 'You're not living – you are merely consuming. And for that matter – what sort of civilisation are you talking about when Western countries, in the twentieth century, only use bombs to solve problems? What kind of culture is that?' Sveta sounds like an echo of Milosevic, despite his professed opposition to the dictator. 'He's a communist and a pagan nationalist. But if only you would just withdraw from Serbia, we'll be able to get rid of him ourselves.'

Serbia's Orthodox Church is built on a traditionally nationalistic and patriarchal system and has always viewed the West with great scepticism. After the NATO bombardment of 1999 the Church stepped up its anti-Western rhetoric. The West was blamed for the loss of Kosovo, for the burning and razing of churches and monasteries by the

Albanians, for the displacement of thousands of Serbs from Kosovo, which in the view of the Church is the heart of Serbia proper and the spiritual birthplace of the Serbian Orthodox Church. This faith builds on the teachings of St Sava, a monk who became the Church's first archbishop in 1219 and went on to name only Serbs as bishops. He further established the doctrine that the Serbian Orthodox Church is identical to the Serbian nation – a tenet that has been used by the bishops ever since to promote Serbian supremacy. This helps explain why so many of them supported Slobodan Milosevic as he rose to power on a wave of nationalist rhetoric. By consistently emphasising the transgressions done to Serbs, and never mentioning the misdeeds the Serbs themselves may have committed, the Church fuelled the ethnic tensions. In return for its support Milosevic gave the Church greater influence. He gave permission for new houses of worship to be built, he allowed public celebration of Christmas and in some schools he even exchanged the teaching of Marxism for religious instruction. When Milosevic broke with the Bosnian Serbs' leadership and the dream of a Greater Serbia was lost, the church leaders distanced themselves from the dictator. They maintained that all Serbs should live in one nation and claimed that the new borders between the former republics of Yugoslavia were drawn up by the West in order to divide the Serbs.

It wasn't until 1999 that the Synod took a public stand and demanded that Milosevic step down. The Serbian Orthodox Church defines itself as a persecuted faith and portrays the Serbian people as victims. It captures people with the myth of the past. It is not about the worldly, but about the heavenly kingdom, and some church leaders claim that the myths are more true than what the history books might say. The church magazine *Pravoslavlje* states: 'The science of history can change the truth with every single fact. Tradition need not change a thing, as it is not built on mere facts, but instead is a representation of the divine truth.'

Bane's voice cuts through the clutter of cheers and shrieks. He wants to tell me about Serbia's glorious past and show me the monuments, the memorials, the monasteries and the churches in the area around Nis. 'You should set aside ten or twelve days,' says Sveta. 'And you have to see our baby,' Jelena adds. 'You can stay with us as long as you like,' they assure me.

Sveta invites me to attend his ordination. The ceremony keeps getting postponed because the Bishop of Nis is busy, out of town or ill. The ceremony is called *rukopolozenje* – the laying-on of hands – and in this the bishop will lay his hands on the new deacon's head and give him his calling.

Then one day Sveta is on the phone. 'Osy, it will be on Easter Monday! How glorious, on such a day of joy!' he shouts. 'You can come over on Thursday, and celebrate Easter with us.' He calls me Osy, which he thinks sounds prettier than Åsne. Sveta meets me at the bus station and we go straight to his church, the St Nikola. We're in time for the evening service and the church is packed. The congregation stands, while a few chairs along the wall are reserved for the old or infirm. Outside, large loudspeakers allow a crowd to follow the service in the soft spring evening. We catch the final two hours of the ceremony, with the choir singing, incense, a communal prayer and the blessing of the priest. Sveta teaches me to make the sign of the cross in the Orthodox style. From the forehead down to the chest and then from the right shoulder to the left.

The thumb, index finger and middle finger must be joined to signify the Holy Trinity – the Father, the Son and the Holy Ghost. The ring finger and little finger must be folded in and kept together; this symbolises the union between God and man.

At the end we receive the blessing of the priest. The priest is Sveta's dad, Father Rasa. 'Just follow me,' says Sveta. We stand in a long line leading to an icon of Jesus. Sveta makes the sign of the cross and kneels three times, kisses the icon, puts some coins in a cup and goes over to Father Rasa, who draws a cross on his forehead with holy oil. Sveta makes the sign of the cross again and kisses his father's hand. I do what he does, and feel a little dizzy.

We head over to Sveta's home to drink wine, discuss Easter, his ordination and the fast that is about to end. Beaming with pride, Sveta holds up his *mantija*, puts it on, checks himself out in the mirror and shows me – several times – how he has to sit down without letting his legs show. He's like a little boy who's just been given his first football strip. Just before midnight the young believer springs up and says, 'We have to drink up in a hurry! We can't drink after midnight – by then it will be Good Friday!' He downs his glass in one gulp, a minute before the clock strikes midnight. 'You can do as you please, of course; you're not Orthodox,' he assures me. I have a feeling that I'd better adhere to the rules anyway, and follow Sveta's admonition about not consuming alcohol on the day of Jesus' crucifixion. I go to bed in the guest room, while Sveta remains standing and praying in front of the icons and the burning lamp in the living room.

Good Friday turns out to be a marathon of church services. The first ceremony begins at eight in the morning and lasts for two or three hours. After that we head straight to the idyllic monastery of Sicevo, which is located on a hillside outside Nis. This service begins at noon and lasts another couple of hours. It ends with the symbolic wrapping of an icon of Christ in a shroud. The congregation lines up to kiss the feet of the icon, a Bible bound in silver and a cross. Then we can kiss the hand of the priest and have another cross drawn on our foreheads with holy oils. Afterwards we drink the monastery's spring water and are fed Easter breads made from holy water and wheat flour. This is the first meal of the day, as no one is supposed to either eat or drink before Jesus has been wrapped in the shroud. On Good Friday many here go without eating or drinking at all. But we head down to Jelena's parents' home for lunch, which consists of cucumbers and a bean stew. Meat is banned. The father offers us *rakija*. 'No, I couldn't drink on Good Friday,' says Sveta.

But he changes his mind when everyone else accepts the offer. 'All right then,' he says.

After lunch there's another service in the St Nikola church. I've come to know half the congregation at this stage. Afterwards we go home to rest before Midnight Mass. The church is again filled to the rafters and another large crowd remains outside. Around the church large boxes of sand have been placed, so that people can put down candles and pray for their loved ones, dead or alive. The first part of Midnight Mass consists of a symbolic *opelo*, a funeral, and then comes the regular service. The congregation joins in with prayers and hymns. The whole thing lasts until half-past three in the morning. At which point I stagger outside, dizzy from the atmosphere, the incense, the hymns and the holy oils of God's house.

I'm off to Belgrade in the morning. By a curious twist of fate I am supposed to catch the end of Belgrade Fashion

Week, which I am meant to cover. A weird change from all the religion, spirituality and devotion that Sveta, Jelena and their friends and families have shared with me.

But Sveta does not forget about me. When I wake up on Easter Sunday there's a new text message on my mobile: '*Osy, Xristos Voskrese!* From Sveta.' 'Osy, Christ is Risen!' That evening I head back to Nis. This time it's Bane who picks me up, and hands me a shopping bag filled with brochures, postcards and small books on the multitude of memorials, monuments, churches and monasteries around the city. 'Some of them are out of date – you'll just have to ignore the communist propaganda,' he says. Sveta is at home, getting ready for the big day. He is visibly nervous about tomorrow's ordination and barely takes note of my arrival as he recites payers in front of the flickering icon lamp.

By six o'clock the next morning he stands again in front of the icons, mumbling his prayers. We're in church by seven, one hour before the ceremony begins. Sveta puts on the black *mantija*, his trousers, the shirt and the shoes he ended up getting. A gold-embroidered red tunic is draped over the *mantija*. The church fills up and the dignified bishop enters to conduct the service. Facing the altar, Sveta stands upright throughout the ceremony. It seems to me that he's swaying a bit, but perhaps it's me who is swaying. A few hours into the ceremony Sveta is called in front of the bishop. He kneels; the bishop puts his hand on Sveta's head, reads from the Bible and blesses him. Sveta kisses the bishop's hand and then slowly walks around the altar three times: once for the Father, once for the Son and once for the Holy Ghost. He kisses all the items on the altar under the stern watch of the bishop and the other priests: the cross, the icons, the Bible. Then the holy fathers return to the congregation, Sveta recites a prayer and the bishop concludes the ceremony with his sermon.

Once the service is over, Sveta is an ordained deacon. And this calls for a celebration. Fifty guests, including the bishop, gather in the Stara Kuca, the Old House, restaurant. The fast is over and a lavish spread of food, *rakija*, wine and beer awaits. Sveta can't sit still and instead bounds from guest to guest. 'I'm so excited!' exclaims the man of the hour. I end up sitting next to his grandmother, who crosses herself throughout the feast. 'To think that my grandchild has become a priest! Jesus says that priests are the light of the world and the salt of the earth,' she sighs as she chews whole spring onions and sizeable chunks of lamb.

The next day Sveta conducts his first service in the St Nikola church. He fumbles only once, when he struggles to put around his shoulders the ribbon meant to signify the wings of the angels. As soon as the service is over we repair to the priest's office to share a couple of Easter eggs, some bread and a few shots of *rakija*.

When we go outside, two lanky, acne-ridden young boys approach Sveta. They make the sign of the cross and kiss his hand. Sveta pulls it back. 'That's not necessary,' he counters, and explains, 'I've only just been ordained.' The boys tell us that they're soldiers on leave and have come to light a candle in the church. To them Sveta, in his black *mantija*, is a figure of authority.

'I don't have anything to contribute yet, so that's why I didn't want them to kiss my hand,' he explains with great solemnity. Standing there in his cassock, he seems to strive to be dignified. And it is the preacher in Sveta who holds court. 'The congregation must grow. It is my mission to ensure that Serbia once again becomes Orthodox. Jesus said, "Go forth and make all the peoples in the world my disciples, in the name of the Father, the Son, and the Holy Ghost.'"

Sveta embarks on his mission with remarkable speed. On his first day in the job he will baptise some twenty babies, children and adults. 'You'll have to come back when you're ready to be baptised, Osy,' he says, and sees me off with the sign of the cross. 'May God bless you!'

In the weeks and months that follow I am continually updated on the doings of Sveta and the Orthodox Church. Their weapon of choice is the Internet. Sveta emails me pictures of bishops on field trips, church missives, prayers in English and Serbian and small personal notes in which he tells me that I am in his prayers and that all is well with him, Jelena and little Andjelina. Towards the elections of 24 September 2000 he informs me that he will vote for Vojislav Kostunica. 'Kostunica is a man of the Church and a true believer.'

A jubilant email greets me when Kostunica finally emerges as the winner following the revolution in Belgrade. A few months later Sveta writes that he is eager for another revolution. 'We need a spiritual revolution. And it will go through the Saviour. We have to cleanse ourselves of what He calls the three enemies of mankind: sin, death and evil. This is the revolution I am trying to ignite, but it is difficult,' Sveta admits.

I travel to Nis to learn more.

'If this change of government was just a changing of the guard, where one set of people was exchanged for another, and nobody desires a cultural and spiritual revolution, then we are on the wrong path,' he tells me.

Wearing his *mantija* in the living room of his in-laws, Sveta looks like an eager apostle. Andjelina has just learned

to walk and as she wobbles around us it becomes clear that
she is the only one able to interrupt Sveta's revolutionary
zeal. Whenever she strays near him he pauses to kiss his
little angel.

'When it comes to the spiritual revolution nothing has
happened,' he says. 'But the Church has been given a larger
position in society since Kostunica took over. Religion and
the Church's efforts are covered more by the media and the
authorities are working to add evangelism to the school
curriculum. Maybe even from this autumn on.' Sveta thinks
it's logical to have priests in charge of this teaching. He also
thinks it's a good thing that the Church is given a bigger
role in governing the nation. 'Kostunica consults with
Patriarch Pavle,' he says. 'The supreme leader of the
Church.'

Even Sveta has become a media figure. He is a regular
guest on a local TV show devoted to debates about spiritual
values and he has his own column in a Nis newspaper. 'I get
a lot of questions from the viewers,' he says. 'But it's always
about what the Church can do for them, or what the government can do for them. Nobody asks what they can do
for the Church or their country. People here have forgotten
what it means to take responsibility. And nothing will
change until we've changed that attitude.'

Later a very pleased Sveta is proven right. The local
paper has got word that an author from Norway is visiting
Nis and that two native sons have been portrayed in a
book – Deacon Sveta and the former mayor, Zoran
Zivkovic. They request an interview, and Sveta escorts
me to the editorial offices. As the clatter and chatter of
typewriters echoes down the hallway, the two of us sit
and wait. The sound of typewriters is like a forgotten
echo of my childhood. We strike up a conversation with

one of the employees, who complains about the lack of everything and the hardships of putting together a newspaper without computers. The woman reveals that they may receive some support from a foreign fund. We're given coffee and mineral water and then told that nobody can find the journalist who was supposed to interview me. Later we're told that she's busy doing another interview. After waiting for forty minutes we leave – without having seen the journalist. We have an audience with the bishop and it wouldn't do to be tardy. A triumphant Sveta turns to me as soon as we're out in the street. 'See that? All they do is complain about everything: never enough of this or that. But it doesn't cost anything to be punctual! The entire population is in need of a great cleansing, as you can see.'

And Sveta makes sure that we pay our respects to the bishop at exactly the agreed time.

In the spring of 2001 I return to Nis to celebrate St Sava's Day. As the founder of the Serbian Orthodox Church, St Sava is Sveta's principal role model. Every family and every institution in Serbia has its own saint, who in turn has his or her own annual day of celebration. St Sava is the patron saint of the schools and the universities.

As usual, Sveta's idea of a celebration takes the form of a relay at high speed. The morning service makes up the first leg, then we pick up the bishop and make the rounds of Nis's schools to preach Sava's message of prayer, learning and hard work. The schools are all decorated with balloons and drawings of the saint, the children sing songs about the man who gave the Serbs their own Church, the bishop tells stories about the life of the saint and Sveta walks around with incense. Candles are lit and at the end of it all the bishop is to bless a large, round cake – a *kolac*. He cuts a cross in the cake and pours wine into it. The red wine seeps into the sponge, and the bishop and a few chosen children cover the rim of it with kisses.

After the school tour we embark on visits to various faculties of the university. Everywhere we go there are hymns and prayers and sometimes we are served *rakija* or cognac and small, sweet biscuits. When we drive by a church under construction, both Sveta and the bishop make the sign of the cross. 'We have four churches in Nis and we're building two more,' the bishop tells me. 'We should have at least fifteen. If Nis had been in Greece this city would have had fifty churches.'

That evening there is a gala event at the military society, with more songs and more speeches. I end up next to the wife of a friend of Sveta. 'This is a song about St Sava . . . This is a poem about St Sava . . . This is a speech about St Sava,' she informs me for the first hour or so. Then she sits quiet for a while, and when I ask what a particularly adorable little girl is singing about, she says, 'Oh, it's a song about St Sava.' I stop asking.

Following the performances there is a cocktail party at the bishop's residence, where Nis's political and religious pillars have gathered. Whisky, vodka, cognac, beer and wine are served and the buffet offers a bounty of delicacies. The choir from the previous event perform a hymn and some people dab at tears, while others make the sign of the cross; but the vast majority don't let any of this interfere with their eating and drinking. At midnight we return to Sveta's parents' place, where we are fed once more. Father Rasa asks me what I thought of the celebrations. I offer my new-found fondness for the choral songs, as I find I've become captivated by the spell the sacred music of the

Orthodox Church casts. 'It contains both mysticism and peace, and it lets the spirit soar,' I tell him.

This pleases Father Rasa so much that he decides to find a husband for me and to convert me.

The next morning it is Rasa who is in charge of the service in the St Nikola church. During his sermon I suddenly realise that he is talking about a visitor from Norway. '*Norvezanka* was captivated by the choirs on St Sava's Day,' he tells the congregation. 'So even people from the frigid north can feel the warmth of our Orthodox faith. Furthermore, *Norvezanka* also said that she felt at home in our faith and that she was well received among us. May we always welcome others with warmth and love,' he ended, and drew the sign of the cross over the congregation.

On the way home for breakfast Sveta repeats the offer to find me a man. 'Or perhaps you already have a sweetheart?' he asks me. 'No, nothing serious,' I parry, as lightly as I can. Sveta is silent for a long time. Then he asks me: 'Osy – how can a human being enter into a relationship that is not serious?'

We ride in silence until the car arrives at Sveta's in-laws' home, where a Sunday breakfast of scrambled eggs, pickled peppers and ham awaits us. Jelena eats porridge; she is feeling queasy. Sveta has already broken the big news to me – they are expecting another child. 'We'll have at least five,' beams Sveta. Over her porridge and peppermint tea, Jelena can only muster a brave smile.

After breakfast there are more tasks for Sveta, Rasa and the bishop to attend to. A wealthy man has built a new house and wants to protect it from accidents and disasters. He has asked the bishop and his entourage to bless the villa. This entails more hymns, more prayers, and the bishop walks around the residence crossing and kissing every holy icon, crucifix and prayer lamp in it. The wealthy man has tithed tens of thousands of German marks to the Church and the blessing is the reward for his alms.

I ask Sveta if this generous man is an example of the spiritually cleansed human being that Sveta desires to see – someone who gives instead of demanding.

'No,' he answers at once. 'This is a man who happens to have money and who shares some of his bounty with the Church. But he has no education and leads a messy lifestyle. The exemplary man must be learned and live by the rules of the Church – he must pray, and of course tithe.'

And under no circumstances enjoy the occasional non-serious relations, I think to myself.

The spiritual revolution is lacking in action. Serbia staggers along; one administration follows another, people struggle, while the Church is continually disappointed to see that none of the new powers that be are willing to open their coffers for new churches or restoration of the old ones. After a while Sveta abandons his habit of keeping me updated by email on the various activities of the Church. Three years go by.

On 17 March 2004 the Serbian Church suffers its very own Kristallnacht. Some thirty Orthodox churches and monasteries in Kosovo are destroyed by Kosovo Albanians. Most of them are vandalised, others blown up. Several of them have their origins in the twelfth century and contained irreplaceable frescos. Icons are defaced, altars are disgraced, bell towers levelled, crucifixes violated. Over the next few, bloody days nineteen people die, of which eleven are Albanians and eight are Serbs. The international peacekeeping forces are surprised and overwhelmed by a mob numbering in the thousands. The rampage is meant to avenge the deaths of three Kosovo-Albanian boys who drowned, their friends said, when they were chased into a river by Serbs with dogs. Later the UN said it could find no evidence of this.

Orthodox Serbs in Nis take their revenge by setting fire to the local mosque, and a few hours later also the mosque in Belgrade. And just as the Belgrade imam didn't address the destructive fires in Kosovo, the Serbian Orthodox Church never expressed concern over the destruction of the mosques. The hatred between Christians and Muslims, where only your own losses and the crimes of the others are tallied, grew a few degrees hotter.

Following the riots of March I want to visit Sveta again and dig out a mobile number from an old notepad. I send him a text message. Half a minute later he replies:

'I await you. Sveta.'

A week later I am standing outside his block of flats in Nis. A single light bulb in the entrance lights my way as I go upstairs and ring his doorbell.

His face is rounder. His belly as well. Life seems to have done well by Sveta these past few years. Even the beard seems fuller. Only a pair of dark rings under his eyes hint at sleepless nights and too-long days.

Sveta showers me with blessings and invites me inside. The living room is almost dark, lit just by the icon lamp below the crucified Christ figure. St Nikola's gaze rests on the sofa, St Mihailo looks out of the window, St Pantokratov keeps an eye on the door, while St Sofia and her three daughters watch over them all.

A figure struggles to get up from the sofa. Jelena goes up on her tiptoes to kiss me thrice, and pats her large stomach. 'This will be our third,' she laughs. 'Seems I'm always pregnant when you come!'

Sveta offers me a seat on the brown leather sofa.

'White wine? Beer? *Rakija*? Coca-Cola?'

'*Rakija*.'

Sveta gets an ice-cold bottle from the fridge. The fast is just over and he can once again partake of earthly pleasures.

'You look younger than before,' he flatters me.

'And you look more holy,' I smile.

'I have been given my own church now,' he says proudly. 'Presvete Bogorodice – the Church of God's Mother. The foundation is from the fourth century! I will show you tomorrow. It's in such a wonderful location, in the countryside just outside the city. I received my own congregation last November, when the bishop blessed me as a full priest. Would you like to watch the ceremony? I've got it on video.'

'Sure.'

Sveta finds the video and then turns to look at me before he puts it in. 'Imagine, it's been three years since I last saw you. Have you got married?'

'Oh, don't start that again!'

There's a knock on the door. 'Father Rasa,' Sveta says, and gets up to open the door. 'He was so looking forward to you coming!'

Sveta's father is dressed in his long cassock, a hat with edges and a sort of large necklace. He enters with great dignity. I know I am supposed to kiss his hand, but I give him a firm handshake instead and curtsy – an attempt to compensate for the absent kiss.

'So you've come to see how we are doing,' Rasa notes, still standing. 'Have you got married yet?'

'No . . .'

'How old are you now?'

'Thirty-four.'

'Alarming! Alarming!'

Rasa caresses his beard with a furrowed brow and examines the space in front of him. He fixes his gaze on the ceiling and delivers his conclusion: 'Your time is almost up. The clock is five minutes to midnight, so to speak. No, one minute to midnight. One minute to midnight.'

I grit my teeth and stay calm until the sermon is over. I'd almost forgotten about this part of it. I decide to regard it as an expression of concern.

'You know, until you are married, you are just a half of a human being. Only through marriage can two halves become one whole.'

I nod and drink my *rakija*.

'I can't tell you how many couples I have introduced to each other. How many weddings I have facilitated. If you would only convert I could find you a husband. A real Serb. What do you say? And remember, a marriage is a duet, not a duel.'

Father Rasa laughs, clearly pleased with his own pun. 'You are Protestant, no?' he continues. 'Luther. Oh yes, Luther knew his business. At the very least he was industrious.'

'Our cathedral was burned down, did you know?' asks Sveta. 'And a hundred monasteries in Kosovo. Hundreds of monasteries.'

Since Serbian forces withdrew from Kosovo in June 1999, approximately 150 churches and monasteries in the region have been destroyed, along with tens of thousands of holy articles.

Sveta leans forward, on the edge of the deep reclining chair. His elbows rest on his knees.

'Islam,' he says, and lets the pause grow pregnant with implied meaning as he waits for me to nod in agreement. 'Islam is the cancerous tumour of Europe.'

Father Rasa has finally sat himself down.

'The cancer is spreading. It can only be vanquished if it is cut out. If we don't start fighting back, Islam will devour us all. Especially you in Western Europe – you're not even watching out.'

Rasa strokes his beard and observes me with a sorrowful look on his face.

'Do you know what the problem is with the Muslims? They have no respect for other faiths. They burned down thirty churches in a single day. They killed priests and nuns. Innocent believers. The only way to deal with Islamic fundamentalists is with violence. That's the only language they understand. Look what we've learned from Israel. Look what they are up against. If we are to vanquish Islamic fundamentalism, we need to show some force. We cannot live with each other – just look at Kosovo!'

The warmth in Sveta's eyes, the warmth that embraced me when he blessed me by the door, has begun to sparkle. A fire has erupted within his corneas.

'Killing is not a sin to Muslims. They murder with complete peace of mind – do you understand? But to us Orthodox, murder is a sin, no matter who you kill. Every human being is a child of God.'

'It is a worldwide crisis,' Father Rasa notes from the sofa. 'Evil is on the march. Globalisation is the Tower of Babel of this age.'

Sveta nods. Jelena sips her juice. I drain my glass.

'Let's go and get something to eat,' suggests Father Rasa, and gets up.

Sveta puts on his cassock. I go along. Jelena stays at home.

'Spreading the gospel is an eternal struggle,' says Father Rasa as we drive towards the centre of the city. 'Fools that we were, we thought the new government would help us – but no. They haven't even given us enough to heat our church.'

Rasa's snort is so disdainful that it turns into a coughing fit. 'I stood side by side with the Democrats to remove Milosevic. But we've got nothing in return. At least my church hasn't.'

The car turns into a dirt parking area. A large sign announces that we've arrived at the Railroad Workers' Football Club. We go into the clubhouse restaurant, a single-storey building with brown tables, folding chairs and a musician who plays old Yugoslav love songs on a keyboard at the far end of the room. The two cassock-clad men are greeted with respectful nods, and the waiter leads us to an excellent table in the middle of the room.

'Pear liquor or apricot brandy? Or the usual, from plums?'

A round of *kruska* – pear liquor – for the table.

Father Rasa orders salads, meats and cheeses, along with a Macedonian red wine for the main course. The waiter appears with a tray, so big that it covers the entire table, filled with a variety of meats. Lamb, chicken, pork and *pljeskavica* – a flat cake of ground meat and spices. Some of the meat is grilled, some is pan-fried. For garnish, perfectly fresh, iridescent green chillies. Rasa offers a quick prayer before we lift our glasses, grab our forks and have at it.

'It might be bloody,' says Sveta.

I'm studying my grilled meat.

'It might be bloody. I know it sounds ferocious. But if we are to avoid getting crushed by Islam, we have to use force, and violence. It is ferocious, but it is what it is.'

I'm puzzled by Sveta's irreconcilable attitude, and his

shift. When I was here last, America and the West was the great enemy. Now it's Islam. Has the US become the good guy?

'Well, they're both our enemies, really. It is the United States that has brought on this wave of Islamic fundamentalism. The Americans facilitated this rise of evil forces,' says Sveta.

'The US created bin Laden,' continues Rasa. 'Now he's come back to bite them. The exact same way they created Milosevic, only to have him turn on them. Just like our dictator, bin Laden has his own agenda. I was very much opposed to the war in Iraq – I knew it would turn out the way it did, a breeding ground for Islamic fundamentalism. Now they're all whetting their swords, and for every day that goes by they have more to avenge. The Americans are drowning in quicksand and I can't see how they'll ever get out.'

'What do you think of Bush saying that he's fighting in God's name?' I ask.

'You shouldn't take the Lord's name in vain,' is Rasa's only response.

'It is a sin to invoke God for the wrong reasons,' Sveta explains.

He puts away his knife and fork.

'There is no God in the West,' says Rasa.

'I think Christians in the West would be inclined to argue that point,' I suggest.

'It is your lifestyle that has no God in it. Being a Christian means to live according to the Lord's wishes – to pray, be righteous, fast, to follow His commandments. The West is all business. Judas was a businessman.'

'God plays no part in your system,' emphasises Sveta. 'This crisis the world is in right now is also a trial. God is testing us. We have to find the righteous path and follow it.'

We've finished off the *kruska* and the Macedonian wine, but the grilled meat seems as eternally bountiful as the Yugoslav love songs on the keyboard.

'Do you know what the bane of Islam will be?' Father Rasa asks.

'No,' I say, expecting some bloodthirsty, apocalyptic prophecy.

'Women's liberation will be the end of Islam,' the priest says. 'As long as the men rule everything, Islamic fundamentalism will survive. But if they had any say in it, the women would not choose this religion for themselves.'

'Why not?'

'I ask you again – what matters the most to a woman?'

'Well . . .'

'What matters the most to women is to bear children.'

'All right.'

'Allah had no children. But our God, the one true God, has a son.'

'Mm.'

'Allah is a cold deity. Our God radiates warmth.'

The meat has grown cold and dry. The marbled fat is stale, and seems to shimmer on the plate. That God, the Orthodox God, is firm but warm may just as well stand as the final word of the feast. We finish our drinks and head home.

Sveta and I say our goodbyes to Father Rasa outside Sveta's building. The old priest jokes that his wife will scold him for not bringing any leftovers home from the restaurant.

'Women!' he laughs. 'Women . . . You'd find something to complain about even in Paradise!'

Up in the flat, Sveta calls us all to prayer. Andjelina and Jelisaveta are asleep. Sveta, Jelena and I stand in front of the icons, each with a Bible in our hands. Sveta points to certain verses and asks us to read. First Jelena, then me, then Sveta. The living room feels sacrosanct. Sveta's low voice fills the room. He has read these lines so many times that the words pass his lips as a hum of sorts. He doesn't just know them by heart – the words know the geography of his mouth, and the muscles move without thought. I can barely make out a word. But God will understand, certainly.

Jelena has made up a bed for me on the sofa in the living room. The guest room has been turned into a nursery since my last visit.

'Will you be able to sleep even if we leave the lamp on?' she wonders. 'You see, the icon lamp has never been put out. Are you sure you'll be able to sleep with it burning?'

I was. At least for a few hours, until I was woken up at dawn, so we would get to church in time. This morning is called Bright Friday – a week after Good Friday.

'In the week after Easter all the days have names,' explains Sveta. He, Father Rasa and a few other priests are to conduct a joint service in one of the city's churches.

We drop by Rasa's. He's getting dressed, and while we wait I have a quick chat with his wife. Sveta's mother is dressed in black, just as she was the last time I saw her. Her grey hair is tied back in a knot at the base of her neck. Coal-grey hairs line her upper lip. She looks at me with round, curious eyes.

'Have you got married?'

'No,' is the only response I can muster. It's barely light out and I haven't had my coffee yet. No drink or food may pass our lips before the service.

'How old are you?'

'Thirty-four.'

'When I was your age I had three children,' she says proudly, almost wistfully, never taking her eyes off me.

'And I've written three books,' I snap.

Rasa's wife can't keep from smiling. 'That's not quite the same thing, now,' she says, in the overbearing manner of someone explaining the difference between right and wrong to a small child.

'It's certainly not – but why do we all have to do the same thing?' I reply.

Her smile dies. Her eyes say: 'Doomed! Doomed!'

Rasa puts a stop to this awkward debate. I jump up as soon as he enters and we can get out of here.

'By the way, what happened to the rich man whose house you blessed?' I ask once we're in the car. 'The one who donated all that money, but was neither righteous nor learned?' I add, when there's no response.

Sveta and Rasa exchange a quick glance.

'Did something happen to the villa? Or to the family? Is there something wrong?'

'He is in prison, in Germany,' Rasa reveals, and pulls his coat around himself. 'Before he left he gave our church a lot of money – as much as fifty thousand marks – which financed the painting of our icons. We even had his name engraved, in gold, on a plaque. One day he came to me and asked me to bless an upcoming business trip to Germany. I tried to explain to him that God can only bless business when it's undertaken with good intentions. Something told me that this trip wasn't, to put it that way. I had a sense that he might very well be involved in something. So he left without having his journey blessed. A week later he was arrested by the German police for smuggling,' recounts

Rasa. Then he adds, with much gravitas: 'We priests must exercise sound judgement in the matter of blessings for this, that or the other. What if I had given him my blessing and he still had been arrested? To think, I would have been an accomplice. I would have taken the Lord's name in vain. And you cannot invoke God for the wrong reasons.' Rasa looks pensive. 'I almost took part in a criminal act. Praise to God, who told me to abstain.'

The church we are heading for has its own spring and today people have come from far and wide to take home a bottle of holy water.

Sveta deposits me in the rear of the church before he disappears behind the triptych. The walls are covered in icons. Some are baroque, some Byzantine – Sveta has taught me the difference. Baroque icons have open faces, pink cheeks and blushing lips. They are painted with curved lines and seem to be in motion. The younger ones seem straight out of an old book of fairy tales – several of them have drawn swords and are pictured in battle, on horseback or even fighting dragons. The Byzantine icons, on the other hand, just stare at you with almond-shaped eyes. They are stern and rigid. The background is painted in gold, or in a deep sky blue if the church can't afford gold paint. In contrast to their baroque brethren, there are no romantic embellishments here that could distract attention from the exalted sanctity of the saints.

'Which do you prefer, baroque or Byzantine?' Sveta wanted to know.

'They're so pretty, all of them . . .'

'I prefer the Byzantine,' Sveta told me. 'They are cleaner. And it is so beautiful with gold.'

I remain standing among the saints and a sea of lit candles, which sends a warm whiff of hot wax into the room.

The church fills up. A large crucifix hangs by the triptych. 'Pay attention to Jesus,' Sveta had told me. 'Wherever you are in the church his eyes are upon you. Wherever you go he will always look straight at you. Jesus always knows what we are up to.'

I follow the liturgy for about two hours. The six priests walk in a procession behind the altar, pick up the Bible, kiss it, put it down, make the sign of the cross over it, then kiss it again. They pick up relics, bless them, put them down. I begin to wonder who came up with the various elements of the liturgy – three kisses, turn around, sign of the cross, arms out, arms up, around again, repeat three times, pass the crucifix to your partner, pass the Bible, kiss three times. It's like a choreographed dance in slow – very, very slow – motion. Two old ladies next to me are whispering and their hushed exchange rustles through the room. Like most of the congregation here, they seem to be on the poor side, and hold plastic bags in their hands. Jesus is looking right at them, too.

Hymns. Prayer. Incense. Blessings. Then the priests trail one another outside, the congregation right behind. Three more times round the church, which is located in a pastoral garden. The holy spring flows into a pond and the sun is just about to clear the tall birches around us. The pond sparkles and I feel strangely happy as I circle the church. Besides, it's almost time for coffee.

People have brought along some round loaves of bread they want to have blessed, as well as lists of people who couldn't make it. The holy men have their hands full with the line of supplicants, mainly women, with their loaves and their lists of names: Slavica, Radomir, Jelena, Vera, Janko, Bogoljub, Drago . . .

Church coffee inside the office. We crack a few Easter

eggs and add a shot of *rakija*. The priests knock their eggs against one another's; the one whose shell breaks first loses. One egg after the other gets eaten, to cheers of *rakija*. Until finally the coffee itself arrives – strong, with lots of sugar.

'Breakfast!' someone hollers. In the room next door there's a feast of *pljeskavica*, lamb meat, cheese, peppers, salads and more *rakija*. The priests take their seats according to rank, with Rasa at the head. The rest of us follow suit. After a few more rounds of *rakija* we switch to white wine. It's made at a local monastery and has a light, fruity taste. The priests mix it with mineral water for a most refreshing mélange.

The conversation returns to the subject of Kosovo, the Muslims, the suffering Serbs, the eternal suffering of Serbs, the ever-unjust treatment of Serbs.

'Something must be done about the influence of Islam.'

'We Serbs have allowed them to run all over us for too long already.'

'We let them take everything away from us.'

'They will devour us.'

'There are only two men worthy of comparison with Karadjordje [who led the first rebellion against the Turks in 1804 and was the ancestor of the last Serbian royal family to hold the throne],' Rasa says. 'Radovan Karadzic and Ratko Mladic.'

Both men are wanted for war crimes, but have been protected by the Yugoslav and Bosnian-Serb armies. Karadzic is believed to spend some or even much of his time hiding in Serbian Orthodox monasteries in Bosnia. Rasa didn't say this much a few years ago, but now it's somehow acceptable to admire him again. Because no one was ever held accountable for anything, people allow themselves to forget – or, rather, remember only the parts they want to remember.

'They fought for us. For the standing of Serbia in the Balkans.'

'And Srebrenica,' someone interjects. 'What was Srebrenica, really? I'll tell you – for a long time the Muslims had terrorised the Serbian population in the area. This time they finally just struck back. It was war. In war civilians sometimes suffer, unfortunately. Very many Serbs had suffered from this war. So very many Serbs had been killed in their homes, or made to flee, so very many murdered in cold blood.'

The men all look at me. They know that the rest of the world has condemned the Serbian atrocities at Srebrenica, the single largest massacre of the war in Bosnia, where seven thousand Muslim men and young boys were killed in just a couple of days. It's as if everyone around the table knows that some line has been crossed here, with the demand for a revaluation of the event. And this is how so many wars have started in the Balkans – through stretching historical facts to fit an emotional state, through lying about everything from statistics to myths. Great wars start out as folk songs and camp-fire stories, and end in genocide and bloodbaths.

'The genocide of Serbs in Kosovo is still going on,' someone says. 'Serbs are getting killed, and have to flee. It's about time that we offered up some resistance. Serbs must retake Kosovo. Serbia has to recover its Orthodox faith. These are the only things that can save us.'

We go outside and sit down on a bench next to the spring. Father Rasa wipes a pearl of sweat from his forehead. A small Gypsy boy comes up with a plastic jug that he fills with the blessed water. He's probably six or seven and has deep, gorgeous eyes. The fingers that wrap around the handle of the jug are thin and dirty, his hair unkempt.

'Are you baptised, my son?' Father Rasa asks.

The boy stares straight ahead at the stream of water going into the jug. He tries to look at the priest when the question is repeated.

'Yes . . .'

The boy holds on to the word, as if hoping it is the right answer.

'Bring your mother and your siblings here, and I will baptise you,' says Rasa.

'Yes . . .' the boy replies, before he hauls the heavy jug away.

Sveta seems lost in thought. Arms crossed over his chest, he looks up at the bell tower and seems not to have seen either the boy or the water.

'How is the spiritual revolution coming along?' I ask him.

'It's coming, it's coming. When God is willing,' he says, his eyes looking up.

Staged Power

Navigare necesse est
Vivere non est necesse
(To sail is necessary
To live is not necessary)

Pompey

Along the road leading out of Belgrade, there's an oasis. A sparkling palace with palm trees, fountains and exotic birds. Beautiful women greet you at the entrance, accompanied by classical music and birdsong.

You are free to wander around within the bright winter garden and marvel at how the flowing water creates compelling patterns on the glass roof. Or you can visit the Indian room and be served a tasty treat. You may indulge in the soft sofas or try the chaises longues. Unless, of course, your preference runs towards deep leather chairs next to one of many fireplaces. Once you've exhausted the entertainment value of a flickering fire, there is a star chart embedded in the ceiling, made up of minute, flashing lights. The waiting staff anticipate your every need before you're aware of it yourself. Perhaps a bit of port before the show?

This is the grand entry of the KPTG Theatre, and the playground *par excellence* of its director, Ljubisa Ristic, noted theatre director and politician. Who joins me, following a performance on a cold winter evening, in front of a brilliant fire, enveloped in soft leather.

'I began construction five years ago, when everyone said you couldn't start anything in Yugoslavia any more. Allegedly, we knew only how to destroy. Now we have three stages and plans for four more,' he says with pride. The theatre, raised from the ruins of a former sugar refinery, was finished in 1999. 'For the first four years, we put plays on outside, or in the condemned factory building, with its broken windows and pigeons in the rafters. In the winter the audience would sit there, wrapped in coats and hats,' Ristic laughs, and looks out over the foyer, which oozes luxury. No detail has been left to chance here. No two leg tables are alike; each one is carved into intricately unique shapes. The parapets along the mezzanine are turned into sculptural art.

'The first performance on a real stage took place during the NATO bombing. The show, of course, had to go on — what if they'd bombed us before we'd even tried out the new rooms with an audience? Years of work would have gone down the drain,' considers Ristic.

'Come,' he says, and gets me out of my easy chair. We walk upstairs on soft carpets, through salons and corridors. Everything is new, cutting edge. The dressing rooms are spacious and the backstage vestibule is decorated with silk-upholstered chairs and pseudo-classical columns. The actors have their own library of dramatic literature, and computers dedicated to 'character research'.

'We've already developed seven thousand square metres,' says Ristic as he points here and there. Gradually, he keeps pointing at castles in the air; at the end of the foyer with the twinkling star charts the wall looks like a large, gold-framed window. Beyond the glass is an actual crater, where ladders and ropes lead down into the abyss. It looks like an archaeological dig, but Ristic speaks of it as an opera hall with five storeys of balconies. 'It will be done in a Gaudí-inspired baroque style,' he insists. In the basement a jazz club will be designed as Scotland's famed architect Charles Rennie Mackintosh might have designed a Chinese ballroom. The building next door is to house a movie theatre with four screens, a large art gallery, a fashion centre with a catwalk and studios for designers. Plans are under way for a fitness centre, beauty salons, spas, and the five-storey emporium will be topped off with a glass-clad, rooftop swimming pool.

While Ristic bounds up and down ladders an alluring whiff of chocolate permeates the frigid winter air of the opera crater. 'They still make some sweets in the basement here,' Ristic explains. 'Did I mention that I will have four restaurants as well – Greek, Italian, Chinese and Mexican?'

Critics have alleged that in order to get his palace built Ljubisa Ristic sold out to Milosevic. Or rather to the dictator's wife, Mira Markovic. In 1995 Ristic surprised Serbia's intellectuals by appearing at a press conference with Markovic, as the recently appointed president of her new leftist party, the JUL. Suddenly the artist, dissident and rebel stood side by side with one of the most despised power-mongers in Yugoslavia. It was an outrage. Ristic had worked all over the former Yugoslavia and was the traditional Yugoslav representative at theatre festivals abroad. During the student demonstrations of 1968 he joined the protests against Tito's regime. He was arrested and beaten by the police, and when he finished his education as a director in 1971, he was banned from producing any plays within a 200-kilometre radius of Belgrade – because of his subversive streak.

He was forced to work in smaller theatres in the provinces and the only thing he ever got to show in the capital was his exam from drama school. 'It is the most seen production ever in Yugoslavia and it's still being done by the repertory at the Belgrade Drama Theatre – twenty-nine years after it premiered!' he brags.

By 1995 he was no longer a subversive. He was the president of the party of the most exclusive establishment in the country. The CEOs of various state industries tended to join the SPS, Milosevic's party, but in the private sector the media barons, captains of industry and entertainment figureheads all went along with his wife. That's where the money was, and the connections. And given the isolated state of Serbia's economy, being on the 'inside' was a necessity if one wanted to get contracts or concessions. Given the rampant nepotism and cronyism involved here, the JUL was never held in high esteem among actual voters. Even with its massive propaganda machine, the party rarely broke the 2 per cent barrier in polls. 'Even people within the party think they've financed my theatre. "This is the fruit of our labours," they tell me. That's as idiotic as saying that the Department of Culture helped finance it; I've paid for everything myself, with money I made through a series of fortunate investments. And I've had the assistance of a group of donors. But nobody has paid me for political support. Besides, the construction has been halted. We haven't built anything after the bombing. There's no money left for culture in Serbia today – not until we've rebuilt all the bridges and buildings that were destroyed by your NATO bombs.'

The multi-tasking artist further refuses to acknowledge that he has turned his back on the revolution. 'I've always fought for the ideas of the left, and for Yugoslav culture – and I still do. Certainly more so than my former comrades in arms, who now are renegade errand boys for the West,' he says, and explains why he decided to go into politics in 1995. 'It was an extremely difficult period for Serbia and the dominant ideology was nationalism. A horrifying war took place in Bosnia. Even to speak of a Yugoslavia was taboo and the parties on the left were marginalised. I had always refused to join any party, but then Mira called me and said her objectives were peace and anti-nationalism. That was something I could throw my support behind. "Do you need my help in any way?" I asked. "Yes – my husband is the President, so I can hardly lead this party myself," she replied.'

Ljubisa Ristic had never met Mira Markovic before this phone conversation took place, but she was well aware of his position as a famous artist. They began seeing each other socially and started to meet on an almost daily basis. Ristic became a frequent guest at the presidential couple's home. 'I've never seen a couple more united than them. They radiate a harmony you hardly ever get to see; the way they listen to each other, brag of the other's achievements, look at each other and admire each other – it's quite exceptional,' says Ristic, and recounts what delicious sandwiches the President makes, how he gives his grandchild baths, how he can recite poetry and sing for hours on end. 'He is the domestic one. Mira is the thinker, Slobodan the practical one. When they come to visit here, he studies the construction and comments on the physical process. She comes to experience Shakespeare.' A typical KPGT production of Shakespeare might please both of their presidential sensibilities, then: in Ristic's interpretation of *Julius Caesar* the Romans are bubble-gum-loving Americans bent on obliterating Egyptian culture, just as, according to him, the Americans have set out to wipe out all things Serbian.

Ljubisa Ristic loves to discuss the human side of Milosevic. He tells of the dictator's envy one evening when Ristic and the chief editor of the government's *Politika* newspaper wanted to follow their dinner with the President with a visit to a nightclub. 'It's well past midnight – surely it's too late to go out,' said Milosevic. 'No, this is when the night begins,' countered a confident Ristic. The two of them left, leaving a frustrated Milosevic at home. 'He wanted very much to come along, but he doesn't have that kind of freedom,' explains Ristic, and you can almost hear his pity. 'Then during the Kosovo War the very evening before Milosevic was to meet the Russian envoy Viktor Chernomyrdin for a round of negotiations, he insisted on sleeping in the residence here, rather than leave town as per usual,' Ristic continues. 'But Mira put her foot down, and the President gave in. That night a bomb landed in their bed in the city.' The theatre director insists that Milosevic is the best man to run Serbia. 'He can't resign now. There's nothing he'd rather do than retire, but he is the only man who can lead this country right now.'

I suggest that Mira could be elected President. This makes Ristic furious.

'This is a normal country, not a monarchy like Norway. You don't inherit power here – please, no more such nonsense!'

Interviewing Ristic is a bit of an ordeal. He's a master of last-minute cancellations as there's always something more important happening elsewhere. The interviews themselves are constantly interrupted by phone calls, choreographers, art directors, actors. Once in a while Yugoslavia's powerful Minister of Information stops by, and I have to wait for him on a sofa somewhere. At other times Ristic simply has to leave in a hurry. But I did get to see a lot of KPGT's productions while I waited. Ristic is nothing if not a gentleman when he wants to be, and picked me up himself, in a silver Audi A8. And, like any Yugoslav gentleman, he celebrated a particularly good answer by kissing my hand. Taking me home one night, he begins cursing at the streets that have had their names changed. Boulevards named for Partisans and communists now carry the names of monarchs and nobles. This is the work of Belgrade's municipal government, led by the SPO, the opposition monarchist party. Ristic is an atheist born into a family of communists. His parents met in the Partisan resistance during the Second World War, when they were sixteen and seventeen years old. His father went on to become a general in the Yugoslav army. I ask if we can continue the interview the next day. But no, he is going to Novi Sad to observe the opening of a bridge, rebuilt after the NATO aggressions, Ristic explains. I ask if I can come along.

'No, it's a high-security trip – we'll be travelling in an armoured train.'

'Who will open the bridge?' I ask.

'That is top secret.'

The next day the first twenty minutes of the evening news are dedicated to the rebuilt bridge and the speech.

'This is a morally superior bridge,' shouts Slobodan Milosevic to applause. 'It shows that we are a superior people, that we are the most European of all nations!' There's more applause and the crowd waves pictures of the Yugoslav President. 'May Europe learn from modest Serbia what historical pride and civil liberties really are. We have vanquished our enemies – not because we are stronger, but because we are better!' hollers Milosevic, and there's no end to the cheering. Afterwards he inspects the train. Extremely serious men and women fill every seat. Clearly they agree that this is indeed a morally superior bridge – not to mention what an honour it is to travel on the same train as Slobodan Milosevic. Suddenly Ristic flashes across the screen – he's got an aisle seat and looks rather bored.

Ristic is easily bored, so almost everything he does is on impulse – even when he directs plays. He can simply walk out of the theatre during rehearsals if he's in a bad mood. Conversely, he might stay all night. He tries to explain his habit of cancelling our appointments: 'It's not that I don't have the time; it's just that I need to be in the right mood.'

On this June day he certainly is. We've landed on a pair of sofas with a vista of the gold-framed opera crater. My subject has two packs of Davidoff cigarettes on the table in front of us, and a waiter makes frequent trips to make sure that we have everything we could want. Ristic is finally to articulate his political philosophy, which is built on the concept of Yugoslavia – 'brotherhood and unity'. Being a Yugoslav supersedes everything else. The name of his theatre, KPGT, symbolises Yugoslav unity; it lists the word 'theatre' in the four languages of the former federation,

Croatian, Serbian, Slovene and Macedonian: *Kazaliste*, *Pozoriste*, *Gledalisce* and *Teatar*. The company was formed in Zagreb in 1978, but it wasn't until 1995 that Ristic's troupe got their own Belgrade theatre.

Much like the government, Ristic views the wars of the last decade as a result of Western manoeuvrings. 'America wants to colonise Serbia because of our strategic geographical position. The main thoroughfare for all traffic and trade between Asia and Europe runs, as it has for millennia, through Serbia. America began to worry that Europe might gain control of this vein and become too powerful. Or, for that matter, that Russia might. So the United States want to position themselves here, just as they did in Panama,' maintains Ristic.

'The wars in the former Yugoslavia were produced by the US, in order to control the trade routes of the region. When the war in Bosnia began, the biggest investment in European history, the Danube–Main–Rhine channel, was just completed. The Americans couldn't stand it. Why do you think they primarily bombed bridges last year? To stop trade and transport. It's the same thing with the sanctions: they are trying to strangle us, so they can colonise us. Look at the other former Yugoslav republics – they're all colonies of the West now. All of them, except for Serbia. We stood up to the Americans, so we were bombed.'

Ristic works himself into a lather speaking of American and Western aspiration to subjugate his country, and of the unyielding resistance of the Serbian people. I try an intervention: 'Don't the Serbs themselves have any responsibility for these wars?'

'Initially Milosevic had a rather naïve notion of defending Serbian interests throughout the former Yugoslavia. I don't think he realised that building a Serbian nation did not at all address the aggressive nationalism that brewed within the other groups. He should have known better; the Yugoslav republic was the only solution to the problem of a Serbian nation, when hundreds of thousands of Serbs lived within the other republics. The Croats had long talked of an independent Croatia, the Slovenes as well, and then the Bosnians, too, wanted independence. But when Serbs began to talk of a Greater Serbia, it was not in our interest. Milosevic never realised how fatal losing Yugoslavia was for Serbia. Now he favours a strong federation, and it was to strengthen Yugoslavia that we formed the JUL,' Ristic explains.

Meanwhile critics of the party maintain the JUL's *raison d'être* was that the presidential couple realised the SPS was too compromised by the Balkan wars at this point. By establishing an alternative party they could garner the population's confidence without losing any real power. They'd keep everything within the family, so to speak; there was no discernible difference in ideology between the two parties.

'This is not the time to haggle over details. We're fighting for our national sovereignty, not over left or right. In the future I hope there will be room for mutual criticism and debate – but now only one thing matters: to be a patriot.'

Ljubisa Ristic's anti-Western rhetoric is as relentless and consuming as that of Mira Markovic herself. Western nations are aggressors and colonists. 'They've now gone so far as to assassinate people, one after another.' Ristic is convinced that the West is behind the political assassinations, in the hope of destabilising the country to the point where it could take over. 'They'll never succeed – not if they've already failed with their bombs. They think

Milosevic is a nationalist, but he doesn't even care about ideology. He's a banker. He's so pragmatic, and they have no idea who they're up against. That's why they'll never outwit him, no matter how dirty their tricks. Milosevic will never resign as long as doing so means handing Serbia to the West on a platter,' thunders Ristic. At least to the extent one can thunder while stretched out, barefoot, on a white sofa with a Davidoff in hand and a cup of espresso near by.

Anti-Western sensibilities aside, Ristic has dubbed his theatre an 'International Art Centre'. 'This will be an international meeting place for artists,' he assures me. But he no longer receives companies from the West and is banned from performing any plays there. His last production abroad took place in London in 1995. Ristic is *persona non grata* in most European countries, as well as the US, owing to his 'close personal ties to the regime of Slobodan Milosevic'. This is the price he pays for serving as Mira's right hand.

He's not losing any sleep over that. 'I can travel to far more interesting places in the world – Latin America, Africa and Asia. Besides, I'm not interested in visiting the West any more; you slaughtered us in cold blood. I'm not a wide-eyed tourist any more, and I see nothing to admire in Europe. We survived, and Europe fell, morally speaking.' If his hatred of Europe seems boundless, his admiration for China seems proportional – 'an example to follow'. Ristic beamed with pride when he was named the official host for Prime Minister Li Peng during his three-day visit to Serbia. And Li Peng returned his warm welcome with a fiery speech in support of Serbia.

Despite his rapid rise, Ristic insists that he didn't go into politics for personal power. 'I've got my career, I am an independent artist. I will remain a member of the JUL as long as there is a need for me there. But never say never – perhaps one day I will develop ambitions on my own, lose control and become hungry for power,' he jokes. 'Honestly, I think it is the absence of personal ambition that allows Mira to trust me – I'm no threat to her position.'

Ristic interrupts himself: 'I'm bored now. Let's go for lunch. Wouldn't you like to meet my mother?' The fifty-three-year-old director lives with his mother, Jelica, and his brother, who is a year younger, in a terraced house on the outskirts of Belgrade. Ristic has always stayed with his mother when he's been in Belgrade, except for the two years when he was married. His brother, too, moved back home after a divorce.

Jelica greets us at the door. She has bluish hair and is wearing a dress with blue flowers on it. Her flat smells of Sunday lunch; a leg of lamb awaits us.

'Norway was always friendly to Yugoslavia, but last year you bombed us. You are traitors – quislings,' she reprimands me, and glares. Her son tries to calm her down. 'Mother dear, be nice to our guest, it's not her fault.' But Ristic's mother keeps dwelling on the treachery of the West while we wait for the lamb to be done. 'I was sitting on this very balcony, watching the bombs drop. Bombs from America, a country that has more people in jail than any other on earth, a country where only five per cent of the population have an education, a country that put the Indians in reservations,' she spews out.

Then the lamb is ready, and we sit down. Jelica, Ljubisa, his girlfriend Danka, me, his brother Branko and his son Sasa, who is on summer break from studying economics and marketing in Brighton. There's not a lot of talk as we eat because we are all watching a tape of last night's football match between Italy and Romania in the European Championships. It ends 2–0, which we knew already. After the meal Ljubisa takes a nap until the next match begins – the quarter-final between Yugoslavia and Holland. I end up with Jelica and Danka, eating chocolate cake and fresh apricots from the garden. At 6 p.m. the entire family gathers in front of the television. Ljubisa and Branko swear loudly whenever the Dutch score. They curse the 'hashish-smoking Dutchmen', who, according to Ljubisa, look like criminals.

'We're leaving,' he announces when the score is a miserable 4–0. He's already on his way out of the door. Danka and I run after him, pausing only to give Jelica a quick hug on the way out. When I get home I catch the final minutes of the match. Yugoslavia lose 6–1. Yet another Yugoslav defeat on the world stage. I wonder how Ljubisa might attempt to spin this disaster into a victory. When I ask him he can't manage more than, 'At least we beat Norway resoundingly!'

Ljubisa Ristic seems tense. He tries to cover this tension with an exaggerated sense of confidence. It's late in the evening of 4 October 2000. Every day protesters take to the streets; the miners have gone on strike and are threatening to shut down the country's power supplies. One profession after the other refuses to work and a general strike is looming. It is the evening before the opposition will make its massive stand. The protesters have accused Milosevic's regime of stealing the election through a fraudulent vote count.

Little do we know that this is the demonstration that will bring down Milosevic. Which in turn will strip Ljubisa Ristic of his position at the seat of Serbian power. We do not know that several generals in the Yugoslav army are struggling with a very hard decision right now: whether or not to hold their fire against the demonstrators if they are ordered to shoot.

'The Supreme Court has just declared that the elections won't proceed,' Ristic tells me when I arrive. 'Because of the opposition's complaints, the election has been annulled. The opposition got just what they wanted. Except that the President remains in power until he chooses to run for election again. Milosevic cannot resign now; the country is much too unstable. I've just called around to all the observers and told them they won't have to return for the second round of voting.'

Election observers from many countries were invited for the initial election, but – except for the odd 'friend of Serbia' from the West – only from supportive nations like Iraq, India and Belarus. The observers pronounced the elections legitimate and fair, despite the opposition's reports of any number of irregularities during the count.

The theatre is empty. Ristic lights one cigarette after the other. His phone won't stop ringing. He is discussing the recent turn of events with party comrades and friends. 'Milosevic is furious about the cancellation. He was looking forward to the second half.'

What Ristic is telling me is a bald-faced lie. The decision of the Supreme Court has just handed Milosevic a final lease of life in the presidential palace. He knows he would have lost the second round of the election.

Around three in the morning Ristic drives me through the sleeping streets, manoeuvring around the barricades the demonstrators have erected. We're driving by election posters such as 'The People Choose – Not NATO', put up by the Socialist Party. But there is also '*Ko*? Kostunica!' *Ko* means 'who', and the implied question here is, 'Who can lead Yugoslavia?'

The next day half a million people stand in front of the federal parliament. We're chased off with tear gas, only to gather again. Chased off, gathered. I can imagine Ristic in his theatre, chain-smoking and on the phone to his nervous buddies from the JUL. On the evening news he can watch as Vojislav Kostunica is named President of Yugoslavia.

In the weeks that follow I have my hands full reporting on the October revolution and its consequences. But one day I make my way out to the theatre and find him in the winter garden. He greets me icily, calls me an agent and a spy, bought and paid for by Western intelligence agencies.

'We should have got rid of them while we still had the chance. Djindjic, Kostunica, the whole lot of them. Thrown them in jail, got rid of them. We should have cracked down on that rabble in Otpor – we gave them far too much leeway. We just stood by and watched them sell out our nation.'

Ristic spits out every word.

'I had never thought we'd see a *coup d'état* in this country. A coup that you and your government are responsible for,' he continues. 'The Norwegian government paid the miners to strike.'

He accuses me of being an informant, pointing a shaking finger in my face. I'm about to leave. Then his anger turns to bitterness.

'Milosevic made too many mistakes and listened to the wrong people. His advisers worked for Djindjic as much as for the President.' Ristic summarises: 'The first mistake was to announce an election a full year ahead of what the constitution required. Given the difficult situation in the country, when we're more or less occupied by foreign agents who poured millions into an inflated opposition, that was irresponsible.

'The second mistake was to trust in the loyalty of the police and the army; after a few hours they changed sides with the demonstrators in the street. But he did manage to avoid the third mistake, which would have been not to give up his powers. Had he not done that, it would have turned into a bloodbath and the foreign-controlled conspirators would have called for an international occupation.'

'How could Milosevic make so many mistakes?' I wonder.

'I think he was sick and tired of ruling. Of the pressure, of always having to battle foreign occupation. He couldn't think straight any more. It's almost as if he stopped fighting.'

We've moved into the bar. It's after midnight and there's no one else here. Ristic fiddles with the espresso machine. He lights a cigarette with his JUL lighter. 'Milosevic is telling the truth when he says he's looking forward to spending more time with his family, and his grandchild in particular,' he offers.

This is not to be. Shortly Milosevic's son Marko will leave the country with his wife and child, for fear of being arrested, or of retaliation. Marko is one of the most hated individuals in Serbia, owing to his thuggish conduct in the Milosevic-controlled village of Pozarevac. Rumours of his ties to the Mafia are legion. He dropped out of secondary school because 'it was impossible to attend school and have a good time simultaneously'. Slobodan's daughter Marija is best known for her numerous and consistently tragic love affairs, the majority of them with a succession of her bodyguards. Her parents gave her a TV station once, so she'd get over one particularly painful heartbreak.

'Milosevic has not had great luck with his children,' Ristic suddenly concludes. But far be it for him to complain of his own lot. 'I have my theatre, and from now on I will fight in opposition.'

Each time I visit Ristic he's more accusatory. So I stop visiting. I hear he's taking an active part in campaigns; at the Serbian parliamentary elections on 23 December the JUL, his party, receives 0.4 per cent of the vote.

When I drop by after New Year half the foyer is closed off. I peep behind the covers. It's freezing in there. 'The power's shut off,' Ristic explains. 'We haven't paid our bill. We're out of money.'

The number of donors has shrunk, it seems. Most of them were entrepreneurs from the JUL, and none of them can see how their interests might be served by funding the president of a party stripped of even imaginary powers. Many of them have left the party, which was anyway more of a business enterprise than a political association. The theatre director has nothing but disdain for the opportunists who've now gone over to the new power base. 'We're rid of the rabble – those who are still with the JUL are those who truly believe in the Yugoslav ideal,' Ristic says. He does worry about his theatre, though. 'The new government do whatever they please. One day they might come here with machine guns, just like they did at the Central Bank, just because I won't collaborate.'

Tonight's play is Peter Handke's *Offending the Audience*. Directed by Ristic, it does indeed consist of a barrage of insults and invective levelled at the audience. The room is half full. I'm sitting in my winter coat and keep digging in my bag for more scarves and mittens. People around me are also wearing their winter clothes, as if it were the most natural thing in the world. Quite likely it is, in this city where Ljubisa Ristic is hardly the only one struggling to pay his electricity bill.

During the spring of 2001 the artist seems to resign himself to his disenfranchised existence. Serbia waits for only one thing: the arrest of Milosevic. Rumours are constantly flying about as to when this will happen – within forty-eight hours, next week, in two weeks.

Ristic is still in close contact with the former President and First Lady. 'Slobodan is fighting for his political future and takes a more active role in the party than ever before. He's not at all afraid; he's innocent. Mira is furious. She is raging at the injustice that's being done to them and at what the country is being subjected to. Criminals and deserters are being glorified, while those that defended the nation are dismissed as traitors. And you, you wait for the end like scavengers – carrion birds,' charges Ristic. 'But they'll never be able to get anything on Milosevic, which is why I fear for the worst – that they'll simply kill him off.

'There's a lot of terror here now,' he continues, and speaks of people who've been beaten by youths from Otpor, or been forced to abandon their offices to the movement. When I ask around about these stories, no one else has heard anything. 'It's because the press doesn't dare to write about it,' explains Ristic later. When I suggest that the international press certainly would cover an organised campaign of terror directed by the new government if such a thing existed, he laughs derisively. 'The foreign press? But you're all agents for your respective governments – you've got exactly what you wanted here!'

One of the waitresses approaches our table.

'We're out of cocoa,' she says.

'Well, go and buy some, then. Or would you rather I do it?' Ristic suddenly says. 'That's actually better, it's rather late,' he decides.

I go with him to the late-night store. Ristic finds the cocoa, gets in the queue and speaks to me in loud English, so that no one can fail to hear us. 'Anything else you need?' he asks me. He may still be on the list of undesirables throughout the West – but he can show that he's being visited, and that he's just a regular chap buying a tin of cocoa at the corner shop.

His girlfriend Danka comes over and we end up talking through the night, over ravioli and wine. We discuss theatre, music and Yugoslav culture. Suddenly Ristic is a discerning, erudite and cultured expert. I wonder what it is that makes him put blinkers on when it comes to politics.

Then Ljubisa and Danka begin to tell me about supernatural phenomena: clairvoyants, magic, healing hands and tarot cards. They outdo each other with stories of inexplicable things that have happened to them. They both frequently consult the *I Ching*, a Chinese book of wisdom several thousand years old which has the answer to everything. A roll of the dice and the *I Ching* interprets hexagrams based on the results. 'During the bombing the *I Ching* informed me that I was in grave danger. The next day I was almost hit by shrapnel from a bomb,' Ljubisa tells me. 'The *I Ching* always has a message or a warning. But often the answers are given as riddles – you are supposed to ponder both the conundrum and your own life,' Danka explains.

By four in the morning Danka and I have got to the 'What is love?' stage of the evening, and Ljubisa puts an end to it. We drive through the streets where he grew up, in central Belgrade. 'This is where we played football,' he says, crossing an intersection near Kalenic. 'In the 1950s you didn't see a car come by more than once or twice in an hour, so when one did we just moved,' he remembers, lost in nostalgia.

Suddenly a policeman pulls us over. The big, burly officer checks the driver's licence and Ljubisa's personal documents. He studies the papers for a long time, as if he doesn't know quite what to make of them. Then he hands them back. 'They've already started to pretend that they don't know who I am. Before, they always made some sort of joke. Now it's as if they're embarrassed to see me,' says Ristic. Quite possibly the deferential police officers are indeed embarrassed by Ristic's long fall from grace – having gone from moving effortlessly through the corridors of power to ending up as a debt-addled theatre director with a dubious past and an arrest warrant potentially looming over his head.

On the evening of 31 March I meet Ristic once more. He's visibly nervous. He tries to hide it behind compliments and charm, and manages to maintain this illusion for a minute or two. He picks some yellow leafs off one of his houseplants.

'These are simply excellent in soups,' he tells me.

'Is that so?' I answer, somewhat absent-mindedly. I'm far more curious to know how he feels now that his dear friends, the Milosevics, are surrounded by police and security forces. The evening before, Ristic stopped by their residence for coffee, but he doesn't want to talk about it.

We take a seat in the Italian restaurant. The other tables are empty, as if people have decided that this is not where anyone wants to be tonight. Ristic lights his first cigarette.

His hands are shaking. 'They are going to kill him,' he states. 'You and your agents have done a splendid job!'

I've never seen him this incoherent before. As he speaks he makes patterns out of his cigarette packet, the ashtray, his glass and a few scraps of paper. Anything he can get his hands on, he starts moving around maniacally. Soon his cigarette packet is torn to pieces. Once that's over with he folds the tinfoil the cigarettes were wrapped in into a small lump, then unfolds it and then makes it back into a lump again. He's feverishly brushing imaginary specks of dust off the tablecloth. 'We should have killed them all while we had the chance,' he repeats again and again. 'And Milosevic should have killed the intruders last night,' he says, referring to the Special Forces. 'Wouldn't you? If someone broke into your house in the middle of the night?'

Any question I ask only sends him further into a rage. The mood is oppressive, and I'm getting ready to leave. But Ristic doesn't want me to go and asks me if I'm at all hungry. It's as if he can't deal with being alone. 'I'll have my favourite pizza,' he says. 'With mozzarella and olives.'

I stay and wait for the drama to get even more intense. But his silence is deafening. I just sit there, wondering what it will take for him to break it, resting my own vocal cords in the meantime. The meal remains completely silent, though, except for the sounds of the cutlery and two people chewing.

When there's not a speck of pizza left on his plate, he finally says something. 'The wind is picking up,' he decides.

His brother, Branko, arrives. 'They'll take him after midnight.'

Ljubisa nods.

'But we'll win the country back. Even if it means starting a guerrilla unit.'

I leave the theatre to catch the capture of Milosevic somewhere else, and call Bojana.

A few days after Milosevic's arrest I'm back at the theatre. Ristic doesn't want to say anything about Mira and Milosevic, except that they are 'angry and saddened'.

'The tragedy is complete,' he says. 'Directed and performed by the Americans. The drama is over, the tragic hero captured. To the victor go the spoils.'

'And what might they be?' I wonder.

'Serbia,' Ristic answers, fixing his gaze on me. 'Serbia is no longer a country, only a territory. That is the tragedy of it all,' he says. 'That is the tragedy.'

The entry gates have almost disintegrated. Vast pools of rainwater have made the floors wobbly. The carpets someone put out to dry off the fluids have given in to the laws of nature and are partially dissolved. The foyer is riddled with buckets and tubs. Drop by steady drop, the rain outside makes its way through the cracks in the glass roof and into the buckets. A huge water tank waits underneath a large fissure along the ridge of the roof.

Other than that, everything is as it used to be. The elegant tables, the artisan chairs – no, actually, the chairs have yielded to atrophy as well. The woven seats are tearing and breaking. Dust and dirt cover the tables and the floors are unwashed. The paint is falling off the walls in large flakes.

It's been three years and there doesn't seem to be a single soul here.

I go through the glass doors to the hall where once a celestial firmament was on display in the ceiling. Now I walk through a series of halls, all dark. Only when a bit of daylight seeps in from the winter garden can you see enough to get an idea of the decay.

There are shrieks coming from the bar farther in. I follow the sound and there they are – lumped together on a table, caged and abandoned. The parrots and the canaries seem to have taken the calamity surrounding them in their stride and can barely be persuaded to give me an arrogant look when I whistle towards their cages.

A sudden jolt tells me that I'm not alone, and I turn around. I can't see anyone. From the walls half-naked Indian dancers watch me. The paintings are as brilliant as they ever were; at least someone didn't skimp on the paint.

On the stairs a young girl stares at me. I stutter something about looking for Ristic.

'He's not here.'

'Do you know where I might find him?'

'Who are you?'

I tell her I'm a friend of his from Norway. She seems not to care and writes down the director's new mobile number on a piece of paper.

'It's Åsne; I'm back!'

'Ah,' replies a spent voice.

'Do you have time to meet me?'

'Sure.'

'When is a good time?'

'When is a good time for you?'

'Any time, really.'

'Just pick a time.'

'Today?'

'Yes, when would be OK for you?'

'Now.'

'Where?'

'Wherever.'

'Just give me a time and a place.'

'No, you pick the time and the place.'

'Well . . .'

'OK. I'll call you in an hour.'

Phone still in hand, I'm stunned. This is the same man who always knew what he wanted, where and when we were to meet, and always wondered if he could even consider squeezing me into his hectic schedule? This, then, is the spoils of losing – time. Now he can't even come up with a place to meet in his own hometown? Why not the theatre, as always? Perhaps it's too symbolic of his stunning decline?

I go for a stroll along the Danube while I wait for him to call me back. The rain turns into a deluge and I am forced to seek shelter in one of the restaurant boats along the shore. Families dressed up for Sunday lunch sit around the other tables and waiters bring a steady stream of steaming fish soup. The broth is made from whole fish – bone, skin and head included – and the enticing aroma of fresh herbs and garlic erupts from the terrines. Shots of *rakija* are hoisted and drained, to the enthralling sound of hushed conversations and bursts of laughter. I head for a table by the windows, with a view of the rain that peppers the Danube like shrapnel. The river devours the bombardment and flows by as silent as ever. The family at the next table orders *Karadjordje* steak – large cuts of pork rolled with white cheese, then dipped in flour and crumbs. The meat rolls are thick and almost half a metre long. The two kids attack their plates vigorously, smear mayonnaise over their cuts and eat. The parents smile and lean against each other.

The phone rings.

'Let's go to Mercator,' Ljubisa suggests. 'Where do I pick you up?'

The Mercator is a new, state-of-the-art shopping centre. I'm puzzled as to why Ljubisa wants to meet there, in the high castle of capitalism. I ask for the bill and the waiter makes a show of disappointment at my leaving without having tasted his fish soup.

Ljubisa bounds out of the car as soon as he sees me, and shoves me into the passenger seat. The car is an ashtray on wheels, cigarette butts and ash covering everything. Two teenagers greet me with indolent nods from the back seat.

'This is Biljana. She's a model. Now she wants to be an actress,' explains Ljubisa. 'And this is Darko, handyman at the theatre.'

He drives down into the underground garage, and parks. I follow Biljana's taut rear and Darko's broad shoulders up the escalator, which takes us into the middle of a large atrium.

'They've got the best cakes in town here,' Ljubisa assures me.

And the ugliest décor in Belgrade, I add to myself.

We sit down to have some cake while the kids go shopping. Ljubisa gives them some cash and asks them to pick up a bottle of Chanel Allure, gift-wrapped.

Ljubisa orders a Black Forest gateau, and I follow suit.

And then we're just sitting there, not quite knowing where to begin. 'She's worked as a model since she was thirteen,' offers Ljubisa. 'There was a big interview with her in the paper today – I've got it in the car. I'll show it to you. She may start working as an actress for me.'

'How are things going at the theatre,' I say, trying to get on track.

'Good. We perform and the audience keeps coming.'

Another kind of audience is milling all around us. Fortunately it doesn't cost anything to look at the expensive items for sale here. The faces of the families around us look haggard in the harsh lighting. I think of the idyllic

scene on the boat and wonder what it is that separates the
families who spend their Sundays window-shopping in a
mall from those who enjoy a long, leisurely meal by the
Danube. Some of the shoppers sit down, drink some coffee
and eat a bit of cake before they disappear back into the
labyrinth of the Mercator. Our conversation stutters.

'More coffee?'

'Yes, please.'

'You remember the coup a few years back?'

Ljubisa always used to refer to the mass demonstration
that brought Milosevic down as a coup, and he obviously
hasn't changed his tack.

'Since then tens of thousands – hundreds of thousands –
have lost their jobs, and their shot at any kind of a normal
life. Instead of building a democracy the "Democrats"
applied Stalinist methods to secure their grip on power.
Foreign powers, their taskmasters, demanded this.
Milosevic was squeezed out and now it's all reruns. The
current government is trying to dismantle the party that
succeeded Milosevic. They'll succeed soon enough and
then the same thing will happen to their administration.
It's the work of foreign powers . . . They only want
chaos . . .'

It's all reruns indeed.

'Do you really think these foreign taskmasters are that
involved these days?' I wonder. 'There are other wars to
engage in right now, aren't there?'

'They couldn't care less about our economy, our culture,
or the attempts at establishing a functioning society here.
They're only interested in the military aspects of this
region – they need a territory under siege,' Ljubisa says.
'We had a strong army, and that turned out to be the problem; our army was too strong, one of the strongest

anywhere. In the end NATO did what NATO had to do, and devastated the entire country. After all these years I've finally figured out what really happened.'

'Offer of the week . . . Serbia's best . . . for the very first time . . . Huge rebates . . . highest quality . . . direct from Germany . . . from Japan . . . Gifts . . . Three for the price of two . . .'

Ljubisa ignores the loudspeakers and continues his analysis in a hushed, imploring voice.

'First Slovenia was to leave Yugoslavia without use of force. Then they were to send arms to the war in Croatia and Bosnia, while at the same time draining Macedonia of all heavy weaponry, to avoid any bloodshed there. They kept the war out of Serbia and postponed the conflict in Kosovo. Remember, nothing happened in Kosovo in all those years that the war raged in Bosnia. The conflict in Kosovo didn't begin until it served NATO's purposes. And now they have achieved the thing they wanted all along: control of the former Yugoslav army.'

A nasty coughing fit interrupts Ljubisa's lecture. 'I don't have any lungs left,' he wheezes. 'Sometimes I have trouble breathing.'

He lights another cigarette before he continues.

'Our history is always tied to the battle for hegemony. During the Middle Ages we were part of the Byzantine Empire. But within the empire the Serbs maintained their language and culture. We built churches and monasteries. Then we were ruled by the Turks and thereafter the Austro-Hungarian Empire tried to conquer Serbia, but failed, just like Great Britain and France and Russia did. But when Tito died, everything changed: Russia supported the unification of Germany and the Germans became obsessed with the idea of creating a Franco-German state, so they could achieve another hegemony. It took the Americans a while to understand what was happening, and they were almost left out in the cold. But they woke up in time to plan the next phase, which was to push all of Eastern Europe into the EU and NATO, so they could control everything. Yugoslavia was not part of this plan, and now we've lost everything. Our borders are fictitious, the economy is crumbling, the culture is vanishing, corruption is everywhere and we are run from abroad. Look around — everything is falling apart.'

'What about you? Have you lost as well?'

Ljubisa purses his chapped lips and twists them into a grimace before he tries to form more words.

'This is not about my personal feelings. Individuals are not important.'

'But everything you fought for is lost?'

'It was all lost years ago. Before I even entered politics. I tried to influence the process, in order not to abandon the idea of Yugoslavia completely. I tried to counter this rampant form of vulgar capitalism that was flooding the country. But I couldn't stop it.'

Alluring offers keep coming over the loudspeakers. From the café we can see any number of store fronts. People sway from shop to shop. But loaded shopping trolleys are few and far between and not a lot of people seem to carry shopping bags.

'Once we produced enough to feed the entire population, but these days we're depending on imports. We had all the energy we needed and could export electricity. Now we depend on donations,' Ljubisa grimaces. 'Our resources are exhausted.'

But Ljubisa doesn't want to dwell on losses.

'I'm too experienced to expect anything. Once you

don't need anything you're free. Once you have no expectations you can't be unhappy.'

'Are you happy?'

'I need nothing,' Ljubisa says.

'There must have been times, moments, when you hoped for victory?'

'Not really.'

Ljubisa wants to light another cigarette, but his matchbox is empty. Instead of asking someone for a light, he puts the cigarette down. I wonder if people recognise him and associate him with the old regime.

'Are you still in touch with Milosevic, or Mira?'

'He calls me now and then, when he can afford to make phone calls. In The Hague they have to pay for everything themselves, you know. I can't call him; there are no lines to The Hague. He calls to consult on his defence. He's defending himself, without any barristers. But there are a lot of us here that help him recover evidence, even among the former opposition. They've realised that this is not about defending him personally, but that Serbia's honour is at stake. He is there to defend our country.'

Ljubisa forces a laugh.

'They still call him Mr President, you know.'

My eyebrows head north.

'They show him a lot of respect. The other inmates on his floor wash his cell. You know, the tribunal is hardly a hotel – everybody has to clean their own room. They cook together, too; help each other out. But he's not allowed any contact with Mira. They are refusing to let them meet. Her passport was confiscated when she applied for a visa for Holland. They say she's in Russia now. Maybe he knows where she is, maybe he doesn't.'

'What does he ask of you?'

Ljubisa looks around and says it's time to find somewhere else to talk. He directs my eyes to the man on the table next to us, engrossed in his newspaper. We move to a table farther into the café. The man keeps reading and doesn't bat an eyelid. Perhaps Ljubisa isn't as interesting as he believes he is.

'You never know. There are ears everywhere,' he says through pursed lips. 'Milosevic is fighting the good fight,' the director continues. 'He has recovered his fighting spirit and understands his historic mission. And that his struggle continues. He is, and always will be, a warrior. Nevertheless, I doubt he'll ever leave the prison alive.'

The model and the handyman return. We decide to go and have dinner at the theatre. Inside the mobile ashtray, Biljana hands me a Serbian gossip magazine in which she smiles at the camera in provocative poses.

'Wow,' I say. 'Gorgeous!'

There are no fancy cars outside the theatre these days. There are, in fact, no cars at all. Ljubisa has traded in the Audi. He enters the former sugar refinery with light, quick steps, checks on the birds, chats with them, even tries a rather forced warble. Like a man on the run, he gives instructions to some actors, leaves instructions with the kitchen staff and then disappears. I'm left sitting by myself in the frigid, cool hall. I light the fire and pull the chair closer. The flames cast a forgiving light on the ruins.

I consider Ristic's words about Milosevic never leaving the prison alive. Well, Milosevic was born in 1941 – most sentences he could receive would in effect be for life.

The longest sentence handed out by The Hague so far is forty-six years. It was given to Radislav Krstic, a former general in the Republika Srpska army, and the second-in-command in Ratko Mladic's Drina Corps in Bosnia. Krstic was the first to be sentenced for genocide by The Hague. More than seven thousand Muslim men and boys were executed in the UN-protected enclave of Srebrenica between 13 and 19 July 1995. In April 2004 his sentence was reduced to thirty-nine years, as he was found to have 'aided and abetted' genocide rather than having been a 'co-perpetrator'.

Slobodan Milosevic is the only head of state to be charged in an international court with crimes committed in office. He is charged with genocide in Bosnia and crimes against humanity during the wars in Croatia and Kosovo.

Behind a glass wall in the courtroom Milosevic makes political speeches. He is trying to prove that foreign powers were behind the Yugoslav wars. His theories dovetail nicely with Ljubisa's.

'What chance does his case have?' I ask Ljubisa when he finally joins me by the fireplace.

'We will see. We will see. He's not guilty of the things he's charged with. It's a political trial.'

'So who is responsible for the deaths of two hundred thousand people during the war in Bosnia?'

'It's sweet of you to ask. What do you want me to say? That the Serbs are guilty, that Milosevic is guilty, that we're all murderers?'

'But what do you think?'

'Things went wrong.'

'All by themselves?'

'The murderers are guilty. Anyone who killed others is guilty. But our President has been defamed as a butcher from the very beginning, without having killed a single person!'

'But shouldn't Milosevic bear some of the responsibility

for the policies that led to the deaths of thousands of people?'

'Look, Åsne – I find it frightfully boring to discuss these matters on your level. You know who broke away from this country, you know who trained people to destroy what was left, you know where the money came from, you know who expelled four hundred thousand Serbs from Croatia, you know who expelled two hundred thousand Serbs from Kosovo. And still you ask these kinds of questions! This is 2004, my dear – your questions belong to 1993, or even 1992! Following this line of thinking is simply disgraceful today, after all that has happened. Again and again and again you do this. What are you saying? What's your point? This trial is a sham to justify the misdeeds and manipulations of outside powers, so they can get away with it. No one in The Hague is interested in the truth. Forget it. All they want are definite statements that they can turn around to feed their propaganda machine, and keep brainwashing people. They could hand Milosevic over to The Hague, but they can't deliver the emotions of an entire people. Come on, you're Norwegian – you know that your country was betrayed, it's part of your history, you know full well what patriotism means. This trial – who really believes a single word of it?'

'Most nations recognise the tribunal in The Hague.'

'Good for them.'

Ljubisa draws breath.

'So you regard Milosevic as the victim here?'

'Milosevic has become a symbol to every side. I know him as a human being. He's neither a hero nor a victim. He's not a butcher. He's not . . . anything like what they say about him.'

'Why do you like him?'

'Did I say that I like him? This is not a matter of likes or dislikes. We discuss politics. Historical events. I was never a member of his party. I had my own ideas. I got involved in politics because there was a need for *my* platform. I had everything this country needed – an anti-nationalist, Yugoslav, leftist platform. It was the perfect platform for those who wanted to end the war without turning our backs on our nation's history and traditions – Yugoslav ideas, leftist ideas; the core of this nation's history. There was a time when I thought it was possible to help, but now I see that it was useless. It's too late now. Too late. Nothing is possible any more.'

'This makes you sad?'

'Yes – it's terrible. And it could get worse. But it is what it is. Things have to hit bottom before they can go up again. Look at Bosnia – it's a bizarre situation. Just a week ago an orthodox priest and his son were beaten senseless by the international forces. SFOR, the UN's Stabilisation Force, claimed that they were hiding Karadzic and wired the doors of the monastery with explosives. The priest and his son are now in a coma, but SFOR never found a trace of Karadzic. These are the methods applied to the 'murderous Serbs'. But through all these years we never killed anyone, we never complained about this international terrorist occupation. The Serbs are misunderstood – we're nowhere near as brave, violent or fierce as people seem to think. Without a word of protest we merely lived peacefully in our homes. And what's the end result of all this? What really happened? Where did this alleged ethnic cleansing actually take place?'

'What do you think?' I ask. 'Where did this happen? Who was ethnically cleansed?'

Ljubisa glares at me, his eyes cutting like knives. His

drooping moustache trembles over the thin, drawn lip. 'Where was there ethnic cleansing? Tell me!' he demands.

'Well, there's Srebrenica . . .'

I'm interrupted by a groan of disdain.

'Srebrenica has nothing to do with ethnic cleansing! A certain number of people were killed. One can argue about who did it, and to whom it was done. The why and how of it. It was mass murder, not ethnic cleansing.'

'But only Muslims were killed.'

'That has nothing to do with anything. Serbs had been killed there previously. Srebrenica was mass murder. And we all know who participated. They all have Schengen visas in their passports, and move about freely. Everyone knows who they are, the tribunal in The Hague knows their names, but nobody arrests them, because they want to pin the blame on Milosevic. So I ask you again: what is the end result of the ethnic cleansing in Yugoslavia?'

Ljubisa's entire body trembles as he leans towards me and asks: 'How large is the population of Croatia?'

'Uh, about four million.'

'How many of them are Serbs – before the war, and after?'

'Well . . .'

Ljubisa answers his own question: 'We're down to a few per cent. Before the war it was twenty. Talk about ethnic cleansing. [In 1991 Serbs made up 12.1 per cent of the population in Croatia. By 2001 a third of them remained.] What about the statistics for Kosovo, before and after the war? Tell me that this is not ethnic cleansing?'

'So you're saying that it is the Serbs who are subjected to ethnic cleansing?'

'Most definitely. The Serbs have been ethnically cleansed. And they are the only ones. This is acceptable?'

'But . . .'

'The Hague certainly thinks so, as does your government – all governments, it seems. How come? Obviously there are two kinds of ethnic cleansing – one that's unacceptable and one that is acceptable.'

The director raises his hand like a master of ceremonies introducing the next performance. The birds suddenly erupt into some communal frenzy. The cages emit a deafening cacophony, only to be drowned out by Ljubisa's basso voice.

'Throughout these wars some eighty thousand Kosovo Albanians have lived in Belgrade. They have their bakeries, their mosque, their lives. Just like they always did. Nobody made any trouble for the Albanians in Belgrade. But they made it incredibly difficult for Serbs in Kosovo. And the Albanians in Kosovo enjoyed full rights under Milosevic. I know: I was born there. Still, the Albanian killed postmen, forest rangers, policemen. And we were just supposed to sit idly by? There's no difference between what they did on 17 March of this year, and what they did ten, fifteen years ago. They were terrorists then, they are terrorists now. In the West you call them freedom fighters. But maybe the West will live to regret its support of these people. Kosovo Albanians have become an increasingly important arm of al Qaeda. They will be the new enemy. They've already begun killing Americans in Kosovo. And remember, Serbs never killed Americans, even though we're arch-enemies. We haven't killed a single German since the end of the Second World War, or any Frenchmen or Brits. But now American soldiers are getting killed in Kosovo. Why aren't you writing a book about that?'

'Well . . .'

'Well, why not?'

'Oh, there are so many books.'

'Indeed – too many. Far too many. This is not the time for books. There is a job to finish. And you and your government are in on it!'

That's about all I can take of Ljubisa. I say my goodbyes. Coldly, he tells me I'm always welcome. He turns away, takes a few steps and says, more forgivingly, 'In a few days Danka comes back.'

'I'll try to make it,' I say, and step out into the winter garden to wait for my cab. The glass roof is getting hammered and the buckets are filling up. Outside the rain is devoured by the darkness. I turn round and look in at Ljubisa and his choir of birds. He ambles over to the computer in the empty bar. He sits down, hits a key and starts playing solitaire. A cigarette dangles from his lips as he sinks into the bar stool and plays the game. My taxi arrives.

The War Criminal's Wife

'If we have to fight, then by God, we will fight.'

Slobodan Milosevic, 1991

'Did you know that he used to make his prisoners bite each other's balls off?' asks Danijela. 'He was one of the worst guards – a sadist who tortured and killed.'

As usual, Danijela's done a bit of research. She is a journalist on *Jefimija*, a kind of Serbian *Cosmopolitan*, where she covers fashion and trends. On top of this she speaks fluent English, and helps me out whenever she has time.

She picks me up outside my house, as usual a bit late, elegant as always. Today it's beige slacks, a white top and white tennis shoes. Danijela is among the blessed few who can look worldly with a bare midriff. 'But you should call Zoran instead – he knows all about him,' she says. We chat about something else for a while and don't give war criminals a second thought until we've reached Pancevo, half an hour's drive from Belgrade.

Dusan Tadic – arrested in Munich, 12 February 1994 – sentenced to twenty years in jail in The Hague on 7 May 1997 for war crimes and crimes against humanity.

Tadic was the first prisoner to be sentenced by an international war crimes tribunal since the Nuremberg Trials after the Second World War. He was convicted for having participated in the Serbs' ethnic cleansing of Muslims and Croats, and for having participated in torture, rape and murder in villages and prison camps in north-western Bosnia.

We are here to visit Tadic's wife. After circling the block a couple of times we spot the alley we're looking for and walk along a dirty hallway. On a door on the third floor a sign reads 'Tadic' in Cyrillic letters.

Mira Tadic greets us with a detached look. She lets us in but does not try to hide her feelings about journalists. We're deceitful carriers of false rumours. I try to stutter some sort of answer to this, while Danijela asks for permission to smoke. We sit down around the kitchen table in the sparsely decorated flat. Not even Danijela is able to lift the oppressive mood.

'I don't generally receive journalists. You're the ones who cooked up this whole pack of lies,' Mira continues, and studies me sullenly. 'But you're here to get my side of the story, aren't you?' Her questions are rhetorical in nature. I look around the living room, full of colourful, Dalí-like paintings. Most of them bear the signatures 'Tadic – 96' and 'Tadic – 97'. 'He paints them in The Hague,' Mira tells us. 'Dusan always dreamed of becoming an artist. But in Bosnia he never found the time. Now he does. Some friends tried to arrange an exhibition in The

Hague, but the authorities refused to allow a war criminal's paintings to be displayed. But he will do the cover of the memoirs of a fellow inmate from Rwanda,' she tells us.

Several of the paintings are obviously symbolic. One is of hands in handcuffs. The handcuffs are about to be cut by a sword decorated with the four 'S's: '*Samo sloga Srbina spasava*'. Also on the wall are photographs of the family from a time when they still had reasons to smile. A couple of times a week Mira gets the long-awaited phone call. She talks for a couple of minutes, then hangs up and goes about the rest of her day. Later she shares these brief minutes with her daughters, eleven-year-old Aleksandra and twenty-year-old Valentina. 'We talk about what we're doing, what our plans are, how things are in school and when we can come for our next visit. Dusan is so sensitive, he can always hear when something's weighing on Aleksandra or when Valentina has boyfriend troubles.' Mira's voice is full of emotion for the man she fell in love with when she was fifteen and he a year older. 'It was winter, he had snow crystals in his hair, and I'd never seen a more handsome boy. And I've never looked at another man since.'

Mira visits her husband twice a year. Once by herself, the other time with her daughters. The Yugoslav Red Cross pay the travel expenses. Set routines shape the brief days she's there. At nine in the morning she is let into the prison, searched and scanned by the metal detector. The guards check her shoes, her pockets, her mouth. She's not allowed to bring anything into the visiting room, except for cigarettes, also subject to a meticulous search. Sending prisoners gifts is allowed, except for food. 'I suppose they're worried that we'll poison our husbands and they'll be deprived of their scapegoats,' she spits. 'Dusan misses my home-made cheese, and smoked meat. The food in The Hague keeps for ever but tastes of nothing. I've had lunch there,' Mira sighs, and makes a face. 'Not that Dusan eats much these days: he's worried about gaining weight. He prefers fruits and yogurt. He's an athlete, so he works out several hours a day: runs on a treadmill and lifts weights. Recently they let him have a boxing pad as well. He does karate and yoga as well; he says the yoga has kept him from losing his mind. He is so strong. They'll never be able to break him.'

Once Mira has passed through security Dusan waits for her in the visiting room. They can stay there until five o'clock, when the guards take her away, and Dusan returns to his cell and waits for Mira to return the next morning at nine. Their meetings always take place in the same sterile room, with no windows, a table and a few folding chairs. 'We haven't seen the sky together for six years now,' Mira says, fixing her eyes on me. She grits her teeth and leads with her chin. 'Dusan usually brings along his cassette deck from his cell and we play some Bosnian music, just so we can feel at home. The music either makes us happy or depressed – it always reminds us of our life the way it used to be. Aleksandra always brings her favourite tapes along, so she can play them for her father. When we have to leave, Dusan always says, "May our next meeting not be in Holland." It's so sad – because our next meeting is always in Holland.'

Dusan Tadic was arrested in Germany early in 1994 while the war still raged in Bosnia. The previous autumn the Tadics had left for Germany. It was a two-stage operation. Mira and the children arrived first, in August after family associates helped them to get a visa. Dusan followed in November, having obtained a short-term invitation as part of a karate delegation. He got a job at his brother's café in Munich. Mira had always dreamed of living in the West, and finally they had managed to get there. When she got a job as a nurse after a few months, everything seemed to have turned out all right. 'I was so happy that finally we had found a foothold in another country.'

For a second a wave of pain flickers across her square face like a shadow. Then she gathers herself and recovers the harsh, sullen expression. 'The day after we celebrated my new job Dusan went to work as usual. He never came home. Just after he showed up at the café the German police took him into custody. Several hours later the police showed up to tell me that he was incarcerated. I didn't understand at all – I was sure it was all some kind of mis-understanding. That evening I watched his arrest on the news. It was unreal.'

Mira had to leave Germany. She first moved into a house abandoned by its Muslim residents in Prijedor – living among another family's bedlinen, china, furniture. At the time, she bitterly complained that refugees from Kozarac lived a better life in Germany while she was stuck in Bosnia. By the end of 1997, after the verdict, she moved with her daughters to Pancevo in Serbia, an industrial town along the Danube. The Serbian lawyer who took over Dusan's appeal against his twenty-year sentence bought them a small flat.

Mira checks her watch – it's time for her night shift. She's a surgery nurse, specialising in children. Her monthly salary comes to thirty-five pounds. We drive her to the hospital and her twelve-hour shift. Usually she takes the bus, which adds another ninety minutes – each way. Mira asks us to drop her off a little way from the gates. 'I don't want anyone to wonder why I came in a car,' she says, and makes us promise not to talk to anyone at the hospital. She hasn't told her colleagues which Mrs Tadic she is.

We agree to meet again the next day. Danijela, in gleaming Capri pants and a grey blouse, is two hours late. 'There's just no petrol to be found in this city,' she explains by way of an apology. We end up getting some on the black market, from a chap on a street corner. When we finally arrive in Pancevo we run into Aleksandra, the eleven-year-old, in the shop next to the block of flats. She overslept this morning and didn't want to go to school. 'I didn't hear the alarm clock and there was no one to wake me up,' she explains. Now she's on her way to a friend's house to copy down everything that happened in class. But she takes us home first.

This time we are greeted in a different way. A barefoot Mira meets us in a blue dress. 'Let's have some coffee,' she warbles. 'I put off my morning coffee until you got here.' There's nothing Aleksandra would rather do than sit on the sofa and listen to her mother talk about her dad, but Mira is firm. 'First homework, and then you're off to ballet – now get going,' she commands. She explains to us that she has to be firm, so the kids won't suffer so much from not having a father.

'It's hard on the girls,' she says after Aleksandra has shuffled off. 'Sometimes I think it would have been easier for them if Dusan were dead. Now they have a dad, but they only see him a few days each year, from nine to five,' she says quietly. 'Valentina asked me the other day: "What about when I marry? When is Daddy going to meet my boyfriend?"' I flash back to the sign on the door: 'Tadic'. Do the neighbours think of her as the war criminal's wife? 'They don't know,' Mira says. 'Why should I tell them anything? I don't want their pity – or glances.

The ones who need to know do.' Aleksandra hasn't told any of her friends that her father is in prison in The Hague. 'Daddy lives in Holland,' she says whenever someone asks about him.

The Tadic family used to live in Kozarac, a small Bosnian town with a bloody past. During the Second World War Serbian men and boys were taken to a field and killed. Only a few got away, and one of them became Mira's father. Not that many Serbs ever lived in Kozarac; it had always been a town with a great majority of Muslims, and only a few Serb families. Ninety-five per cent of the town's population of 27,000 were Muslims before the war in Bosnia. Now Kozarac is in the Republika Srpska, the Serb part of Bosnia.

Mira and Dusan used to have a good relationship with their Muslim neighbours until the war broke out. Dusan ran a café and was a known athlete with a black belt in karate. 'When things began to get tense, in 1990, our family received threatening notes telling us to leave Kozarac. Everything changed in 1990. Suddenly friends became enemies.'

The couple joined Radovan Karadzic's Serbian Democratic Party, the SDS. 'It was the only party that could protect us Serbs,' Mira explains, and gushes about Karadzic. 'His ideas were good and he did a lot of good things, but then he lost control. Once the war came everything was just chaos. Brother killed brother, neighbour killed neighbour.'

Dusan became increasingly involved in the SDS. The neighbours began turning their faces away when they ran into Mira. Dusan was convinced that the populations needed to be moved so that each village was ethnically pure. And he maintained that Kozarac should be a pure

Serbian town. The threats increased. In May 1992 the Tadic family left Kozarac for the Serbian town of Banja Luka. Dusan reported for duty with the local police, joining the traffic division.

That month Serbian forces began to launch attacks on Muslim and Croatian towns. Dusan Tadic took part in raids on the villages around Prijedor in Bosnia, including Kozarac. Throughout this area Muslims and Croats were forced from their homes and taken prisoner. Thousands were transported to three camps: Omarska, Keraterm and Trnopolje. They were tied together and marched in a line, if not killed on the spot. Kozarac was cleansed of its Muslims – every single Muslim home was first looted, then burned to the ground, until only Serbian houses were left. Dusan Tadic was convicted of taking part in this ethnic cleansing of Kozarac. He was also convicted of killing and torturing his Muslim neighbours in the Omarska concentration camp. (The indictment can be found at www.un.org/icty).

The Hague Tribunal described conditions in the camp as brutal. The prisoners were crammed together and there were no hygienic facilities. They were given pitiful rations once a day and had three minutes to eat them. There was no change of clothes, no bed linen, no medical treatment. The camp consisted of three buildings: the administrative building, where the interrogations were conducted; the white house, where the torture took place; and the red house – prisoners who were taken there rarely came out alive. Torture was common and the guards used wooden sticks, metal rods, electrical cables, rifles and knives. Both men and women were raped and sexually abused.

'He was convicted of having been a guard in the

Omarska camp, but he only worked in the traffic division, and the only thing he ever did was to escort prisoners inside,' Mira swears. 'He wasn't even anywhere near where the crimes he was convicted of took place. The Hague Tribunal listened only to the Muslims, and a lot of them were paid to lie. Whatever the Serbian witnesses testified to was never considered. I sat there myself and listened to the lies of our Muslim neighbours.' Mira tells of one witness: 'That man is psychologically unstable, he's had sex with animals, he stole, he was retarded. How could a court believe such a man?' she wants to know. 'They listened to such terrible lies.' Her voice cracks. 'Dusan is innocent – he's serving a sentence for other people's crimes. He couldn't possibly have done any of the things he's convicted of. Dusan is kindness itself, he's charming, handsome and has the soul of an artist. Everyone who meets him falls for him – he could have any woman he wanted. It just doesn't add up – why would he ever rape Muslim women, when he could have any Serbian woman he wanted?' Mira asks. I just nod, listen and take notes. I'm not the Hague Tribunal – or one of the women who testified against Dusan Tadic.

Mira maintains that the court didn't have a single piece of evidence against her husband and that the whole thing is a conspiracy, that they needed to find someone guilty so that the real criminals could go free. 'None of the real leaders has been caught.' Tadic was represented in court by an international team of lawyers, two British, one Dutch. This team conducted the investigations on which the court case was based and made several trips to Bosnia. Milan Vujin, the Serbian lawyer, worked with them at the outset, but after he handed a list of defence witness names to the police in

Prijedor, they concluded that he should not be involved with the investigation and Vujin was removed. However, about a week before the verdict was due to be delivered, Tadic sacked his international team and replaced it with Milan Vujin.

A great deal of money could be made from representing clients at the Hague. The daily fee for counsel was more than a month's salary in Belgrade. The agreement was that if Vujin could take over the defence and launch an appeal, then Vujin would use some of the money he made to buy Mira a house in Serbia.

During the appeal, the Serbian lawyer pursued a new line of defence which the Tadic family had always favoured (but the international team had investigated and rejected as implausible) – that the crimes had been committed by a doppelgänger of Dusan. Charges were later brought against Vujin for his general conduct. Some of the witnesses were allegedly paid to give false testimony, or given signals in court to indicate how they should respond to questions. Vujin was convicted of contempt of court and of having hindered the work of the tribunal, for which he was disbarred from future tribunal cases and fined.

'They'll probably never overturn his conviction,' thinks Mira. 'There's so much money and prestige behind it, and the Hague Tribunal would never admit to having made any mistakes. But it's just absurd that the lawyer can be convicted without that having any effect whatsoever on Dusan's sentence,' she sighs, ignoring the fact that it was Dusan himself who had sacked the international team and replaced it with Vujin.

It's now late afternoon, and we sit there deflated and look at each other gravely. 'I need some air,' Danijela says. 'Let's go for a walk, shall we?'

We walk to a nearby park. It's sparse and unkempt, and

we walk under the trees in silence. Flowers and weeds battle for supremacy and the silence becomes increasingly oppressive. It's as if we've brought the horrors of war along with us. Even under the burning sun it seems dark. The sun can't reach where we are and we don't see the flowers.

Mira breaks the silence by telling us of the Bosnian town she grew up in. They kept cows, sheep and goats. 'Before the war I always used to take my girls there every summer holiday. Now I haven't been there in years,' she sighs. 'But my parents still live there.

'Are you hungry?' She suddenly asks.

'Yes!' shouts Danijela.

Mira wants to cook us a real Bosnian meal: cheese pie, green onion and sour cream salad and pickles. While Mira prepares the meal the conversation takes a different turn, as if none of us wants to get back to the war, or The Hague. Danijela and I lounge on the sofa with the photo albums, while Mira keeps up a running commentary from the kitchen. There are pictures from her childhood, wedding shots, photos from when the kids were small and several series of Dusan practising karate in Kozarac, striking poses for the camera.

Danijela wonders about a picture of Mira and Dusan in which Mira is wearing a long, elegant evening dress. 'It's from our graduation party. I still have the dress,' Mira says. She goes into the bedroom and comes back with a silk dress. 'Isn't it funny? – when we left Kozarac I brought this dress along, even though I hadn't worn it in almost twenty years. I took this, the baby blankets from the girls and the photo albums. Can't remember anything else. It's always been with me – this dress has survived all these wars,' she smiles.

The phone rings. Mira disappears for a couple of minutes. 'That was Dusan. He sends his regards,' a happy Mira tells us. 'It's a good thing you are here; I've just reminded Dusan of how we fell in love, the graduation ball, the black dress and our wedding. It's so rare that we remember the past,' Mira says. 'He said he was fine and wondered when my next visit would be. He'd heard that there is a bus you can take to Amsterdam now, which is cheaper than flying, so maybe I can visit outside of the Red Cross trips.' Surviving on a nurse's salary is hard.

'I worry about what I am going to put on the table every single day. Aleksandra has told me three times now that the strawberries have arrived at the market, as if I haven't seen them myself. But I just can't afford it.'

Over dinner Mira opens up and even reveals to us the secret of how to find and keep the perfect man. 'Find one that's a little bit uglier than you are, because then he'll never leave you,' she assures us.

'Great,' a happy Danijela blurts out. 'Zoran is definitely uglier than I am.'

'Also, he should have a little bit of money and be kind and tender,' Mira instructs us. 'That's what I always tell my daughter.'

From then on our conversation is confined to men and love. At the end Danijela tells our fortunes from the coffee grounds. We leave when Mira's favourite soap opera comes on. 'It's incredibly exciting!' she says of the Latin American series, and follows us out into the run-down hallway. 'Come back whenever you like,' she shouts as we go down the stairs.

'Did you see how beautiful she was when she was young?' Danijela asks as soon as we're outside. 'She looked totally hot in some of those pictures. And I wouldn't mind that black dress; a few minor alterations and it would've fitted me like a glove.' Clearly she's back in her own world. Mira Tadic is left in hers, or in whatever escape the dreamy world of soaps might offer her. I glance up at her window and can see the ghostly light of the television through the curtains. Behind them sits an ordinary, slightly overweight woman of forty, in a blue cotton dress, whose husband is in Holland.

In September 2000 Dusan Tadic is transferred to a prison in Germany to serve the remainder of his sentence. The visiting rules get more restrictive. He can phone home once a month and Mira is allowed to visit him once a month, but only for an hour. 'One hour,' she repeats. 'It's like reliving his arrest all over. I'd got used to talking to him several times a week.'

Dusan has been in the new prison for five months when I meet Mira again. She has only visited him once. 'I can't afford to travel back and forth to Munich for just one hour,' she sighs. 'But I'm thinking of going this spring. Dusan is trying to find out if we can get credit for the hours we haven't used, so that I could be there for five or six hours next time.'

Mira pours coffee and counts hours and months. Dusan has fourteen years left of his sentence. On the table waits a freshly baked Bosnian cake. Valentina and a cousin sit on the sofa, watching TV. Mira looks in now and then, but fortunately it's not her favourite soap she's missing owing to my and Danijela's visit.

'So now we write letters to each other,' she says, and goes to get the last letter she received. She begins to read out loud about how much Dusan misses her and the kids, what they talked about when they last spoke and what he was thinking when they did, or about the other inmates, about his workouts. 'He writes so well,' Mira says. 'He's begun writing his memoirs now. He let me read some of it the last time I visited. It's very poetic; everything he touches becomes romantic. He lives his life by romantic ideals. It's as if he's trying to write *War and Peace* all over again,' she laughs. 'To me some of his writing is sometimes a wee bit florid – for instance, he went on and on, for several pages, and with great passion, about these birds he saw through some trees. In the middle of a war!'

Dusan enclosed a picture of himself in his last letter. He's sitting with his hands in his lap, wearing a striped T-shirt and a seductive look. 'I'm sending you this to remind you that I still look pretty good,' he writes in his letter, and on the back of the picture it reads: 'I will always love you, Mira. Your only one, Dusan.'

Mira lingers over her memories of the last talk with us: the dress she showed us, what we said about the various photos. Obviously reminiscing is a rare indulgence for her. She tells us she never wants to return to Bosnia, because things will never be the same there. She wants to wait for Dusan in Serbia and then start a new life with him here.

'Poor Dusan,' she says, and tells us how much he hates the new prison. In The Hague he made friends with the other inmates. He and a condemned war criminal from Croatia even agreed to go into business together when their terms were up. But in the Munich prison Dusan spends most of his time by himself. 'He's got some problems with the Muslim inmates and has had to change cells several times. They threaten him, the Albanians too, and they keep the other prisoners away from him. They lie about what he's done, so nobody else wants anything to do with him. But he's stopped telling me about all this in his letters. All it did was make me have nightmares about Muslims again,' she says and closes her lips tightly.

'To think, he's doing time with ordinary criminals!'

She pierces us with her glare.

'Ordinary criminals: killers and rapists,' she repeats, to ensure that we fully appreciate the injustice of this predicament. 'Not with other political prisoners.'

'You consider Dusan a political prisoner?' I ask.

'What else?'

Mira's mouth is agape; then she rushes to explain why her husband is a political prisoner, and even a prisoner of conscience. 'The tribunal in The Hague is set up to punish us Serbs, to blame us for the war. It's funded by American money and does America's bidding. Why is it only Serbs that are jailed there – there's plenty of room for Croats and Muslims and Americans, too,' she says. 'A war is like a marriage – it takes two to start a fight.'

During the spring of 2001 a debate about war crimes and guilt takes place in Serbia. For the very first time the state media asks critical questions about Serbian warfare in Croatia, Bosnia and Kosovo; documentaries and debates are aired. Mira won't hear of any debates. When I ask her what she thinks should be done with Milosevic, she responds that we should leave him alone. 'I don't want to speak ill of our leader. We should stand by our leaders when everyone else gangs up on us. Other people defend their leaders from attacks – we Serbs spit on them.'

Mira doesn't believe in confronting the past. 'It would be much better if we just let it be and started all over again. If we begin to talk about who is to blame we won't be done for another hundred years, and the world will have passed us by.'

Mira is tired of all this talk about governments. She's redecorated her living room since our last visit, and moved the TV and the sofa to the opposite side of the room. She asks if we agree that this is much better. 'It certainly is,' we say, as is expected of us.

On TV, Mira's soap has gone and a talk show with music and chitchat drones on in the background. Mira isn't at all happy with the change in programming. 'They're forcing these Croatian and Muslim pop stars down our throats. It's all well and good that they come here, but why aren't any Serbs going to them? With all these singers from Croatia and Bosnia, there's barely any room left for Serbian artists on TV any more,' she points out indignantly. 'But I do have a very pleasant Muslim colleague at work, from central Bosnia,' she suddenly adds.

This reminds her it's time for her shift. Valentina is on her way to her evening class. She's in the first year of law school. 'It was an obvious choice after all the injustice done to Dusan,' says her proud mother. 'Valentina will fight for justice.' Aleksandra stays at home to do her homework and then has to put herself to bed.

We drive Mira to the hospital. In the car she talks about how hard it is to raise the kids alone. 'Aleksandra came home from school crying the other day. She'd argued with a friend who shouted, "May your father never get out of jail!" Aleksandra, who thought that nobody knew about her dad, was crushed. I would not wish this on anyone – being a poor, single mother or having a dad in jail.'

We've reached the hospital. Just like the last time, she wants to be dropped off a little way from the gates. These last metres she wants to walk alone, so she can throw off 'Mira – the war criminal's wife' and become 'Mira – the nurse'.

'Do you have champagne?'

'No, but we have whisky.'

Belgrade is showing its saddest side, and even the street-lights look like they'd rather be anywhere else than here, casting a mute glow on to the muddy puddles we splash through. People lurch along, heading home. The wipers keep up a monotonous beat on the windscreen, while a suffering voice croaks over the airwaves. Tormented and wretched, the post-Yugoslav balladeer seems on the verge of utter despair. Plum brandy can be bought on every corner here, but the nectar of the gods is conspicuously absent from the shelves.

'And what is it again that we are celebrating?' Danijela asks. 'That her husband is still in jail? That her nurse's wages aren't enough to feed her family? That her daughter never made it through law school?'

'That's exactly why we need something to lighten the mood,' I argue in the dark streets. The rain is coming down sideways. Even this far south, April is the cruellest month.

Finally we spot a store with a pair of faded bottles of Yellow Widow in the window. By the look of it they've spent a few years there – but it's still champagne.

'Great gift.'

Danijela looks as if she's serious. I've just told her that I've brought along a basket of soaps, creams, salves, bath oils and perfumed candles for an aroma bath.

As soon as the bottles have been wrapped in brown paper and stuffed in a crêpe-paper bag, we hit the road. Danijela searches for a less depressing radio station and finds U2. Great driving music. Suddenly we feel like driving all night, just keeping going and not stopping until we're far, far away from here. It's as if we're dreading our visit to Mira and would rather go anywhere else but there. But we leave the main road at Pancevo, like we're supposed to, and find her street, her flat, her door. The brass plate with the Cyrillic letters is the same. We ring the bell.

The same appraising stare.

'It's been a long time,' Mira says. Her eyes are apprehensive, reserved.

'Three years,' I tell her.

'Right. Well – would you like some coffee?'

'We've brought some champagne,' suggests Danijela.

'I don't know anything about champagne,' Mira counters. 'But thank you anyway. You shouldn't have.'

'We should celebrate our reunion first, and then we can have coffee later,' Danijela proposes. Mira goes off to find glasses. I open the bottle, with a small *pff*, and fill the glasses Mira returns with.

'You have proper champagne flutes!' exclaims Danijela.

'Cheers!'

'Cheers.'

We knock glasses and look at each other. One suspiciously, one curiously and one straining to be cheerful. First Mira wants to hear what we've been up to since our last visit. Danijela has been out of work for a while but just started working for the Red Cross. It's over between her and Zoran; he's about to get married to some actress. I talk about my vagabond life around the world. Danijela and I drink fast. Danijela fills our glasses again and tops up Mira's. She's barely touched her champagne.

Aleksandra, now fifteen, sits on the sofa. The bouncy little girl has turned into an awkward teenager with bad skin. She sits stiffly and stares at MTV, where Britney Spears slithers across the screen. Britney is a sexy stewardess on a plane, about to seduce a blond Beckham lookalike in the toilet. After which she returns to singing and serving drinks.

'Your turn to talk,' says Danijela.

Mira fixes her gaze first on Danijela, then me. She's put

make-up on and had her hair done. She's wearing a pretty, colourful sweater and black trousers. She appears to have prepared herself for this visit and already decided which version of herself she wishes to display.

'I take on as many night shifts as I can to try to make ends meet. I make sure that Aleksandra and Valentina have decent clothes. I try to feed them proper food without spending too much money. I'm all right.'

Her words are designed to emphasise that she's not one to complain, not one to buckle under pressure.

'How is Dusan doing?'

'Fine,' she says. 'He's on kitchen duty now. He likes it. It helps kill the time. He works out, eats healthily, counts the days. But that's all. He's stopped writing. Suddenly he ran out of words, so I suppose there won't be another *War and Peace* after all. He can't afford to call me any more.'

'What about letters?'

'What about them?'

Mira glares at me as if to say, What could you know about letters?

'Do you get a lot of letters?' I try.

'Not so much any more.'

'Do you write yourself?'

'I don't like to write.'

'Why not?'

'Åsne, I'm sure you enjoy writing, since you write books and all that. But I don't like it. That's just the way it is.'

'But his letters – do you read them often?'

Mira holds my eyes for a long time. Her expression grows into one of disdain. 'Is this where you want me to say that I read his letters five times a day, and that my tears fall on them and dissolve the words? That I've read them to pieces? Would that work for your book?'

The champagne bubbles have all but died. Nobody touches their glass.

'I'm not a fifteen-year-old girl any more. Everyday life takes a lot out of me. I read the letters and put them away. How much do you think he can really tell me about prison? I can tell you one thing: I haven't lived since Dusan was arrested. Sometimes I have nightmares. I dream that I'm being chased. Or I just lie awake and think.'

'What are you thinking about?'

'What do you think?'

'Dusan?'

'I've slept alone for ten years now. That's what I think about.'

Kosovo Serbs – No Admittance

'Serbia without Kosovo is like a human being without soul.'

Verica, Serbian refugee from Kosovo

'The men drink and smoke, the women weep and smoke.'

Verica crushes a cockroach under her foot and lights another cigarette. 'Nobody needs us here, nobody wants us here.'

It's early morning and Verica is already waiting for the day to be over. She's got all the time in the world. For almost a year now she's been waiting to be returned to Kosovo. 'Kosovo is Serbian; we will return there,' she says. 'If I didn't think we were going back I might just as well kill myself.'

She stares into thin air. Her husband Radovan pours the first *rakija* of the day. Breakfast is still some way off. 'If we have to stay here for another year I'll go crazy,' he says.

Verica and Radovan are Serbian refugees from Kosovo.

They left in a hurry when the Serbian forces abandoned the area on 11 June 1999, with the KLA in hot pursuit. 'We had to flee or die. The only things we could take were some clothes and our photo albums. We had a few minutes to pack. The Serbian leadership in town said we could return in a few weeks, so we locked the doors and left. Now we've been here for almost a whole year,' says Verica.

She and her husband live with two of their daughters, Aleksandra, three, and Dragana, seven, in a room at a refugee centre in Adrani, in southern Serbia. Their two elder daughters live in a hospice in Nis, a couple of hours away. The family's room contains a bed, where all four of them sleep, a table, some chairs and, in a corner, a chaotic pile of cardboard boxes and plastic bags. They have no cupboards and there's nothing on the walls except for a circular mirror with a red plastic frame and a calendar with an image of a holy man. St Nikola keeps his blessed watch on the family as they sleep, eat and live. 'This is no kind of life,' Verica mutters, and shows me how a typical day goes by. 'Like this,' she says, folding her arms across her chest and lighting another cigarette.

Her family escaped the Albanian avengers, but coming to Serbia was a bit of a shock. For the first few months they were put up in a school, sharing a classroom with thirty other people. In the autumn they were sent to the centre in Adrani, outside Kraljevo. Kraljevo is the first town you get to once you cross the Kosovo border, and in June 1999, over a few days, some thirty thousand Serbian refugees arrived there. Already Kraljevo was home to twenty thousand Kosovo Serbs who had settled there over the past decade, along with several thousand other refugees from Bosnia and Croatia. Originally the town had about sixty thousand inhabitants; in short order this number doubled.

Verica dreads going outside and prefers to stay in her room with her cigarettes and memories for company. The Kosovo refugees are not welcomed in Kraljevo. '"Go back to Kosovo – nobody wants you here," this woman told me at the market the other day,' she tells me. '"Why couldn't you just go to Albania?" the bus driver asked me when I went into town last week. We're unwanted in our own country.'

'Kosovo Serbs – No Admittance' reads a sign on the door of one of the town's most popular cafés. 'They're rude and arrogant. I began to lose customers as soon as they showed up,' says the proprietor, while the owner of the Mataruska Banja spa outside Kraljevo blames the refugees for a drop in tourism. 'People stay away from here because of these filthy, troublesome refugees,' he says to a newspaper. The locals have threatened violence in order to expel the refugees from the municipal buildings they've been housed in, be they concert halls or barns. 'We've decided to take the law into our own hands. Blood will flow if they don't get the hell out of Mataruska Banja,' the hotelier threatens.

The average citizen of Kraljevo is equally contemptuous. 'They're more like Albanians than Serbs,' is a commonly held sentiment. 'They speak Serbian worse than Albanians do,' people say of the Kosovo-Serbian dialect. 'They act like Albanians, speak too loud, park wherever they feel like it. They sell their humanitarian aid at the market, they've got money that they hide so they can beg for more, they have as many kids as the Albanians, their kids are noisy and vandalise the schools.'

The crush of refugees had led to clashes in Kraljevo and

the surrounding villages. Cars with Kosovo number plates have been smashed up. The village of Lazac was the scene of large demonstrations when the local authorities wanted to house refugees in the cultural centre. Another village, Vitanovac, refused the refugees access to the water grid. There was already a drought and the local Department of Water feared that their network would collapse. The number of pupils per class has risen from thirty to fifty in some schools, local health services are overwhelmed and property prices have gone through the roof.

'I'm met with animosity wherever I go,' Verica tells me. 'I got along better with my Albanian neighbours in Kosovo than I do with my Serbian neighbours here. Until the war broke out we lived peacefully with the Albanians. Our kids played together, we would visit and help each other out all the time. When the war came, and our neighbours fled to Albania, my kids stood outside crying and wanting to go with them. Dragana spoke better Albanian than she did Serbian,' she says of the seven-year-old. Verica won't accept any blame for the Albanian exodus from Kosovo as the war began. 'I don't know why they all left. Nobody forced them – I think they were worried about the bombing,' she says of the several hundred thousand Albanians who flooded over the borders to Albania and Macedonia when the Serbs began their campaign of ethnic cleansing in March 1999.

A few months later it was Verica's turn to flee, along with thousands of other Serbs from Kosovo. As soon as she was on the other side of the Serbian border she called her neighbours back home. At first the woman wouldn't say anything. But then she told Verica that her and Radovan's house had been burned to the ground. 'She didn't ask about anything. Not where I was, not how the kids were, nothing. Everything is ruined,' Verica says. 'How can we live together after this?'

She sits on her bed as she talks. Women from the other rooms here have come to listen to her story. Verica talks about the house they'd built themselves, about the washing machine she misses more than anything else, about the food they ate, about her job for the Mayor of Urosevac, where she registered births, marriages and deaths. 'The hardest thing now is not having a job – nobody needs me any more,' she says, and breaks down crying. The other women just look straight ahead or leave the room. There are so many tears in the Adrani centre.

'Enough of that,' Verica says, and dries her eyes. Dragana has to get to school at one o'clock. She attends school in the afternoon because the school is full in the mornings. Her freshly laundered school clothes are nicely folded in a bag. Verica borrows her neighbour's iron and leans over the bed, which serves as ironing board and sofa in the daytime. Soon the red T-shirt and the blue trousers are impeccably ironed, not a crease anywhere. 'Even if we live this way my daughter will look decent,' Verica says.

The town's animosity towards the refugees includes their children as well. Dragana has not made any friends among the locals. Verica carefully brushes her daughter's beautiful, wavy hair, adds a yellow pin and sends her on her way. She looks like a little princess, freshly scrubbed, wearing a perfectly clean outfit. Dragana strikes me as the happiest member of the family, perhaps because she has something to do every day. And even if her classmates won't have anything to do with her, there are always other refugee kids to play with.

When the kids are off to school there's still a couple of hours until the Red Cross lunch truck arrives. Everything's already washed, cleaned or tidied, so it's just a matter of waiting and smoking. 'I'm glad you're here,' Verica says. 'Helps pass the time.'

She brings out a photo album and shows me pictures of her past: her wedding, the girls' baby pictures, family gatherings, holidays, the house in various stages of construction. 'Fortunately we managed to save the albums,' Verica sighs, then lights a cigarette and offers me more coffee. Outside a horn bleats – the lunch truck. The refugees receive one meal each day. It consists of rice, beans, potatoes or macaroni. Today it's bean soup. The refugees line up with buckets or pots, and each household gets its share. Usually this comes with half a loaf of bread, and today two hundred grams of cheese is being distributed as well. 'Aid from Czech Republic,' it says on the cheese. In addition the refugees receive a daily newspaper, *Politika*, the faithful mouthpiece of Milosevic's regime. 'Beijing Warns Washington Again', reads the main headline on the busy front page. Others read, 'Support in EU for the End of Sanctions', 'Putin Sworn in as President', 'American Imperialism Condemned' and 'Thousands Protest against America in Athens'. But nobody cares about the newspaper and the things the regime considers of utmost importance – it's feeding time. Another *rakija*, and then we can sit down.

Verica apologises for the modesty of the meal and drifts back to Kosovo. 'We had meat every day, we had both pigs and chickens.' She doesn't eat anything herself. 'I just want to cry and smoke,' she tells me. 'The only thing that keeps me going is the kids. I always tell the two eldest girls that they have to keep their spirits up – they're young, they have to study hard, and then we can go back to Kosovo,' she says. 'And begin living again.'

After lunch everyone gathers in the corridor, which is the social nexus of the centre. Two benches and a few chairs line the walls here, and at the end of the corridor is a communal hob. Hours are killed here. The door to the sunny courtyard is open, but nobody cares about sunshine and they have no business outside anyway. We're nursing our coffee and it's my turn to answer questions: 'Have you been to Kosovo? What do you think of Albanians? What do people say of us Serbs? What did the Albanians tell you about us? When do you think we can go home?'

Everyone is hanging on my every word.

'The situation in Kosovo is very complicated and tense and it's difficult for me to judge anything,' I try, and feel like an idiot. 'I really don't know any more than you do,' I finally admit, and have to register the refugees' disappointed faces.

A man shows me pictures from his village. He was in Kosovo the day before and was driven in a KFOR escort to see his hometown. 'It's all burned down. That's my house right there – it's just a ruin now. That's where my uncle lived, that's where my godfather lived, that's my parents' house,' he says and points to the pictures. 'The church was burned down, too. But we'll go back and rebuild everything.'

I ask if they think they can live alongside the Albanians after something like this. The room grows quiet. 'We'll have to kill those Albanians that are guilty. The others we can live with. And we'll have to do the same thing to the Serbs,' says an elderly man. This is the first time I've heard anyone even mention that the Serbs might be guilty of anything. Not that anyone here will admit that any sort of abuse was ever directed towards the Albanians in Kosovo.

'They had full rights,' someone says. 'They terrorised

us,' says Slavica, Verica's sister. She lived in an Albanian
neighbourhood in the village of Brezovica, and worked as
a phone operator. 'After a while the neighbours stopped
saying hi. They turned away whenever they saw me. One
day I met a colleague on the street and I turned away.
"Slavica, why don't you say hi to me?" he asked. "I didn't
dare," I said. He told me not to worry about politics.
That was the last time I heard a friendly word from an
Albanian.'

The refugees are unyielding in their version of the war:
there was never any ethnic cleansing and the Albanians left
of their own accord. The Kosovo Serbs' unwavering support of Milosevic is part of the reason they're viewed here
with such scepticism and animosity. The refugees are his
staunchest supporters. And because the Albanians boy-
cotted the elections, almost all the Kosovo seats in the
Serbian parliament went to the SPS. The Serbs in Kosovo
trusted Milosevic to protect them against the growing
Muslim population. In a demonstration the Kosovo Serbs
mounted in Kraljevo to protest their miserable conditions,
passers-by would shout, '*Uzivaj!*', which means something
like 'Enjoy!' In other words, 'Serves you right!'

'He did manage to protect us until now,' Radovan says of
the Yugoslav President, and pours his third, fourth, fifth or
perhaps sixth *rakija* of the day. Maybe the only thing more
prevalent in Serbia than *rakija* is the way Serbians see themselves as eternally suffering. 'We've always been victims,'
Verica thinks, once more on the verge of tears and once
more with a cigarette in her hand. 'America started the
war in Kosovo by riling up the Albanians,' goes a familiar
refrain among the refugees. They insist that the mass graves
are in fact filled with Albanians who died from the bombing and had to be buried in a hurry. 'It's Bill Clinton,

Madeleine Albright and the KLA's Hashim Thaci that should be in The Hague. Milosevic is innocent,' maintains Radovan, and proudly displays his SPS membership card. 'He's the greatest leader ever, except for Tito,' he concludes.

Nor will the refugees blame their own pitiful circumstance on the regime. Again this is all America's doing. 'Serbia is getting hammered by the economic sanctions; it's a miracle that this society still functions and that we're getting any help at all,' says one.

But on one issue the Adrani refugees part ways with the party line. Slobodan Milosevic insists that the Serbs emerged victorious from the war in Kosovo. When I ask if anyone agrees with this, it goes quiet. 'No, we've lost,' one man says. 'We've lost everything. But we'll win it all back,' another is quick to add. 'As soon as KFOR leaves we'll be able to deal with the Albanians ourselves. We'll need weapons, though. We'll have to go back in with the Serbian forces and demand our rights.'

Radovan claims that they will all be able to return on 11 June 2000. 'That's when KFOR is leaving,' he says, without seeming entirely convinced himself. Among the refugees this misunderstanding is prevalent – that the deal Milosevic signed only holds for a year. Newspapers controlled by the regime frequently write that the KFOR deal is valid for 'an initial year', without adding that it is automatically renewed. Still, it appears that the refugees themselves realise, in their heart of hearts, that a quick return is just wishful thinking. The Serbs who remain in Kosovo live in enclaves, protected by heavily armed soldiers from KFOR. If they move outside their villages it's open season on them. The children get a military escort to and from their schools.

When their current circumstances become too depressing for words, the refugees engage in the Serbian national pastime – reliving the past. They tell me stories of Tsar Lazar, who was made to choose between divine and earthly kingdoms in the battle against the Turks in 1389. They tell me about their many churches and monasteries, and talk of Kosovo as Serbia's heart and soul. 'Kosovo is Serbian, has always been Serbian and must remain Serbian for all time,' Verica says. 'If I am not to make it back, and my children don't make it back, then my grandchildren will have to fight to win Kosovo back.'

This day is a particularly sad one; it's St Marko's Day, when one is meant to visit the family's graves and light candles. 'Ours are all in Kosovo,' Verica says. She doesn't know the state of her parents' graves. Many Serbian cemeteries have been vandalised and destroyed. 'I can't bear to think about it,' she says. One of the other women changes the subject. Having lost everything else, their families are all they have left and the main subject of all conversations. '*Nisi udata*? You're not married?' The stunned refugees stare at me, with eyes that read something like, 'You'd better hurry up, girl . . .' In the very next instant I'm bombarded with offers of marriage. I could have my pick of the young men of eighteen and upwards. The candidates themselves remain happily ignorant of their impending nuptials, but their mothers are fully engaged. 'My son is twenty-four and studies technical engineering in Nis – how does that sound to you? You could take him to Norway,' an elderly woman proposes. 'Is it easy to get work there? Can you help us?'

Again everyone's eyes are on me, and waiting for an answer. Verica breaks the silence: 'Leave her alone! Come on, let's go and look at the photos you haven't seen yet.'

She takes me by the hand back to her room, where we sit on the bed and leaf through her past. Verica cries again. Unwanted by the local population, ignored by the government. To them she's only a reminder of another war that the Serbs lost.

It takes me almost a year to get back to Adrani. The March sun bathes the courtyard between the white brick buildings in a cheerful glow. Some kids play football, a few girls skip. By the gate I meet a young girl carrying a pair of water buckets and ask her if Verica and Radovan still live here.

'They are my parents,' she replies, before putting the buckets down and following me inside. This is their second-eldest daughter, Duzica. I greet some of the familiar faces on the way to Verica's room at the end of the corridor. Verica has dark rings under her eyes, a lot of new wrinkles and a reddish rash on her chin. Life as a refugee has made her ten years older.

I'm pushed down on a sofa and offered coffee and cigarettes, Verica's recipe for survival from last year. 'Yes, we're still here,' she answers before I've even asked. 'And we're not four to a room now, but six.'

A month ago Radovan's mother came from Kosovo. She used to live in a Serbian village near Brezovica, but even with the protection of KFOR, killings still took place. She saw her brother murdered, before their Albanian neighbours stripped her house of valuables, including their animals. Despite this, she wanted to remain in Kosovo until last month, when a Serbian bus exploded, killing eleven people and seriously injuring many more. Finally she decided she'd rather share a room with Verica and Radovan in Adrani.

The mother-in-law, who has remained on her stool in a

corner, interjects her creaky '*ai-ai-ai*'s in a whimpering voice as Verica recounts her fate. Her eyes are blue and watery. Sixteen-year-old Duzica sits on another stool; she came here from Kosovo along with her grandmother. She attended secondary school in Brezovica, after completing junior school in Nis, but after the bus was bombed Verica wouldn't let her live there any more. Because it's the middle of a term, the school in Kraljevo refused to let her pick up where she left off, so now Duzica has nothing to do. She's bored and just waits for the next term to begin.

There are no books in the small room at the refugee centre. When I suggest to Duzica that she could go to the library in Kraljevo to read something, she just looks at me. She spends her days helping her mother with breakfast, lunch and dinner, and then helps clean up after breakfast, lunch and dinner.

Everything else in their room is more or less as it was last year, except that the St Nikola calendar now reads 2001. And the family has added a new icon, the Virgin Mary with Infant Christ, and have been given a cupboard and a fridge.

A year ago Verica was determined to return to Kosovo. Now she is resigned to a different fate. 'I don't think I'll ever be able to go home. Things are just getting worse there. The Albanians want a state of their own, free of Serbs. They terrorise us at will, while the KFOR soldiers just watch. Even the children know that KFOR are on their side. The soldiers and the Albanians are the best of friends. Now we're trying to sell our land in Kosovo, so we can buy something here, but it seems impossible.'

Verica shows me pictures of the burned-out house, of which only the foundations remain. The ruin is framed by unharmed buildings on each side, the homes of their

Albanian neighbours. 'I still have my house keys,' Verica tells me in a voice dripping with sarcasm. 'It never occurred to me that I wouldn't come home again. I remember I watered my houseplants before we left.'

They were sent the photos a few months earlier. Radovan had asked an Albanian neighbour to take pictures of his father's grave and their house, so they could see that it was really burned down. The man took the pictures and sent them off. A few weeks later he was found in a ditch, killed. 'We don't know why, but they've begun to turn on one another now, if someone has attitudes that aren't totally anti-Serbian. The Albanian community has some harsh, unwritten rules,' he says. 'It's sad, really. This neighbour was a nice guy and only thirty-two years old. He left a wife and three small kids. All of Kosovo is engulfed in hatred,' Verica says.

The relationship between the refugees and the Serbian neighbours in Adrani hasn't improved either. 'In the two years we've been here not a single neighbour has dropped in to see us. Not one child has played with the kids here and none of ours have been invited home by any of their classmates. We're shunned,' Verica says. 'I suppose there are just too many of us.'

The lunch truck honks outside and Duzica goes out to get bread. Just bread. Verica doesn't want any more of the prepared food. 'It rotates between rice, beans and macaroni every three days. In the end I couldn't stand it any more.'

I go with Duzica to get the bread. Like last year, people queue up with pots and pails, into which a hodgepodge of rice in dirty gravy is ladled, along with the odd, symbolic piece of carrot or meat.

When Verica insists on cooking her own food it's not just

because she's tired of the dull diet. It's also a matter of
dignity. Having to wait for the truck to honk some time
between one and three every day, and then to walk outside
with a pail and have something or other scooped into it
only makes her feel as if she's an animal, being fattened up
for slaughter. She'd rather spend her meagre income on
buying her own food. As a government employee she still
gets paid for her job in Kosovo, although it's less than
twenty pounds a month.

Radovan has begun to sell cigarettes on the black
market. Neither of them has tried to get a job. 'There's no
point. The unemployment rate here is high enough as it is,'
Verica says. 'Nobody's going to hire anyone from Kosovo.'

Getting a job would mean taking another step away from
Kosovo, too.

Radovan returns from the market, a few packs of cigarettes lighter and a few dinars richer. He's brought salad
and radishes in a shopping bag. The *rakija* makes its appearance on the table. It's served from a plastic bottle of
unknown origin, but tastes just the same as always. The
neighbours from down the hall drop in to visit.

When she's not pouring coffee or attending to something or other, Verica crouches on the floor. I look around
and understand: there are not enough chairs. Once in a
while, when it gets too painful, she'll put her knee down.
Sometimes she'll pick invisible specks of dust off the
carpet, or just have another cigarette.

'What do you think – will we ever be able to go
home?' asks Radovan. I figure I might as well tell them
what I think, and say it doesn't look good. And that if
they do get the opportunity to go back they'll find themselves in a very different Kosovo from the place they
left. A Kosovo where they will be governed by

Albanians. 'Is that something you could live with?' I ask.

Radovan gets up to pour more *rakija*. 'As long as nobody stops me living my life, in my house, or doing my job, it's all the same to me who the government is,' he says. In the next instant he talks about the importance of Kosovo remaining a part of the Serbian state. Then he changes his mind again and says that nationalism and ethnicity never mattered to him.

Radovan has kept up his membership of the SPS, even after Milosevic's fall.

'Everyone here voted for him,' says Duzica.

'Now he's accused of being a war criminal, just because he tried to protect us Serbs. The whole world blames him for the Balkan wars. What about Tudjman and Izetbegovic and Thaci? It's not fair that we're being blamed for everything,' Radovan feels.

'If he is guilty of something, of course he should be punished for it, but he certainly shouldn't be sent to The Hague. The trial must take place here. What did Milosevic ever do to the Dutch?' Verica wants to know. 'The West is against us Serbs, so it can never be a fair trial.'

Nobody at the centre has a TV, and people rarely listen to the news on the radio, preferring stations that play only music. 'The news just makes me depressed,' Verica says. The daily delivery of *Politika* ended on 6 October. 'New regime, no paper,' Radovan laughs.

After a while Verica doesn't want to talk any more about politics. 'I don't know anything about it. If I'd known anything about politics, I wouldn't be sitting in this room, would I? And if I say anything more now, I'll probably be charged with war crimes, too, and have to rot in jail along with Milosevic,' she says, and laughs in a way that sounds like a cough. 'We just want what's ours,' she adds after a long pause, while she rubs on an imagined speck on the oven with a rag, even when the appliance sparkles as if brand new.

Despite the brilliant spring weather, we remain indoors. The room is thick with smoke. When at long last I bring up the wonderful weather, Verica just says that the sun doesn't warm her any more. Silence descends. Nobody can think of anything to say. Everyone just looks into the air, or down at the floor, in a way that indicates that this is how they spend most of their time. Radovan tips his chair back against the wall and drinks beer. Verica is hunched over on the floor, smoking. Even I end up with a blank stare, not thinking of anything. It's as if the boredom of the refugees is contagious. My head feels empty, bereft of thoughts to hold on to. Time to go home.

On the drive back to Belgrade it occurs to me that Verica didn't cry any more. It almost felt better when she cried.

Five years have passed since Verica watered her houseplants for the last time, locked the door and left. I'm back in Belgrade and wonder how she's doing. There were no phones at the refugee centre, and I can't find the notepad where I had written down their surname. Without it there's no way I can track down the family through any sort of refugee register. They could have gone anywhere by now, been transferred to a different centre or moved into a flat somewhere. Maybe someone helped them build a house. I don't even have the address of the centre in Adrani, but I think I'll find it once I'm there. Then I can ask someone if they've gone – assuming that the centre itself still exists.

I ask Drago if he wants to come along, and he promises to pick me up early the next morning. He doesn't and his phone is dead. There's an angry buzz at the door late in the morning. A dishevelled Drago stands outside my house, greeting me with a haunted look. His clothes are smeared with blood and mud. He's spent the night in jail, following a fight the previous evening. I tell him to go home and shower.

Two hours later we're on our way.

'You know that something always goes wrong when you go out! Why did you have to hit the town on this very evening? You said you were going straight to bed!'

Drago grits his teeth in silence. He drives fast and harshly. He jerks the wheel back and forth and slams his brakes on for red lights, coming to a halt at the pedestrian crossings. This is by no means the first time Drago's got into trouble, and I'm in no mood for pity. Neither of us says a single word until we're out on the main road, where Drago can drive as recklessly as he feels. As it turns out, he broke his mate's nose in the fight. Now he's worried about his wanting revenge. The guy is well connected to the Mafia.

'Can't you fix it?'

Drago just snarls at me in response.

'Let me know if there's anything I can do to help you out,' I add. Pity wins out after all. I remember Drago as an effective, up-and-coming Serb. Three years ago he had a good life, a good salary and great hopes for a future without Milosevic. Now his phone is cut off because he can't pay his bill. What money I pay him for interpreting and driving me around goes straight to his creditors — his landlord, his bar bills and, not least, to his friends and his family. Last night, he added a bloodied ex-mate to his list of troubles.

'I'll get myself together, I'll get better. It's just that these are difficult times. But, hey – let's talk about work. Who did you say we're supposed to meet today?'

I tell him about Verica and Radovan and the girls and the grandmother, of their neighbours and their house that was burned down.

'I hope they're still there,' I say. 'Or, rather, I really hope they're somewhere else, that they've found something better. In any case I hope we can track them down.'

Drago nods. He's happy to get out of town. 'It's probably safest if I stay away for a few days.'

By the time we get to Kraljevo it's dark. From there on we keep getting lost. We stop and ask for directions, drive on, check the map. It's raining and the car angrily negotiates its way over potholes and stones.

'It's on the right side of the road. Just after we cross a river,' I recall. 'Or, if we're coming from this way, maybe it's on our left. I think.'

'Wouldn't you rather stop and ask for better directions?' Drago suggests when we remain lost.

'No, we've asked enough times already.'

'Maybe we should try this tomorrow, in daylight,' he groans. Obviously the lock-up in Belgrade didn't provide the most relaxing respite before a journey like this.

'No, I want to find them tonight. I'll know it when I see it.'

We cross a bridge. 'Here!' I shout. 'Turn here.'

The courtyard is empty. The rain keeps coming down, as it's done throughout April. Drago parks and we knock on the door. There's no response, so we let ourselves in. Shoes and boots are lined up several rows deep in the hallway. We take ours off, turn left by the communal hob, and there, behind the first door on the right, is where they used to

Milan Djukic, of Croatia's minority Serbs

From wire reports

ZAGREB, CROATIA — Milan Djukic, a prominent leader of Croatia's minority Serbs and a former deputy parliament speaker, died Monday. He was 61.

He died of an illness in his home village, Donji Lapac, in central Croatia, his family said. His family did not disclose the cause of his death.

Djukic led the Serb People's Party since the early 1990s, representing Croatian Serbs who did not join their compatriots' armed rebellion against Croatia's independence from the former Yugoslavia, which triggered a six-month war.

As a representative of a minority, he was deputy parliament speaker in 1992-1996 and a lawmaker from 1992 until 2004.

Djukic often was targeted by both Serbs and Croatians. Many Serbs disliked him because he was part of Croatia's political establishment at times when rebels fought against it; Croatians because of his continuous criticism of Croatia's treatment of its minority Serbs.

His influence diminished, with other ethnic Serb leaders attracting more minority votes.

Arrangements by
YURCH FUNERAL
HOME
216-398-1010
www.cleveland.com/obits

Death Notices

ALBERTONE

MIKE ANGELO ALBERTONE, age 86, of Wickliffe, formerly of Mentor and Euclid. Beloved husband of the late Edith "Edie"; dear father of Dominic (Jane) Albertone, Grace Maloney, Connie Whelan and Michele (Skip) Creighton; grandfather of 12 and great grandfather of 21; son of the late Dominic and Grace Albertone; brother of the late Antoinette Vaccariello, Lillian DiLillo, Josephine Santoni, Dolores Angeletti, Frank, Joseph, Donald and Jack Albertone. Mike was a Co-Founder of Albertone's Jewelers. Funeral Mass will be held 10:45 a.m. Saturday at Our Lady Of

BOBER

MARY T. BOBER (nee Knobl), age 93. Beloved wife of the late Stanley A. Loving mother of Joan Dianiska (Jack), Linda Dodge, Janice Berg (Doug), and Jim Bober (Gail). Grandmother of nine. Great grandmother of 14. Sister of the late Elizabeth Gruber, Joseph Knobl, and George Knobl. October 10, 2007. Funeral Mass Saturday St. Angela Church at 10 a.m. Interment Holy Cross Cemetery. Friends may call at CHAMBERS FUNERAL HOME, 29150 LORAIN RD., NORTH OLMSTED FRIDAY 2-4 AND 6-8 P.M. Memorial contributions

consultant and volunteered in that capacity at Kibbutz Hatzor and Todiron in Israel. A world traveler, avid skier, ice-skater, gardner and philanthropist. He loved Baroque and Classical music. He played the recorder and entertained a group of Baroque musicians at his 50-acre farm in Twinsburg for many years. He was the founder of the "Peace Library" at Givat Haviva in Israel, a cultural school for Arab and Israeli children. He was a strong supporter of of the local Jewish Community through his life-long contributions to the Jewish Community Federation, The JCC and many others. He was a staunch member of the ACLU and a contributor to the Cleveland Institute of Music and many other civic institutions. Well read, he spent his life in learning and was an inspiration to all who knew him. Services will be held Friday, Oct. 12 at 11 a.m. at the BERKOWITZ-KUMIN-BOOKATZ ME-live. I look at Drago, who nods eagerly, and I knock on the door.

A beautiful girl opens the door. It must be Dragana. Behind her I can see Verica's back, bent down as she kneels to pick something up off the floor. She turns round and jumps up with a scream. She's got me wrapped in an embrace in one single bound. Radovan just stares, disbelieving. His mother rocks back and forth on a stool, then looks up and back down again without ceasing her swaying motion.

Many kisses and soft hugs later, Verica shoves me down into a chair.

'Yes, we're still here,' she jumps in. 'It'll be five years in June, but tell me — what's new with you?'

The *rakija* appear on the table. Drago lights up.

'Do you remember Åsne, Mother-in-law?' Verica shouts to the rocking woman, who just shrugs and looks at me with empty eyes. 'She's had two strokes in the last year. Such grief,' Verica whispers. 'She doesn't talk any more.'

The room seems even more cramped than before. Verica has added a hob, so she no longer has to use the one in the corridor. And they've got a TV now. 'We sold the car and bought a TV,' she explains.

A Brazilian soap flickers on the screen. St Nikola is where he always was, but now a host of other icons keep him company. Every surface is covered with stuff — a porcelain puppy, a glass bowl with water and snowflakes, a teddy bear the worse for wear, a cardboard icon, a worn-out greeting card, a bouquet of fake flowers in a vase.

'I was almost hoping I wouldn't find you here. That you'd moved somewhere else.'

'If only we could,' Verica says, and lights a cigarette. 'Yes, I'm still smoking,' she apologises. Radovan offers

Drago one as well. 'Another *rakija?*' he asks. 'I've given up the stuff myself. It became too much, I began drinking every day. A lot . . .'

Then the lights go out. Everyone remains still. Radovan lights a match. Nobody gets up to check the fuse box. We just wait for the power to come back on. Radovan continues: 'In the beginning it helped. It was a comfort. Then everything got worse. My nerves were shot, I grew afraid of everything, began doubting everything. I drank even more just to calm myself down, but then I got nervous again, so I drank even more, and finally I was just a nervous wreck . . .'

The power comes on again. The TV jumps back into action and the ceiling lamp once more emits its barren light.

Radovan has changed the most. He must have lost twenty kilos. When I first met him he was a big, strong guy. Now his cheeks are hollow. Shoulders, stomach, chest – it's as if he has imploded.

'I came close to losing my grip totally, and realised I had to put aside the bottle for good.'

Drago nods in sympathy. 'Losing your grip, yeah,' he says, through bloodshot eyes.

Verica on the contrary looks much better this time. Her skin is clearer, her eyes have regained some of their spark. 'Maybe you're right,' she says when I compliment her. 'I was most depressed in the beginning. The first year was the worst. It was just one shock after another: that they burned our house down, the return that never happened, the situation in Kosovo. Back then I remembered all too well what it was like to live in your own house, where everybody had a room of their own, where we had a washing machine and . . .'

Suddenly everything goes pitch black again. 'Ooh,' Verica groans. 'You see? This is how we live.'

The glowing cigarettes do a slow dance up and down in the darkness. Nobody gets any candles; we just wait. It's hard to speak in this darkness; it's almost too intimate. As if you have to say something important, or nothing at all.

'The washing machine,' Verica continues when the lights are back on. 'That's what I miss most. Doing laundry is worst in the winter. We stand outside over our wash tubs until our hands are red and swollen,' she says, and shows me her cracked fingers. 'Imagine, just five years ago doing laundry was the easiest thing in the world.'

I remember her having told me this before – but a washing machine remains an impossible dream in a building with no running water and only one tap in the courtyard. To wash themselves, they take turns with a plastic bowl in the same room where they eat and sleep.

Several of their neighbours stop by as the evening goes on, and those who remember me nod carefully before leaving again. Verica retrieves cheese, eggs and cucumbers from the fridge.

You can't visit a Serbian home without eating what is offered, and a tasty smell of frying bacon accompanies our chat. 'You used to like bacon,' Verica recalls.

'Our two eldest daughters are married now,' she beams, blushing, over the glowing hob, and points with the spatula to two photos on the wall. 'They both married Serbs from Kosovo, so I think we'll be sticking together. The eldest one is in the process of building a house – with aid from the Norwegian Refugee Council, actually.'

'The Norwegians are helping a lot of people, they're doing a good job here,' Radovan notes.

'Are you hoping for your own place?'

'How can we get a house without any money?' asks Radovan. 'We'd need a plot of land first, then building materials. We won't have any money until we can sell our plot in Kosovo. The house is burned down, worthless – but the land is good. But how can we sell it when we can't even go there? Why would anyone want to pay for something they already could help themselves to for free? They've divided our garden up like some sort of war trophy.'

Visibly bitter, Radovan lights a cigarette. His hand is trembling.

'Only when we can sell there will we be able to build something here.'

'But the thing we want most is not to build here but to return to where we were born,' Verica tells me. 'Where our ancestors lived and are buried. I think the only solution for Kosovo is partitioning. An Albanian part and a Serbian part. It would be declaring defeat, since all of Kosovo is really Serbian, but at least it would be better than it is now. Here I doubt we'll ever be able to make anything for ourselves.'

'But, if so, the international community has to do something, and investigate KFOR. They didn't protect us. They don't care. Now, during the troubles last month, they just stood by and watched as the Albanians set our churches on fire,' says Radovan who's still a member of the SPS. 'They've got a good policy for Serbs.'

Verica seems to be far away. It's always struck me how quickly her expression can change from bitterness to tenderness.

The food is all gone. It's late. The two youngest girls come in from the corridor, where they've been playing. Night is about to fall on Adrani. Beyond the door you hear hushed voices, doors closing, splashes of water, the odd shout or steps coming and going.

'I dream of walking in the fields again,' Verica says, with a faraway smile. 'Those beautiful hills and valleys.'

Her thoughts remain in Kosovo. She lights a cigarette.

'But I have to stay here, trapped in this room. We once had a large bathroom, with a new shower and a bath. And here we are, lining up to brush our teeth at the tap out the back. For five years. We do our business in an outhouse behind the building. Not that I really care any more. When you saw me last I had just one thought in my head – to go back. Now I just try to make the best of it, really. I've almost forgotten what my life used to be like. It's better to forget. Don't they say humans can adapt to anything? As long as they forget.'

Mayor for Democracy

'Freedom is the awareness of the harmony within the dissonance created between imperfect people.'

Dzoni Stulic, Croatian rock star

'We'll colour in every house in this town! Red where there are Milosevic supporters, yellow for the Democrats, blue for the Draskovic faction and white for the undecided. Every household must be registered, and we'll find out how everyone intends to vote. As soon as we know, we can plan our strategy.' So says the Mayor of Nis, Zoran Zivkovic, who is planning his next campaign. Not that he or anyone else knows when there is to be an election, but whenever Slobodan Milosevic makes up his mind Zoran will be ready.

Nis is a city of 280,000, and I express curiosity as to how Zivkovic thinks he can learn the voting intention of every single household here. He looks at me, not quite comprehending. 'This is a small town, and everybody knows everybody. Besides, we have a long tradition of surveillance in this country – if there's something we really know, that would be it,' he laughs, and then tries to explain: 'I know more or less who everyone on my street will be voting for, and on top of that I know people all over town. The party spokesman can colour his street, the general secretary another one. Every single party member gets assigned his or her own street to cover – how hard could it be? You can colour your block,' he tells his secretary, Aleksandra. 'Well, actually, colouring in tenement buildings might be tricky – they'll end up rather multicoloured.'

There's a staff meeting at the mayor's office. Four of his closest aides sit around a table, studying municipal maps, polls and possible electoral scenarios. 'We'll spend two weeks registering every household, two weeks on making the map and two weeks planning the campaign. By May Day everything should be set and ready to go. We'll concentrate on the areas with the highest concentration of undecided voters – they're the ones who'll determine the outcome anyway. There's no point in trying to convert the Communist faithful or Milosevic's people.

Zivkovic's team studies a poll that suggests a union of opposition parties would defeat Milosevic, if the election took place now, in the spring of 2000. If they are not able to unite behind one single candidate, they'll lose. The poll further indicates how best to influence voters; a third never read newspapers and get all their information from television, while only 8 per cent of the population believe anything that the government's *Politika* says.

'The best way of running an election campaign is the "*dobar dan, dobar dan*" method. "Hello, how are you? Hello, how are you?" We'll go from door to door and talk to people,' Zivkovic explains. 'We will need two thousand volunteers for that. We'll need to explain and persuade. Then we will have to figure out how to make sure that the most persistent anti-Democrats are locked in on election day,' he laughs. 'I used to threaten my parents with that when they still believed in Milosevic. But, fortunately, in the last election I didn't have to resort to such methods – they came to their senses and voted for me!' The energetic mayor promises to go after Milosevic in his advertising. 'We're going to list all the promises he's made in the last decade and then show people how things have turned out instead.'

Zoran Zivkovic is one of Serbia's most popular politicians. Not yet forty, he is among the precious few who aren't compromised by the broken promises of the past. In his three years as Mayor of Nis he's proven himself an efficient advocate of the city's interests. He's the Democratic Party's number two, after Zoran Djindjic, and is one of the most outspoken opponents of the regime in all of Serbia. In Nis the opposition is well organised and the city has become a vanguard in the fight against Milosevic. Previously it was known as a 'red stronghold'; along with the rest of southern Serbia, the regime enjoyed solid support here. While the rest of southern Serbia remains in Milosevic's camp, Nis has chosen a different path. Seeing one government-run enterprise after another get shut down or downsized, people lost faith in the authorities, and Zoran Zivkovic became the city's first non-communist mayor since the Second World War. He has not been able to turn the tide on the local economy, but he has convinced the voters that rising unemployment is the fault of the regime's policy and not his.

Local authorities have little real power in Serbia, and a mayor from the opposition is by definition subject to active interference from the regime. When Zivkovic took office the government reduced Nis's budget to a quarter of what it had been when Serbia's Socialist Party ran the city. The authorities never felt obligated to explain why the funding of cities run by the opposition was cut far more drastically than that of cities administered by Milosevic supporters.

Budget cuts are not the only tool in the regime's arsenal of dirty tricks. In the winter of 2000 none of the opposition-controlled cities in Serbia received any heating oil for their schools, hospitals and homes. The cities managed to stave off the cold through the 'Energy for Democracy' programme, in which several Western European nations sent oil to the 'democratic' areas. The government also did its best to hinder this effort, and in several instances convoys of heating oil were left standing on the border between Macedonia and Serbia for weeks on end, before they were allowed to pass through customs. Zivkovic spent most of December 1999 shuttling back and forth to the border trying to negotiate entry for the precious cargo.

'There's absolutely no contact between the authorities in Belgrade and our municipal administration. In my time as mayor here, some fifty ministers have visited Nis – but only one of them stopped by my office. Everyone else only visited the local headquarters of their parties.

Until the overthrow of Slobodan Milosevic in the autumn of 2000 his government was dominated by members of three parties: the SPS, Serbia's Socialist Party, led by Milosevic; the JUL, Yugoslavia's leftists, led by his wife, Mira Markovic; and Serbia's Radical Party, led by the ultra-nationalist Vojislav Seselj.

In order to put down troublesome initiatives, the government also uses legislation. Zivkovic risks up to three years in prison if he is convicted of 'spreading false information'. This law came into effect after Zivkovic criticised the armed forces during a rally. He could be tried at any time, having renounced the immunity elected officials here usually enjoy.

Two further charges hover over Zivkovic's head. One accuses him of having arranged a spontaneous demonstration for a local TV technician, who was jailed for having encouraged people, during half-time in a live broadcast of a football match, to show up for an anti-Milosevic rally. The second charge concerns comments Zivkovic himself made about the judge who sentenced the journalist Nebojsa Ristic to a year in prison for having put up posters supporting a free press on the exit door of his television station. Zivkovic said the judge did not deserve to be a citizen of Serbia. 'I knew better than to make slanderous statements – I stuck to making a few recommendations. I recommended that he put a dirty plastic bag over his head, and that people should turn their backs on him when they saw him in the street. On top of which I suggested he should be ashamed of himself.'

All of which added up to a libel charge. The investigation is in full swing, but Zivkovic doubts they'll put him in jail. 'It would be doing the opposition a favour,' he says, not without pride, and then shows me the poster the journalist was sentenced for displaying. 'I'm having them framed – one will hang in my office, one in the foyer downstairs and the rest in our conference rooms. Without a free press we'll never be a democracy.'

The politician has also been physically attacked by his opponents. A security guard from Milosevic's party knocked him down in a café in Nis, and the night after

Zivkovic renounced his immunity the police came to his house to arrest his wife. They said it concerned some accounting figures that she had never turned in to the firm she worked for. 'We had no idea what they were talking about and she refused to go with them to the station in the middle of the night. She showed up the next day, only to be told it was all some sort of misunderstanding. Of course, there never was any misunderstanding; they'll do anything to scare us off.'

The mayor is confident and resolute. He radiates energy and doesn't fit in among the dark, heavy pieces of furniture in the solemn office in city hall. This morning he is checking his email and the news on the Internet; the server has been down for a few days, so there's a lot to catch up on. He tells his secretary which of the emails require immediate attention and which can wait.

Later there's a meeting with the city's comptroller about the loan Nis took in order to pay for the heating oil it bought from the state. The 'Energy for Democracy' oil covered only half of what it needed, so the rest had to be bought from the Belgrade government, at soaring 'federal' prices. The bank's terms stated that Nis would repay the price of the oil plus 1 per cent per month. However, as the price of heating oil has quadrupled since last winter, it now has to pay back four times as much. Zivkovic is trying to renegotiate the loan, but given that the bank is owned by the state and controlled by Milosevic's people, he's having a tough time. 'One more way to choke us off,' he sighs.

Then the running of Nis's theatre tops the agenda. 'Half the staff loaf around all day not doing anything. The repertoire is outmoded and the directors are terrible,' Zivkovic explains. He's being visited by a theatre executive from Belgrade who's had great success reorganising several playhouses in the capital. The two men have some *rakija* and the Belgrade executive outlines for Zivkovic how he thinks the local theatre should be run. They soon agree that the best solution is to dissolve the current company, reorganise and then have people reapply for their old jobs. 'But it'll have to wait until after the election. I don't want to risk such an unpopular move right now.'

Zivkovic places a call to the current theatre director to get an update. The director wants to know if he has made arrangements for the new cleaning lady they need. He rolls his eyes after hanging up. 'The administration is fast asleep – they think they're still living in a communist state, where everything is done for them!'

The mayor is a heavy smoker – Yugoslav Moravas without filter. 'They're made here in Nis,' he says. 'I have to support what little is left of the local industry, despite the fact that the director of the tobacco factory is a Milosevic supporter. If I were to boycott everything that the regime controlled I couldn't use a phone or electricity or buy petrol.'

Zivkovic admits to being a very good customer for Moravas. 'On a day without stress I'll smoke a packet. But if I get stressed I'll get through two. And I haven't had one day without stress for at least four years now.'

When he's not smoking he chews nuts, raisins and dried apricots, washing them down with Turkish coffee. Zivkovic is a sturdy fellow of around a hundred kilos. When I meet him he's fasting – not to lose weight but in order to follow the Orthodox custom of a seven-week fast leading up to Easter.

The local bishop is on the line. The mayor uses the opportunity to ask for advice: 'Is it in the third week that we're not to use any oil in our food?' he asks. 'No, that's in the first and last week of the fast,' he is told.

Zivkovic was raised as an atheist but let himself be baptised three years ago. He collaborated closely with several priests during the massive demonstrations against the regime in 1996 and 1997, when Milosevic refused to acknowledge the election results in any city where the opposition did well enough to win – which included most of the larger cities, Nis among them. Milosevic eventually had to back down, and Zivkovic became a mayor and a Christian.

He invites me home for lunch. The bodyguard follows him to the car. After the assaults Zivkovic got a bodyguard, but usually he only comes along when Zivkovic walks around town or is at large gatherings. 'He was a soldier in Kosovo and when he came back he couldn't find a job. Since I know his mother I hired him,' Zivkovic explains. We get into a small, bright-yellow Yugo. 'I don't have a car, I have a Yugo,' people say of the car, once the pride of Yugoslavia. 'I've got to do something about the roads here. There can be no real progress on roads this bad,' he says. 'Asphalt for Democracy' is another project waiting in the wings.

His wife, Biserka, is waiting on the doorstep when we arrive. The mayor's family live in a house they share with his parents. The family includes Milena, nine, and Marko, two, and they have seventy square metres at their disposal – a small living room with a kitchenette, and two bedrooms.

'One of my most important battles is the fight on corruption. I could bring in several thousand German marks a day if I wanted to, as could my co-workers. But I'm trying to clean up this crooked country, and it's a matter of great importance that I don't have any material goods I haven't earned on my own.'

The mayor estimates that about 80 per cent of the

economy in Nis is black or grey. Bribery is rampant. 'I have to make sure I'm clean,' he says.

The icons are the first thing he shows me of his home. One of them is the family's patron saint, St Michael. Another is the patron saint of the Democratic Party, St George. He is commemorated with a huge picnic each year, in addition to a liturgy in a church. A crucifix, and the city's saints, St Constantine and Empress Helen, complete the display. 'I try to pray now and then; the fast isn't only about eating properly – you're also supposed to turn your attention to God, to pray and atone, and keep away from earthly pleasures. But I'm not fanatical.'

On the wall is a worldly caricature as well. It portrays St Peter in a boat, headed for modern times along with a rock star, a devil and a woman wearing nothing but sunglasses.

The *rakija* is served to the tones of Lajko Felix, a young Serbian-Hungarian violinist. The wide range of appetisers that Zivkovic's wife has prepared for us go sadly ignored, for the mayor has hit upon his favourite subject for discourse: Milosevic.

'Getting rid of him is of the utmost importance. Anything else is secondary. As long as he is in power we will remain a pariah state in Europe, hampered by sanctions and excluded from investment. Exiled and isolated from progress,' Zivkovic thunders. 'He's obsessed with Milosevic,' say his critics. 'Give him an hour on TV and he will spend fifty-five minutes ranting about Milosevic and five minutes on his own policies.'

Zivkovic is almost as irate when he talks about the West's position on Serbia. 'The West should be ashamed. The bombing presented the opposition with enormous difficulties. At the last election I urged people to vote for a democracy styled on Western Europe, and then these very same democracies attack us. How am I supposed to justify this? I asked people to put their faith in the EU flag – and the next thing we know, we're bombed by the EU!'

Thirty-four people in Nis died from the bombings – the last one just a few days earlier, when an elderly man was blown to bits after coming upon an unexploded bomb in his vegetable garden. Several hundred people were seriously maimed when blocks of flats were hit. NATO apologised and explained that they were aiming for the airport but miscalculated their coordinates. 'Since when do you use cluster bombs to take out an airstrip?' an angry Zivkovic wants to know. Cluster bombs are designed to kill and maim. They contain warheads with shrapnel that does fatal damage to human bodies but hardly has any effect on a landing strip.

'The sanctions are a boon to Milosevic,' Zivkovic continues. 'If it was up to him he would build a Berlin wall around all of Serbia. Now he can blame the sanctions for everything that's wrong here. Besides, this gives Milosevic and his inner circle full control over all imports and exports, without any supervision whatsoever. The West argues that the sanctions will weaken Milosevic because people's suffering will become insupportable, but that doesn't hold water. People have no idea that Milosevic is the reason for the sanctions. They believe, because that's what they see on TV, that it's part of a Western conspiracy,' he laughs bitterly. 'Serbia is like an old cripple with all kinds of ailments, barely able to crawl around on crutches. The West is a doctor who ponders how best to cure this patient and decides that a few hard whacks with a baseball bat ought to do the trick. He hires three strongmen to do the job, and then waits for the cripple to get up and walk,' Zivkovic mocks.

'We've had sanctions on the import of petrol for nine years now, but there's always petrol. It's smuggled in, and expensive. People lose, the smugglers win. These policies have led to a boom in the black-market economy: smuggling, drugs, prostitution. The weird thing is that when I am visited by foreign ambassadors they always agree with me. But I suppose governments don't really listen to diplomats – only to their own experts,' Zivkovic says. He stops to breathe, looks at the forbidden appetisers, pours another shot of *rakija* and picks up where he left off: 'This is a society on the verge, and anything this close to the edge is inherently dangerous. Milosevic can declare a state of emergency at any moment. If he keeps up this oppression people will revolt, and then he can call on the army. But if he does want a civil war on his hands we'll make sure that it begins in Dedinje [Belgrade's most exclusive enclave, where Milosevic has his residence]. People will be on his doorstep demanding his resignation. He'll be in jail before the year is over,' Zivkovic assures me.

'Do you really believe that?' I ask him.

'Well . . .' He hesitates. 'I have to believe it. Otherwise I might as well pack it in. But, let's eat.'

I help myself to stuffed eggs, ham and cheese, while Zivkovic chews on green salad and radishes. Afterwards there's beef ragout and several kinds of grilled meat. Zivkovic casts longing glances at the forbidden delicacies. He has to settle for bean stew, boiled peas and carrots, washed down with numerous mouthfuls of beer; the Church hasn't stripped him of the pleasures that the Serbian brewery Jelen can provide. Biserka barely takes time to sit with us. Like a perfect hostess, she keeps an eye on everything.

'We got married ten years ago: 1990 was the last good

year in Yugoslavia, just before we ran off the cliff. We could travel wherever we wanted to, we had money, anything was available,' Zivkovic remembers. 'I imported medical equipment, but my company was squeezed by the socialists. I lost my licence to import in 1995. The regime gave these licences only to its supporters, and at that time I was vice-president of the Democratic Party and elected to the Serbian parliament.' His wife and father-in-law found themselves without jobs when Zivkovic became a member of the parliament. They didn't get work until he was elected Mayor of Nis.

His wife is a lawyer. Only when the coffee has been served and Zivkovic is distracted by a phone call does she begin to talk. 'I'm both a mother and a father, a housewife, a wife, a party worker and a lawyer. I'm struggling to keep this family together. This isn't a normal life. Zoran never has any time for his family. But these are not normal times in Serbia and that's what the struggle is all about – to make Serbia a normal society again,' she sighs.

On the floor, two-year-old Marko is playing with his big sister's Barbie dolls. Barbie slaps Ken, and Ken strikes Barbie back. 'Wartime children in the Balkans learn quickly,' Zivkovic laughs, before he has to take another call. Making himself available is a point of pride for the young politician, and every journalist in town has his mobile number.

When his dad is on the phone Marko talks into his toy phone. But the mayor would hate to see his son follow in his footsteps. 'I hope that when Marko is a man we've managed to get this country to a place where politics is boring. I'd much rather see him apply himself to building something of his own, so that Serbia can once again be a modern nation in Europe, where we belong.'

Then he has to dash off to a strategy meeting with the party. Biserka stays at home to put the kids to bed.

At the beginning of May I drop into city hall to check on the coloured-in map and get an update on the campaign strategy. Zivkovic sits behind his desk, unshaven and wearing a tracksuit. An American thriller flickers on the TV. It's Easter Monday. 'The map isn't done yet. To be honest with you, we haven't even started it yet, or gathered more data or plotted a strategy. Nothing happens on time in this country. There won't be any election until September, at the earliest, if there is one at all,' Zivkovic sighs. He's been in the US for a week. 'A failure. I suppose my expectations were too high. My goal was to convince the Americans to lift the sanctions, but they tightened them instead.'

Several days' of growth makes Zivkovic's beard itch. It looks as if his Easter celebrations took a lot out of him. 'I can't stand shaving. I used to have a beard, but was told by Zoran Djindjic to shave it off. 'People don't trust politicians with beards,' he said. When I'm through with this madhouse I'll grow a huge beard.'

He laughs and empties his glass of ouzo, which he administered to himself as a morale booster. It doesn't appear to have done the trick.

'The maps are done,' Zivkovic brags when I visit him again towards the summer. 'They are at the party headquarters. We ended up making about ten smaller maps, so we could fit every household in. More than a thousand party members helped collect all the information. Now we'll analyse the results. 'The political situation in Serbia is more dismal than ever. The opposition fight among themselves, while more and more TV stations are shut down and journalists are arrested. Political activists and demonstrators are being jailed as well. The local TV station in Nis is still on the air and Zivkovic is fighting any way he can to keep it going. 'We've got armed guards around the broadcasting tower and I've said publicly that we've turned the area surrounding it into a minefield. Whether that's true or not is not as relevant as whether people believe it's true. It could be,' he says, and offers me a *bon voyage* shot of home-made plum brandy. 'This bottle was given to me by the father of a soldier who was killed in Kosovo. He called by the other day just to chat,' Zivkovic tells me. During the war he wore fatigues and inspected the troops who were heading to Kosovo – despite the fact that he opposed Milosevic's war as strongly as he did the NATO bombings.

We sink into a pair of deep leather chairs in the rather chilly mayoral office. Outside it must be forty degrees. Zoran Zivkovic has just returned from Norway. Twelve mayors from cities run by the opposition undertook a two-day visit. Zivkovic praises the efficiency and the beautiful scenery, and was impressed with how clean the streets in my hometown of Lillehammer were. 'But no wonder Lillehammer looks like a showcase,' he says. 'The municipality has a budget forty times larger than ours and the city is a tenth of the size. With that kind of money we'd be able to keep our pavements clean as well.'

The Norwegian government presented Zivkovic with a going-away present – dustbins and containers. 'Those dustbins will hold a lot of votes,' he laughs.

He looks tired and, like so many of the people I meet in Serbia in the spring of 2000, he seems to have lost faith. 'I have trouble sleeping and when I wake up I'm just as tired as when I went to bed. I come home after the kids have gone to sleep and leave before they get up. Now I haven't seen my children in three days. I need a holiday,' he sighs, and looks hopeless. Then he pours another shot. 'But this autumn we're getting rid of Milosevic,' he assures me. 'Just wait and see!'

The Zivkovic family do finally allow themselves a holiday, in Montenegro, but as far as Zoran is concerned it's a rather brief one. At the end of July Slobodan Milosevic announces national elections, after having altered the constitution so he can run for another term. Local elections, parliamentary elections and the presidential election will all be decided on 24 September.

Zoran Zivkovic heads the campaign in Nis. The Democratic Party trounces its opponents in the local elections, and a large majority of the voters here end up supporting the opposition's candidate for President, Vojislav Kostunica.

'We won so resoundingly I just knew Milosevic had to go right then and there,' Zivkovic smiles over a glass of whisky. It's a few days after the street revolution in Belgrade. I'm meeting the victorious mayor at the restaurant of the Democratic Party.

'What did I tell you? That Milosevic would fall this autumn!'

He laughs, obviously pleased.

'I took a convoy of hundreds of vehicles from Nis – cars, lorries, tractors. Along the way others joined in. On the road north, to Belgrade, we met people from Vranje, Leskovac, Pirot and Kragujevac. Whenever we came to a police barricade they generally just waved us through, and when they did stop us we only had to intimidate them a little. We were too many to stop, too many to be afraid of anything. When we reached Belgrade we marched as one to the parliament, where we met demonstrators from all over the country. We got there just before the parliament was stormed.'

But the events of that glorious October day are already history, and Zoran Zivkovic is not happy with the new President whom he helped get into office. 'Vojislav Kostunica has kept too many of Milosevic's men. He let the notorious Nebojsa Pavkovic, the chief of the armed forces, keep his job, not to mention the security chief, Rade Markovic. He negotiated with Milosevic without consulting the coalition. And as long as these people from Milosevic's inner circle are still in place, victory is not ours. Kostunica has a short window of opportunity to get rid of everyone whose hands are dirty. But he has to do it now, because it'll be more difficult later on. There's still a good chance the army might falter, because a lot of the generals have strong ties to Milosevic.'

General Pavkovic later recounted how the President had asked him to have the army subdue the demonstrations and, if necessary, shoot to kill. Pavkovic refused to obey and was allowed to keep his job by Vojislav Kostunica.

Zivkovic has to hurry off for an interview on RTS. 'Imagine that – I will be interviewed on Milosevic's former network!'

A few days later I visit him back in his office in Nis. Once more he expresses his dissatisfaction with Kostunica. 'Milosevic must be arrested at once. We have to show the world that we are a nation with a rule of law and that we are able to conduct a fair trial against the man who has led us from one disaster to another for the past decade. Right now Kostunica is alone. We've all told him to seize the moment. But he's a lone wolf. He always does what he wants.'

The phone rings. It's his party's boss, Zoran Djindjic, the

brains behind the unified election strategy of the Serbian opposition. Zivkovic grows serious. 'Where? How many?'

Djindjic has heard a rumour that a division of the army is on its way to Belgrade. The mood in the mayor's office is tense. 'There's still a good chance that there will be a minor counter-revolution. But, even if it's true, it will be defeated,' says Zivkovic.

I go back to Belgrade that same evening and see no troops anywhere.

Following these heady, early October days, the situation settles and the army remains loyal to the new President.

At the end of October a meeting is ordered to negotiate the various cabinet posts in the new Yugoslav government. These are to be divided between Serbia and Montenegro. On the Serbian side of the table sit Vojislav Kostunica, Zoran Djindjic, Goran Svilanovic and Zoran Zivkovic. It's already agreed that the Democratic Party will get the post of Interior Minister. They've put together a shortlist, but found them too light, too willing to compromise or lacking the necessary qualifications.

'I have a proposal,' Zivkovic says to Djindjic.

'You mean yourself? Fine – it's settled,' Djindjic replies.

And it is settled. Goran Svilanovic is named Foreign Minister. The cabinet is announced at the beginning of November and Zivkovic leaves his mayor's office and moves to the capital.

'What does the Mayor of Nis know about politics?' the journalists ask. 'He has no education and no qualifications for the Ministry of the Interior.'

'I'm good at knocking down doors and tearing down walls – and an expert at solving problems,' is the response of the new Interior Minister.

*

A few months later I meet the rookie minister again at a cocktail party at the bishop's residence in Nis. He offers me a lift back to Belgrade the next day.

The speedometer hovers around 220 kilometres an hour. Within the minister's armour-plated car, it's as if we're flying. Zivkovic is on the phone half the time. He gravely listens to himself on Radio Belgrade. It's the crisis in southern Serbia that tops the news these days. Three soldiers from the Yugoslav army have been wounded in attacks by Albanians. Several villages in the buffer zone between Kosovo and Serbia have been occupied by Albanian rebels, who are demanding their independence from Serbia.

'Interior Minister Zoran Zivkovic has given the extremists in the Presevo Valley one month to reach a diplomatic solution with the Yugoslav authorities and KFOR,' the radio announces.

'What happens if they don't reach an agreement?' I ask.

'Then the Yugoslav army goes to work,' Zivkovic answers.

'What does that mean?'

'That means that the Yugoslav army does what it's good at – obliterating terrorists. But we won't do it unless we get a green light from NATO. Or at the very least a yellow light,' he adds.

With the new situation Zivkovic's security is radically upgraded.

'Is it necessary with an armoured car?' I wonder.

'Well . . .' says Zivkovic.

'Yes,' the driver interrupts.

'Still, in the end only God can protect me,' Zivkovic adds, and invites me this coming Sunday to visit a friend of his who has become a monk.

Zivkovic has to attend, late in the evening, a meeting

of the Democratic Party, and drops me off at my house. A few hours later I see on the news that the driver of Serbia's new head of intelligence has been shot. The car was parked next to Zivkovic's outside the headquarters of the Democratic Party. The incident is understood as a warning to the government as they decide who to arrest for crimes committed under Milosevic. The driver survives.

The following weekend I come along to visit the monk in Sopocani. Our journey begins with a cup of coffee in Zivkovic's new offices in the Palace of the Federation. In Nis I could walk right into his office. Here I'm stopped by a policeman outside the building, then escorted inside by a security guard and then taken upstairs by another guard. I have to wait with a secretary until I'm led by another secretary through two armoured and soundproof doors into a huge office — at the far end of which I can just about make out the Minister of the Interior. The décor consists of large, heavy furniture in green velour, a massive desk, several empty tables, and lots of space. A gigantic portrait by the famous artist Petar Lubarda shows the Kosovo battle of 1389, while a map of Yugoslavia and the flag are displayed behind the minister's back. The Danube can be seen flowing by through a dozen windows.

I ask him if he's scared now, after the attack on his colleague's car the week before. 'We can't give in to fear — it might even have been a petty car thief,' he jokes as we head downstairs to the waiting car. Both his chauffeur and his bodyguard are experienced police officers.

In the back seat we discuss recent events. Zivkovic has just met the chief prosecutor of the Hague Tribunal, Carla del Ponte. She wants Milosevic tried for war crimes, while most Serbs want him to be tried in a Yugoslav court. 'We are the primary victims of his policies,' is the main argument. This is the attitude of the new President as well, but Zivkovic is not so sure. 'We have to cooperate with The Hague. We're obligated to, as members of the UN.'

It's February 2001. Deciding Milosevic's fate takes a long time. 'I guarantee that he will be arrested during this month,' Zivkovic says.

The monastery we are to visit is in Sandzak, a Muslim-dominated area on the border with Bosnia. Almost 80 per cent of the population in Novi Pazar, the largest city in the area, is Muslim. We're travelling on steep carriage roads that have never been used by a minister's armoured vehicle before. The beautiful monastery sits on the top of a ridge. We make the sign of the cross, then admire the remarkable murals inside the church, make another sign of the cross, then one more, and finally we are led into the monastery proper. The monks have invited some local Serbs to meet the minister. For refreshments we're served rose-petal jelly, coffee and *rakija*.

The first thing the monks want to know is when Kosovo will be returned to Serbia. Then they want to know what the authorities are planning to do about the Albanian guerrillas in southern Serbia. Then they'd like to hear what steps Zivkovic will take in Sandzak to ensure that the Muslims won't take over. The discussion quickly becomes animated and everyone wants to recount just how terrible the Muslims are, with their corruption, their bribery, their international funding. Zivkovic eventually grows tired of the accusations.

'But can you live with them?'

'Well, yes,' people murmur.

'We'll just leave it at that, then,' the minister says.

The abbot concludes the discussion and invites us to lunch.

I end up between two men eager to continue the talk. They complain about the corrupt Muslims who care only about money.

'What do you care about, then?' I ask.

'We care about more spiritual things. Like the Church and stuff,' they mumble.

On my right, Mica has a different perspective. He speaks English, so the others won't understand. 'They're a bunch of hypocrites. One moment they demand money from the West, the next they complain that the Muslims care only about money. The truth is that Muslims work five times harder than Serbs do, and are better off as a result. And the reason is very simple: all state-owned businesses and all administration have been closed to Muslims, so they've had to survive in the private sector. Corruption may very well be rampant – but who is it that receives these bribes? Serbian public servants.'

Mica sighs and tells me this sort of discussion reminds him of what Bosnia and Croatia were like before the wars broke out: the level of suspicion and distrust just grew until people went to sleep with guns under their pillows at night. 'The authorities have their work cut out for them,' he notes, and casts a troubled look at the Interior Minister at the end of the table.

Zivkovic gets to his feet and thanks the monks for their hospitality and the open dialogue.

After the visit to the monastery he is to meet some of Novi Pazar's most important men. A group consisting of both Muslims and Serbs awaits us in a café in town. There's a surgeon, a judge, a few CEOs and some shopkeepers. They've all realised that it's the Democratic Party that's running the show now, and they want to enlist as members. They chat for a while, and another meeting, this one in Belgrade, is agreed for a few weeks later. 'They have to understand that it pays to cooperate – not just with us, but with one another,' Zivkovic comments once we're back in the car.

We're on our way to the next item on his agenda. The minister is scheduled to participate in a live broadcast from Krusevac, and we're running late. It's grown dark and it's snowing hard. The armoured Audi isn't fitted with winter tyres, and the driver races along on roads slippery with ice. Zivkovic tells him to speed up where it's not icy.

On a bend leading into a bridge the driver loses control of the car. We skid sideways down the road and slam into the crash barrier. The car punches through the barrier and ends up suspended over the bridge. Some twenty metres below, the river rages. As the car dangles over the river, none of us moves. Nobody dares to blink for fear we'll tumble into the abyss. We exchange quick glances and then Zivkovic very slowly opens the door on his side – the side facing the road. He puts a foot down and pulls me to safety. The driver and the bodyguard are able to get out as well. A few centimetres made the difference – otherwise we would have been crushed against the rocks below or ended up in the freezing water.

The bodyguard crosses himself. Zivkovic lights a cigarette and I stand there shaking. The chauffeur tries to call for help but there's no coverage in this area. A man in a lorry arrives and takes us to Usce, the closest community. We show up at the local police station, where the small-town cops are rather stunned to receive such an unexpected nocturnal visit by the Interior Minister.

While the practicalities are sorted out and arrangements are made to get another car for us, the policemen waste no time. They tell the minister about their lousy salaries and their useless equipment. They've got a point – there's no mobile-phone coverage in Usce and the police station can only make local calls, so it took some time to organise our return. 'Ridiculous,' says Zivkovic. 'We will do something about this – only don't expect results overnight,' he adds. An hour later we're told that the transport to Belgrade is ready.

The live broadcast in Krusevac is long since over. It's quiet in the car; we are all deep in our own thoughts.

'Good thing we did all those signs of the cross up at the monastery,' says the bodyguard.

'Hm,' responds the minister.

I make a note of Zivkovic's guarantee that Milosevic will be arrested in February. In March I call him and we meet at his office.

'The investigation is ongoing,' he tells me. 'But we don't have enough evidence. Even though we know we're dealing with a criminal, we have to follow the law. Al Capone walked around with impunity for twenty years, even though everyone knew who he was and what he had done. The police just didn't have the evidence. Hopefully, we won't have to wait that long,' he laughs. 'We *should* have him by the end of March.' He is now unhappy about the collaboration with the West. 'I'm disappointed because I had expected more help and a better atmosphere. I hadn't expected that they would engage in extortion when it came to The Hague. The US is threatening to stop all aid unless we arrest Milosevic by 31 March. We've assured them that we are cooperating, and they ought to believe us. They caused billions of dollars' worth of damage with the bombings, so they should be obligated to help us,' reflects Zivkovic.

'The years ahead are like the road to Krusevac, whether we're talking about the conflict in southern Serbia,

Montenegro, the Hague Tribunal, the social situation here or the economy – everything. The road is long and it's dark and slippery. We're driving with bad lights and know there are all manner of curves, potholes and ice. We're in a hurry and have to go as fast as we can, but we can't really see what's ahead of us. It'll come down to a matter of being lucky – or unlucky. Just as it was with us. The crash barrier saved us. I don't know that the crash barrier exists that could save Yugoslavia.'

'We may have been going a bit fast . . .'

It's been three years. Still larger than life, Zoran Zivkovic is sitting behind an empty desk in an empty office. We're in one of Belgrade's darker alleyways, within a passage even cab drivers don't know about. If you're heading there you have to tell them you need to go 'behind the petrol pump at the café on the corner between Street X and Street Y', and then just keep your eyes peeled.

'The crash barrier couldn't hold us,' Zivkovic says. 'On the other hand, we knew how dangerous the road was. Still, we crashed into the abyss. Most transitional governments do, I suppose, and certainly that's been the case throughout Eastern Europe before it came to our turn. Now we have a new driver. A driver who doesn't go as fast as we did. A driver who, in fact, may try to turn around.

'Few countries have tried to change so much so quickly, and so radically, as we did. We wanted to cut through all the old stuff in one fell swoop. Or perhaps just outrace our past.'

Zivkovic's life these past few years has hardly left the fast lane. After a couple of years as Yugoslavia's Interior

Minister he was meant to be named Serbia's Minister of Defence in 2003 – a more powerful position. The former mayor had become Zoran Djindjic's closest collaborator, and a perfect number two: loyal to his boss, a tireless and energetic worker and someone who would never dream of challenging number one for the top spot.

Just as he was about to be named for the new post, Zivkovic's political fortunes took an unexpected turn. It was on 12 March, his wife Biserka's birthday. He was in his car when the mobile rang. He could see from the number that it was her, and thought he would let her know which restaurant they were to celebrate at that evening. He was soon by the government's offices, where a large crowd had gathered. Another demonstration, he told himself as he lifted the phone to his ear.

'They shot the boss!'

'What?'

He was a hundred metres away from the buildings.

'They shot him!'

'What?' he shouted again. But he knew right away what had happened. They had talked about it often enough: the risk of getting assassinated. The security detail insisted on wearing bullet-proof vests.

'Who'd dare shoot at us?' they had joked to one another.

'The heart of democracy can't go around in a bullet-proof vest,' Djindjic had said.

'Besides, they don't make them in my size,' Zivkovic would joke back.

The chauffeur stopped the car outside the government buildings. Zivkovic saw stunned faces, trembling shoulders, people crying. He headed for the side entrance, where he usually went in. There was blood on the stairs. The shots had been fired just minutes earlier.

He drove straight to the hospital. The doctor who met him told him right away that the Prime Minister had no chance of surviving.

On his way home Zivkovic recalled their last meeting. 'We talked about the new changes to the constitution. Zoran was on crutches. He had injured his Achilles tendon, and this day it hurt more than usual, hence the crutches. Usually he left them at home. He got up with an effort once our meeting was over. The secretary came in to get the coffee cups and asked Zoran if it was hurting badly. "Kennedy lived his whole life with a bad back; I think I can handle an aching foot," Djindjic replied.'

Soon after the murder Zoran Zivkovic was named Serbia's new Prime Minister.

'I had to try to continue what he started. After a tragedy like this you know what has to be done. My first act was to launch an investigation. We caught the little fish but not the big ones; we got the gunman but not the ones who ordered the hit. It was the old guard that killed him,' Zivkovic believes. 'A combination of Milosevic supporters and the Mafia. It might have been revenge by Milosevic's inner circle, or even family, or it could have been an attempt to keep Milosevic from being deported to The Hague. That Monday, two days before he was killed, we'd found a witness who could take down several of the big Mafia bosses in Belgrade. We decided that we would arrest the whole lot of them on Friday. By Wednesday Zoran was dead.'

The new Prime Minister was given credit for his attempt to clean up the Mob-dominated kleptocracy. A state of emergency was declared and hordes of criminals rounded up and arrested. But soon afterwards the criticism mounted. Zivkovic was accused of arresting his political opponents and of abusing his power. He couldn't get the coalition to cooperate, so the reform process soon stalled. 'He isn't good enough, not wise enough, not brilliant enough,' went the chorus of disapproval. Everyone compared him unfavourably with Djindjic, the greater thinker, the superior strategist. 'He could not run an entire country,' the politician and professor of psychology Zarko Korac told me later. 'Zivkovic is a kind and sensitive man. After the assassination he would sometimes come to my office and cry. He couldn't deal with a challenge like this. It's not that he's not a good leader – he'd make an exceptional Prime Minister in a country like, say, Norway, where everything is defined – where there is a national infrastructure in place, where there is the rule of law, where the police do their job, where you can trust the intelligence apparatus and where hospitals, schools, social services run on schedule. But for a country like Serbia, where nothing works? That takes a greater man than Zivkovic.'

'We lost precious time when we lost Zoran,' Zivkovic reflects. 'He was someone who could have seen the reforms through much better than I ever could. He got people to cooperate. The coalition included fifteen parties. Zoran excelled when it came to patting others on the back, talking with everyone, listening to other points of view. I never had his patience. And eventually we became utterly paralysed.'

When the next election came round, the Democratic Party lost heavily and the nationalist parties gained ground.

'I wasn't surprised. We were extremely unpopular. People don't realise the need for shock therapy. Serbs, like most other people, don't want to hear that they'll have to do the job themselves. They welcome the changes but don't want to pay the price for them. They're lazy,' he says, echoing what Zoran Djindjic had told me in the back of his car just after Milosevic's arrest.

'We knew we ran the risk of losing the election. I remember Zoran and I having intense discussions about this before he was killed. But we always agreed that we'd continue, even if the reforms made us unpopular. Zoran was ahead of his time. He was both a visionary and a pragmatist, a philosopher who understood politics and social science. Only in death did he become beloved. "If people think they can stop the reforms by getting rid of me, they are sorely mistaken," he said, just weeks before he was shot. But he was wrong. The reforms died. God knows when we'll be able to resurrect them.'

As a consequence of the election results Zivkovic had to relinquish the position of Prime Minister to Yugoslavia's former President, Vojislav Kostunica, in the spring of 2004. Kostunica had lost his position as President the previous year, when Yugoslavia had officially ceased to exist.

Zivkovic received Kostunica in the government offices and handed over the keys, which was a first in Serbian history. Usually a minister clears out his office before his successor arrives.

'I'm not expecting anything positive from you, but I pray to God that I'm wrong,' Zivkovic told Kostunica during the meeting. Kostunica didn't answer. 'He usually doesn't respond. Now it's been two months. I hope someone has told him he's the new Prime Minister,' Zivkovic adds sarcastically.

Then came Zivkovic's next battle. Following the worst election he'd ever run in, where the Democratic Party received only 12 per cent of the votes, the party was in disarray. During the annual party conference in March he lost his chairmanship to Boris Tadic, the Defence Minister. Zivkovic promptly resigned from all other responsibilities as well.

'After holding office for twelve years I just wanted to be a loyal, well-regarded citizen again!'

Zivkovic's large body shakes with laughter and he scratches his beard, which he has grown, just like he said he would when his political career was over. The former Prime Minister pulls out a sheet of paper and draws a curve. It runs upwards sharply, only suddenly to plummet straight down.

'This is my political career. I was a regular party member for only five days before I was elected to the board of the local party chapter in Nis. Then I won a seat in parliament, then I became vice-president of the party, then mayor, then Interior Minister, then Prime Minister, and then, meaning right now, nothing!'

He strokes his beard and looks out of the bare windows.

'The party has to go through this. Just as the country threw out the Democratic Party, the Democratic Party threw me out. We made a lot of mistakes. The party had almost complete power after Djindjic's death. During the state of emergency we even controlled the army. People started to think we were omnipotent. That they lived in a one-party system again.'

'Have you lost friends?'

'Oh, after middle school you don't really make friends. You just have colleagues and associates.'

'Are you in contact with Boris Tadic? Does he ever call on you for advice?'

'No,' says Zivkovic, visibly surprised by the question. 'Never. Besides, I'm on holiday now. I've granted myself a hundred days of silence. People won't have to listen to a single word from me for a hundred days, and then I'll start to think about my return.'

'You want to return to politics?'

'Eh . . . I've talked only politics for a dozen years now. I think it's time I tried silence. I'm building a house in Nis. It'll be great to get out of Belgrade. I mean, I lived in the most dangerous neighbourhood in town, you know — Uzicka Street, number 16. The people who lived there before me have already been sent to The Hague!'

'What are you going to do now?'

'The first thing is to let my kids get to know me again. They've barely seen their dad and they've lived with their grandparents the past few years. Biserka and I didn't want them living in Belgrade, since we were both so busy here. My daughter was one year old when I entered politics and my son hadn't been born yet. Politics is a heavy drug. It grabs you and chokes you.'

The bearded giant looks out through the cracked window. From his office in the basement, the view consists of the feet of those who pass by outside. He turns to face me again.

'Now I go to bed without worrying about what tomorrow will bring.'

But Zivkovic looks too tense for me to believe him. His flickering eyes betray him. Could he be plotting his revenge here, or is he resigned to his fate in the basement?

'How will you make a living?'

'I'll become a businessman. Start a business. Or maybe lease a plane. So we could have non-stop connections between Nis and the rest of Europe: Paris, Zurich, Athens, Amsterdam. What do you think? Or maybe set up a firm for exports.'

'What would you export?'

'Anything.'

'Like what?'

'There's a Norwegian company that I'd like to export goods to.'

'Which one?'

'It starts with a "T". "T"-something – I can't remember.'

'What do they do?'

'They do vegetables. Or, they need vegetables. They need freeze-dried vegetables, large volume – carrots, peppers, onions, beans. We could grow and dry them, and then export them to Norway.'

'What do they do with dried vegetables?'

'They make soups and sauces and things like that. It starts with a "T" . . . t, t, t . . .'

'Toro!'

'Yes, that's it! Toro!'

On my way out to the alley nobody knows about, I stumble over some junk by the basement door and think to myself that some politicians become statesmen. Others become vegetable dealers.

Stylish Resistance

'He is finished!'

Otpor's slogan, 2000 election

'He is guilty!'

Otpor's slogan, 2001 election

'The truth well told!'

McCann-Erickson Group's slogan, 2004

With her subtle make-up, shiny black mane of hair and sunglasses casually resting on her forehead, Katarina resembles an Italian movie starlet. When she raises a clenched fist she looks like an Italian movie starlet playing a demonstrator. But Katarina's struggle is real enough. When she is pushed around by riot police in the streets of Belgrade, when she receives threatening phone calls and when she's tailed at night, on her way home from her watch at Otpor's offices, it's all too real. Katarina is an activist in Otpor, or Resistance. She is among those whom the Serbian state media refers to as fascists and terrorists. 'Criminals, drug fiends and freeloaders,' was Information Minister Goran Matic's description of the Otporists.

During the spring and summer of 2000, each week activists were jailed, beaten and threatened. Their offices were searched and closed. Otpor was accused of being behind the murders of both political leaders and members of the Mafia. Given that the political opposition frequently engaged in endless, internal debates and arguments, many came to see Otpor as the regime's only credible opponent. Several political leaders took to wearing T-shirts and badges with the organisation's logo, a clenched fist. In turn the regime regarded Otpor as a growing threat, while the opposition exploited its popularity to regain lost credibility.

Katarina joined Otpor in the autumn of 1999, when she was twenty. 'I saw the fist everywhere, on posters or on walls, as graffiti. I didn't know what it meant but I liked it. The fist recalls both fascist and communist iconography, but it really represents resistance to them. I like the fact that it's in black and white, the hateful and the pure. It represents unity. When the regime advertises itself it always uses pink colours and flowers. And that's exactly the sort of oppressive dishonesty that we're fighting.

'I'd been curious about the fist for a long time when I learned about Otpor. I went to a meeting and decided that I wanted to do my part in the struggle for a free Serbia. I like our campaigns. It's so obvious what we stand for: you have to struggle, you have to resist.'

The similarity between Otpor's fist and the fascist symbol is not lost on the regime. One morning Belgrade was covered in Nazi-like posters, showing an SS soldier with a clenched fist and the Otpor logo on his chest. 'Madlen Jugend,' read the text. Madeleine Albright, the US Secretary of State under Clinton, was the regime's favoured object of loathing, and with this poster they tried to make their point that Otpor was bought and paid for by the 'Fascist Mrs Albright'.

'It's too stupid – they aim too low and don't have any style,' moans Katarina about the regime propaganda. 'I get so mad when they go on TV and brag that Yugoslavia is the country of progress and development. We're completely cut off from the rest of the world. All I want is to live a normal life. I'm fighting for democracy, for free universities, a free press. And of course that he goes,' she adds; 'he' being Slobodan Milosevic.

We're at a table in Plato, a pavement café next to Belgrade University's philosophy department. Katarina is a second-year psychology student and has an exam in a couple of hours. She doesn't seem all that nervous. 'It's a simple exam, just a few English translations,' she explains, and returns to the subject of resistance. Like Katarina, most of Otpor's members are students, but a growing number of older people have joined the organisation, along with various celebrities. It's become hip to be an Otporist.

Katarina's account is interrupted by a woman anxious to share the latest rumour. 'Did you hear that the Education Minister will close all the faculties tomorrow? My daughter just heard it on the radio,' says the woman, a professor of psychology. 'Where will it end?' she sighs.

Katarina takes this in her stride. 'So maybe I won't be able to take my exams this year. What's the big deal? I'm happy to sacrifice a few terms to my resistance struggle. If I don't fight now, and get my degree in a few years, then what? Who's going to pay me? It's right now that we can do something for our future.'

Morning coffee turns into lunch. We order salad and a pizza Margarita to share, and then Katarina will head off to her exam. Perhaps her last exam for some time, if the universities are to be closed.

When we meet up the next day the plaza in front of the university is teeming with students. It's a demonstration against the Information Minister. Katarina is wearing Otpor's colours: black Capri pants and a white T-shirt. Once again she looks as if she has stepped out of a fashion spread despite not having slept a wink all night. 'I got an anonymous warning yesterday telling me to lower my profile. And they told me not to sleep at home,' she says. 'I stayed away from home, but the police never showed up. Maybe they called because I sat here talking to you all day yesterday. A lot of the waiters are government informants. That guy who sells popcorn across the street is as well,' Katarina says, pointing him out.

After the threatening phone call she went to a party that, as usual, continued until dawn. She was among the last to leave. Thus was solved the problem of where to spend the night. 'In all likelihood they had no intention of arresting me. But this way they are at least able to intimidate people.'

During this week hundreds of activists are arrested, most of them in the early hours of the morning at home.

The crowd keeps growing. We've found a table beneath a parasol and have a front-row seat for the demonstration, with some protection from the glaring sun's thirty-five-degree heat. It's a bit cramped, but we're in good shape and ready, with an ample supply of espresso, to listen to the numerous speeches. Representatives from various university departments take turns, all of them saying the same thing: 'Resist, resist, resist.' The drone of words is punctuated by bursts of heavy rock music. But the demonstration doesn't really kick into high gear until someone shouts, 'Tear down the wall! Tear down the wall!'

This refers to the hated fence that closes off the larger part of the university plaza. It was erected by the authorities in the summer of 1998 to keep students from gathering to protest at the new education law that stripped the learning institutions of their autonomy. Under the new law it was the government's job to name deans and chancellors, who in turn could hire and fire staff and faculty at will.

The students hurl themselves at 'the wall', pushing and shoving until the abhorrent structure collapses into planks and sheets of corrugated metal. The jubilant students rush in, some doing cartwheels on the overgrown lawn. Left to its own devices, the lawn has turned into a verdant wilderness, full of wild strawberries, red poppies and flowers in white and lavender. Katarina adorns herself with flowers and dances to the rock music. And then it's time to leave. The student leader gives advice in case the police come to stop us. 'We'll divide into small groups, take the side streets and meet up at the city hall,' he shouts. 'Save Serbia – Slobodan, go kill yourself!' the crowd roars, using an old football chant. Sometimes Slobodan is replaced by Mira, his wife, but it's the Slobodan chant that gets the loudest response. Milosevic's father, mother and uncle all committed suicide during his early years, and many in Otpor think it would be a splendid idea if he were now to follow suit. But not Katarina. 'I don't really like that song,' she says, and only half-heartedly adds her voice to the crowd's. 'It's too primitive.'

Several thousand students march through the streets, and not a single policeman can be seen. The march first heads to Saborna Crkva, the Patriarchate Church, to ask for the Church's support in the struggle, then to the city hall, where they demand that the mayor come outside to answer their charge of cowardice. Belgrade's city council is led by the Serbian Renewal Movement, Vuk Draskovic's party. Draskovic, a former member of Milosevic's cabinet, is not above striking the occasional secret deal with the authorities.

Having yelled themselves hoarse in the burning sun for hours on end, Katarina and her friends have had their fill. 'Let's go and drink *Gazozo*,' she suggests to her crowd, who respond with cheers. 'You have to try *Gazozo*; it tastes so silly that you just have to laugh. It's a fizzy drink with bubblegum flavour,' they tell me. We drink the iridescent yellow tutti-frutti drink on the pavement, and it does indeed have a ridiculous taste. We toast the sunshine, and the clenched fists relax for today.

Katarina wants to go back to Otpor's offices to see 'if anything's happening'. She is to help organise activities for the following day, when a massive demonstration in Republic Square is planned. 'I hope it's not at noon,' she mumbles. 'There's this cosmetics convention I'd like to check out.'

It's understood that the demonstration takes precedence if she is made to choose. A few hours later she calls me with the happy news: 'The demo's not until five. We'll make the convention just fine.'

A brand-new Katarina meets me outside the Intercontinental the next day. She fits right into the exclusive hotel's rarefied atmosphere, wearing a tight sea-green skirt and a blue blouse. She has brought along her equally

gorgeous friend Jelena. But despite their elegant appearance, the two students have little disposable income, so
instead of shopping we just drift from stand to stand, try
things, smell things, laugh and flirt. Pretty soon there is not
an inch of their flesh that isn't covered in various shades of
lipstick and eyeliner or immersed in a cornucopia of per-
fumes. We attend demonstrations of anti-cellulite
massages, wrinkle-removing creams, hair removal and nail
extensions. We spend a lot of time on lip gloss, which can
be found with glitter, in pink, blue, yellow, gold or silver,
and costs one pound. Katarina and Jelena take note of the
shades they really like and tell the salesgirls that they'll
think it over. We allow ourselves a breather in the swish
lobby.

'Over there is where Arkan was killed.' Katarina points,
almost in awe, at a section in the corner set out with chairs.
'They've blamed that murder on Otpor, too. It's absurd. It
was a Mafia hit,' she assures me.

Jelena is examining the testers and the brochures she's
collected; a law student, she is far more concerned with
make-up than with politics. 'I can't really get engaged –
this country's going down the drain and I'd rather just
watch from the sidelines.' Katarina is beyond trying to continue this discussion with her friend.

At the end of the day Katarina decides on a perfume for
her mother's birthday, while Jelena allows herself the lip
gloss in pink glitter. An exhausted Katarina sinks down
into the purple-leather extravaganzas in the lobby. I remind
her that the opposition's mass demonstration is about to
start. She's not moving.

'It's against my principles,' she announces, almost dis-
missive in her certainty.

'What?'

'The opposition doesn't deserve my presence.'

'When did you acquire this principle?'

'Last night,' she reveals with complete confidence. 'The opposition is a mess, they can't decide on anything, everybody's got their own agenda, everybody wants to run the show and everyone's negotiating with Milosevic behind one another's backs. I've attended every single demonstration the opposition has arranged this year and I've gone to city hall every night at seven to hear them read the news aloud. And what have these eternal demonstrations achieved? Nothing!'

I'm surprised. Maybe even Katarina is about to be engulfed by the treacle of apathy that seems to overwhelm most people. Or maybe she's just bored with it all.

'From now on I'll only attend Otpor's protests,' she decides, not without some relief at not having to rush along to Republic Square in the afternoon heat.

This way we have lots of time to get ourselves pretty for the evening's festivities. Katarina and her friends are going to a *splav*, a disco boat. 'You should get dressed up,' Katarina tells me. 'You can come as you are, of course, but you'll have more fun if you dress up a bit and put on some make-up.'

I get the message and spend the rest of the afternoon trying to become young, fun and fashionable. Pink top with silver patterns, a shiny grey skirt, sandals in fake gold, blue eyeshadow and pink, glittery lip gloss. To top it all off, I put my hair up in a ponytail. As soon as I'm in the taxi I understand that I've pulled it off – at least the young part.

'Are your parents diplomats here?'

'No.'

'Are you a student, then?'

I tell the driver that I'm writing a book about the Serbs.

'I'm sure it will be very interesting,' he responds graciously. Down by the waterfront he stays to make sure that someone's meeting me before he risks leaving.

As soon as I spot Katarina I realise I'm wearing all the wrong things. She glides towards me in an ankle-length, steel-blue evening dress showing ample cleavage, and subtle make-up. She looks like Liz Hurley. I can go as her clumsy cousin. Along the glittering Danube the boats lie like a string of pearls – restaurants, discos, cafés. Each has a distinct style, its own clientele. The *Prestige* suits Katarina and her friends: beautiful, stylish kids in their twenties.

'Looking good matters more than anything here,' Katarina explains. 'You may not have money for food or your phone bill, but you can't let it show.'

We have a window seat next to the railing and pay close attention to who comes and goes. The clenched fists are out of sight, out of mind.

'A lot of my friends in Otpor, that's their whole life. They seem to live at the office. I like to socialise with all kinds of people – except for those that support Milosevic, of course; I wouldn't want any of them for my friends. But it's important for the cause that we recruit people from all kinds of backgrounds; only then will we be victorious,' she tells me, and interrupts herself for a rousing singalong with the rest of the boat. The house band seems to specialise in Yugoslav disco classics. Apparently, running around in the streets chanting, 'Slobo, go kill yourself!' isn't the only way to let off steam in Belgrade.

Eventually Katarina and Bojana's attention turns to the railing. 'I saw their car pulling up,' says Bojana. 'Maybe they're on a different boat. But I'm sure they'll get here eventually,' they assure themselves. The girls have crushes on two players in Yugoslavia's youth football team. They flirt with them on the *Prestige* every Saturday night. But the hours pass and the two boys never show up. At long last Bojana goes ashore to investigate. 'The car's gone,' she reports, downcast. 'Maybe they have a big match tomorrow,' I try, by way of encouragement. 'Nah, the season's over,' they both inform me. Once the two footballers are out of the picture, the evening doesn't quite have the same sparkle. Some of the air goes out of the girls, and around three we start walking back.

Over the weekend we meet up at the usual café outside the philosophy faculty. A large demonstration has been arranged to protest at the closing of the universities. But as it turns out, the faculty remains open, so the demonstration is cancelled. The dean refused the government's orders, and was joined by his colleague at the linguistics faculty.

'The police have brought dogs to guard the entrance to the law school,' says a guy. 'Let's go there to demonstrate!' he urges us, but Katarina only shakes her head. 'I have to defend my own faculty,' she answers, and stirs sugar into her espresso. 'Besides, I really have to study for my exams,' she adds, a bit sheepishly.

Later that week she calls me again: 'My grandparents are joining Otpor! Want to come along?'

Katarina comes from a family with a long tradition of rebellion. Her grandfather, the philosopher Ljubomir Tadic, was one of the first opponents of Tito. He helped found the dissident journal *Praxis* in 1964 and was a vocal critic of Tito's socialist regime. Later he became concerned with the plight of the Serbs and inspired and supported Milosevic's nationalistic rhetoric in the late eighties. Tadic fought for the rights of Serbs in Kosovo but eventually turned his back on Milosevic. Katarina's grandmother, Nevenka, is a well-known psychiatrist. Now the two of them join their old friend Dobrica Cosic, who had joined Otpor a week earlier. This former President of Yugoslavia was a novelist and intellectual credited with being the original inspiration for the resurgent Serbian nationalism of the 1980s and 1990s. For that he was called 'the father of the nation'.

In articulate French the professor of philosophy explains to me what sort of country Serbia has become: '*Le despotisme, la dictature, la stupidité.* I have always been a dissident, always been against the regime. This is simply a continuation of Tito's rule, although without the ideology. Tito at least had one. The current regime has but one goal: to hold on to power. They have no ideas, only old slogans. This regime is pure violence,' Ljubomir Tadic concludes. '*La pure violence!*'

Katarina listens in silence. 'I'm pleased to see that you are continuing this family's revolutionary traditions,' her grandfather says. 'Today it is exactly thirty-two years since I was beaten by the police here at the university,' he says, recalling the student riots of 1968. By the Otpor stand at the university plaza, the grandparents take out their glasses and write down, each in a meticulous hand, their name, address, age and which faculty they belong to. 'I'm still at Philosophy?' asks the retired professor.

The grandparents are given their Otpor badges and a brochure. They are now among thirty thousand registered Otpor members.

'Just one more thing – you have to learn to use the clenched fist as our greeting,' their granddaughter suggests. She shakes her fist to demonstrate. The grandparents follow suit. '*Otpor, Otpor, Otpor!*' the grandmother shouts softly.

'I still can't believe it,' shrieks Katarina in my mobile. She can barely be heard over the rock music and cheering in the

background. The Serbs are celebrating their sudden freedom for the second night in a row, and Katarina has danced
along Belgrade's streets singing victory songs for more than
twenty-four hours, until she hardly has a voice left. 'It's a
dream come true,' she croaks. 'We've won! Slobo is gone!
This means I can stay in Belgrade and get an actual job,
instead of thinking I should emigrate!'

The psychology student has found a spot where the
music is less deafening. 'But I'm a bit angry as well,' she
suddenly says. 'Vojislav Kostunica has yet to mention Otpor
in any of his speeches, and I just know that we delivered at
least half the victory. Last spring the opposition clamoured
around us because people trusted us, while they just
engaged in all kinds of infighting. But now that they've
won they're tossing us aside.'

But Katarina can't dwell on the bitterness for too long.
'It's the oddest thing. Today it's a year to the day since I
joined Otpor. And this is our first day of freedom!'

She soon grows impatient and wants to return to the
revelries. 'I'm really looking forward to seeing you again –
just not tonight.'

A few weeks later we meet again at Plato. 'I've decided
to leave Otpor and become a normal student again. All I
really want to do now is study,' she tells me.

At the table next to us some of the leaders of the student
organisation remind a reluctant Katarina of a meeting at
five o'clock.

'The battle is won,' she says. 'The best thing now would
be to disband the organisation completely. We could resurrect it later, if it's needed. To continue fighting would
just be about nostalgia. We need to get on with our own
lives instead.'

She puts out her cigarette and returns to her studies.

There are several exams coming up over the next few weeks. At some point this autumn she leaves Otpor behind.

Otpor arranges its second congress in February 2001. Activists from all across Serbia are bussed to Belgrade. They gather in front of the federal parliament, which they took part in storming, and wave their banners, raise their fists and take pictures of each other. The crowd plants flags by the statue outside the Trades Union Building, where the congress is taking place. The security guards are unable to process the huge crowd in a timely fashion, and soon enough everything is a chaotic mess. Journalists, cameras and VIPs are teeming within the conference hall.

The assembly starts with an emotional movie about the struggle for freedom. Everything from footage of the war in Bosnia and shots of policemen beating up demonstrators to scenes from the storming of the parliament and the election victory in December is mashed together and set to a rather dramatic piece of classical music. Then there's a speech honouring the many activists and ten young men are called to the stage. They are supposed to be the ones who risked most in the struggle against Slobo. 'All in all, we've spent forty-two thousand hours in Milosevic's jail cells,' the speaker announces.

The next speech details, with much pomp and circumstance, how Otpor now will transform itself from a revolutionary movement into an evolutionary movement. The fist has to go, as they no longer have an opponent worthy of such a gesture and this is a time to be gracious to the vanquished. A torrent of words flow over the crowd, but nothing really indicates exactly what the purpose of the evolutionary movement is meant to be, beyond a host of slogans. Still, the ten men on stage outdo one another in glorious mutual assessments.

A voice from the floor shouts out: 'Otpor was not made up of ten people!'

'Let the winner speak,' replies a stout young man on the dais. He seems to delight in the spotlight, and continues to speak of this 'house' that Otpor is to build. 'It will be resistant to storms and bad weather, because it will be built by *us*.'

Much applause. The speaker leaves the podium and the audience wait for the next item on the agenda, but nothing happens. The stage is empty. Evidently the congress is over before it began, without any debate, any floor votes. Not that Otpor ever demonstrated any sort of democratic leanings on an organisational level. After a while a janitor takes the stage to begin the clean-up and asks the stragglers to leave the building.

I meet Katarina soon afterwards. She nods when I recall the grand, yet hollow speech. 'There's no creativity left in the organisation – only big words. They're relying on the same rhetoric as they used against Slobo, but these days it just sounds ridiculous.'

Only now does Katarina reveal that the inner workings of Otpor were far from high-minded. 'A lot of money came in from abroad, and some of it disappeared. People had their own agenda. Some of those that remain are trying to milk Otpor for anything that might be left. I didn't want to believe the rumours about the money at first, but I'm afraid they're true.'

Katarina has other bones to pick with the organisation. 'Male chauvinists. The fact that only guys were called to the stage is symptomatic. All those who had any power in Otpor were men. They made the decisions. I didn't notice at first, because I felt very welcome, but after a while I noticed that girls were more than welcome to help out, but you wouldn't get to participate in making decisions. They asked me to be the model for a poster – that was the part they envisaged for me.'

Still, Katarina thinks the organisation played a crucial part in bringing about the fall of Milosevic. 'We helped diminish the fear. We showed people they could take chances.'

The transition from Milosevic's totalitarian regime proved more difficult, on a mental level, than many had expected. 'People became depressed. The struggle had given their lives meaning, and now they had to find something else. That feeling of unity and energy is why so many of them recall the struggle against Milosevic as the best time of their lives. You have no idea of how many couples broke up afterwards. These relationships that seemed so perfect, in reality they were only about Otpor. Suddenly they had nothing in common any more, or anything to talk about. So they split up.'

And while Katarina is done with Otpor, she's not done fighting. 'Some friends and I are going to start an organisation to encourage peace and reconciliation throughout the former Yugoslavia. It's high time we all find our way back to one another, so young Croats, Bosnians and Serbs, who were all kids when the wars started, don't end up making the mistakes their parents did,' she explains to me.

'You know why this matters to me?' she asks, and grows serious. 'I'm afraid for my brother. He's only sixteen, but he reads all these books about Serbia: history, myths, all about the great Serbian nation. He's turned into a rank nationalist and believes that Serbs are superior to anyone else. It scares me to talk with him now. He said the other day that he couldn't fathom me having a Croatian girlfriend and that we ought to hate Croats. I just hope he'll grow out of it, that it's just some kind of teenage rebellion thing,' says Katarina.

I attend one of the very first meetings of the 'Peacemakers'. We're meeting in a *pivnica* – a beer hall – in the centre of Belgrade. One of the boys has already proposed a logo: a heart cut in half held together by two hands. 'The logo is a play on "pacemaker", and that we have to join together to make the heart beat again,' he explains. A girl suggests that the background might consist of a red map of the former Yugoslavia. 'No, that's too banal,' someone argues. 'It's Yugonostalgia,' concludes another.

'Yugonostalgia' is a word heard more and more in Belgrade. It is meant to evoke the sorrow and melancholy surrounding the dissolution of the republic. 'I am a Yugonostalgic,' Katarina admits. 'We'll never get Yugoslavia back, but at least we can try to get people talking and living with one another again.'

The Peacemakers' first order of business is to conduct a seminar on war crimes. 'We want to gather young people from the whole region, invite researchers and politicians, and try to understand more about what really happened during the war. Our primary goal must be to establish a peaceful dialogue with kids from the other states, so that we'll never have another war here. We have to make a distinction between collective and individual responsibility,' Katarina says. 'I was ten when the wars began, and I don't want to accept any guilt for what Milosevic and Karadzic did, just because I'm Serbian. Nobody asked me if I wanted to go to war.'

The Peacemakers fall apart over the spring months. Their plans for a war crimes conference is the first casualty:

it's simply too large an undertaking for the eight activists. Then they are unable to agree on other projects and can't decide on what methods to proceed with. Katarina half-heartedly attends a few of the meetings. 'Truth be told, I'm tired of trying to make the world better – I'd rather focus on my own life for a while,' she says, and talks with great enthusiasm about her studies, what books she is reading and the discussion group she leads at a mental institution outside Belgrade. 'You should see the condition this place is in. There are no activities for the patients, the paint is peeling off the walls, they haven't eaten meat for years. The highlight of their week is my Wednesday-evening group. They pick the topics themselves. When I'm there I feel like I'm actually doing something, something real, to create a kinder Serbia.'

The espresso has been replaced by green tea. Katarina's fashion sense is geared more towards a hippie-ish style and she's a bit paler than she used to be. She's wearing a grey knitted sweater with a green scarf tossed casually over her shoulder, and declines sugar with her tea. Her health regime is not, however, of the extreme sort; it doesn't take her long to light her first cigarette. It's 2004, and we're back at Plato. After a raucous reunion embrace, Katarina sits down. 'The situation is more depressing than ever,' she sighs. 'I want to move.'

'You?' I say. 'You, who always wanted to have a future in Serbia?'

'Well, I can't really see any future I'd want here. And at least I would want to see something else before it's too late. I would like to go to graduate school in Great Britain. But it's next to impossible to get into any schools there, get a visa, money to live on. I'm almost a fully fledged psychologist now; my finals are this spring. But I have no idea what I'll do after that.'

In the wake of the democratic dream crumbling, perhaps nobody has had their illusions broken quite as hard as recent university graduates. They had the highest hopes of anyone, aspiring to jobs, travel, flats. When it became apparent that Serbia couldn't be turned around overnight, they fell the furthest.

'The party ended soon enough,' says Katarina. She herself is privileged: she lives with her parents, who have good jobs and do well. She has been able to focus on her studies. 'A lot of my friends have drifted off course. People drop out of school, talk about emigrating. You remember, when Milosevic fell, everyone talked about staying here after all. But now everyone wants to leave again.'

Katarina smiles and waves to several people who pass our table. Friends keep coming over to give her a hug, relive the last party, give her a message from someone. The fledgling psychologist has an astonishing ability to slip in and out of conversations, to share her attention equally, only to pick up just where we left off.

'My best friends are all politically active. On the same side as me. You know, for the Democrats. But I attended my middle-school reunion the other day and among them there were quite a few who had voted for the nationalists – can you imagine?'

The twenty-four-year-old rolls her eyes. Her gestures are as dramatic as they ever were. She flails her hands like an Italian, only to catch my eyes again.

'Nationalism is coming back. It's scary. It's as if we've forgotten everything that happened during the war in Bosnia. Especially following the unrest in Kosovo, it's suddenly become acceptable to speak of Serbian greatness again. That's where the Radicals find their votes now. The new government is playing on this sentiment as well. They've retracted Djindjic's reforms in education and other areas. A representative from the Ministry of Education recently informed us that English will no longer be taught from the first year of school onwards, as the Democrats had decreed. "It is not in our national interest – it might disrupt the study of Serbian," he said. It's like living under the communists again, when the leaders feared foreign influences.'

Katarina draws deeply on her cigarette.

'And more recently, when the Ministry of Culture presented their priorities, can you imagine what they put in first place? Protecting the Cyrillic alphabet! As if that is endangered in any way . . .'

Katarina is unwavering in her belief that her future lies in Europe. Subsequently she's found a youth organisation sponsored by the EU, which educates people about European integration and European values. 'I got a spot on a five-day seminar in Strasbourg! Imagine – I get to go there,' she smiles enthusiastically. 'The seminar is titled "Politics, Society and State". Oh, I wish Serbia could join one day, but I'm afraid that's a way off. If we were in the EU the university library wouldn't have just one of the books on the required reading list, but maybe twenty. Only a few of us can afford to buy books and the reading list for the curriculum is almost impossible to get hold of. We copy off each other, but the copies are poorer each time. And then there's the notion of having soap in the university's toilets. Or just toilet paper. You know, even that is just too fancy for us: soap gets stolen right away.'

Katarina sighs.

'In this organisation we try to educate people, but it's

not easy. People don't get the EU thing. They say, "I don't have a loaf of bread to my name, and we're going to join Europe?" Or, "Never mind not getting a visa to Italy; I can't afford a bus ticket to Nis." People don't have money for food, and someone like Seselj becomes alluring, with his promises of free bread and the resurrection of a Greater Serbia. We need more optimism, a new energy, but we have neither right now.'

'Well, you do.'

'Yes, but a lot of my best friends don't care. They're just concerned with their own lives. They take classes, think about themselves and wait for something to happen. I'm astonished by all those who have no interest in shaping their own future. What could be more important than that? On the other hand, I can understand that people give up; we've been disappointed so many times. But we can't give up the dream of a better world,' she says, and looks around at the crowd at the tables around us. Students and professors sit side by side, drinking tea or whisky, or eating pizza. Posters cover the walls, every ashtray is overflowing and the smoke is thick throughout the café.

'This is a confused society,' Katarina decides, still observing her fellow guests. 'Nobody understands what's going on, or who's in charge. But I do believe that young people here are about to wake up, and realise that it's not nationalism and Kostunica that they want, but that this will only lead us further away from the rest of the world. We're at a crossroads,' she says. 'Anything can happen. Sometimes I wonder what I'm doing here. I see my friends moving abroad and wonder if I should do the same. But are their lives better there? Maybe they can get a job as a waitress or a dishwasher. They'll have to fight for their survival there as well.'

'What do you yourself want?'

'If I truly could pick and choose, I would go to London for my postgraduate studies and then come back here. I want to be a human resources manager.'

'What's that?'

'Human resources manager? It's like . . . You really don't know?'

I shake my head.

'It's, it's . . . Wow, look at the time! I promised my professor I'd help pass out some tests. Sorry, I have to dash off – I'm already late as it is.'

Katarina flutters out of the door, with me hard on her heels. Outside in the street, she greets people left and right, but pauses only for the briefest of exchanges. We run up the stairs to the lecture hall where the students await their papers. Katarina sweeps into the hall and takes command of the room. She shouts out instructions, hands out the papers and tells everyone to hold their questions until the professor returns. I take a seat and study Katarina for a while. She has a natural, almost arrogant, authority. Intelligent, beautiful and decisive, she is among those who will always land on their feet, I think to myself. Those sitting in the rear rows are a different matter. It's as if Katarina's words from the podium have nothing to do with them. When they have to go and get their papers they are slow to get out of their chairs.

I have to leave, and wave discreetly to Katarina by the door.

'I will email you,' she shouts back, over a forest of fellow students, as I sneak out.

But it is the students on the back row that linger in my mind afterwards. The ones with the dull gaze, leaning back on their chairs, wondering when their lives are supposed to start.

Back in Oslo a few months later, I get an email:

> Dear Åsne,
>   I have a surprise for you! I got a real job, and I am starting on Monday! I will work in one of the biggest advertising agencies here – McCann-Erickson Group – and I will do some kind of strategic planning. I am very excited!
>   Write when you have time!
>   With Love,
>   Katarina

June, a week ahead of the Serbian presidential election. After the initial round two candidates remain: Tomislav Nikolic from the Radical Party and Boris Tadic from the Democratic Party. Nikolic, standing on a platform steeped in nationalism, received most votes in the first round. Katarina is involved in the Democratic campaign for Boris Tadic, her uncle. 'We're trying to get young people to vote,' she writes in another email. 'That's the only chance for a Democratic victory. The Radicals have a very mobilised electorate, and they will show up at the booths.'

Katarina has rediscovered her enthusiasm for politics. Her email is bursting with optimism and hope: 'Now I am also involved with one GOTV [Get Out To Vote] campaign, with my NGO – Centre for Modern Skills . . . The motto is "Where are you going out on Sunday?" And the answer is, "To the elections, to choose myself a President!"'

The point, she explains, is that young people should choose a President for themselves and not leave it to others, to their elders, to do it for them.

'As you know, we have a problem with all the young

people who've been disappointed before and don't want to vote any more. But they're the ones we need right now!'

I follow the international news agencies' coverage of the 27 June election. The Democrats win, with 54 per cent of the vote, beating the nationalists.

In Belgrade Katarina parties all night long and shouts herself hoarse to me on the phone: 'The energy is back!'

Slobodan's Apprentice

'We did not win the war because we were stronger than the enemy, but because we were superior.'

Slobodan Milosevic, May 2000

Each morning a car from the party waits outside Branko Ruzic's house. Unless, of course, he decides to drive himself. 'I like to feel free,' he says. 'I don't like anyone waiting on me.' The twenty-four-year-old has risen quickly to a position of prominence in Milosevic's Socialist Party. In his position as the chairman of the Socialist Youth section of the party he enjoys privileges like a large office with a leather chair, a massive desk that oozes intimidation and the obligatory portrait of his boss on the wall. 'I've met him three times,' Branko proudly recounts as we share a table in the Siesta restaurant on the first floor of the party's offices in central Belgrade. The sound system blares Yugoslav Top Forty stuff. It's barely noon and Branko orders a vodka with a twist. 'Wonderful,' he says of his meeting with Milosevic. 'Fantastic. He's an impressive man, and enormously charming. It's incredible that he should be accused of war crimes – it's beyond belief. When we've met he always tells a few jokes and then we talk about the youth of Serbia. He's rather informal and says all the right things. He is a man with a vision.'

The 'vision thing' is a pronouncement Branko is prone to make frequently. In fact, he uses it when he's not quite sure of what else to say.

'What sort of visions?' I wonder.

'Visions of creating a just world, a world with more than one centre of gravity, unlike now, where the US dictates everything. The US has broken every single UN resolution when it comes to Yugoslavia; they'll break any rule that doesn't serve their interests. Two-thirds of the world's population is against the US,' Branko reckons, and he lists China, Russia, Cuba, Vietnam, North Korea and a few African nations.

'In your opinion, would you say Milosevic has been successful these past ten years?'

'Of course! He's had some difficulties, owing to outside pressure and the conflicts within the former Yugoslavia, and we've lived under sanctions for eight years now, but we've managed to keep the nation together. Even if the Serbs who lived in Croatia were subjected to ethnic cleansing and had to flee from there to here, they are at least still alive. Milosevic did everything he could to help them. We have almost a million refugees today, but we have not ceded any territory. Yugoslavia still exists,' Branko assures me. 'There are no statesmen in the world that can hold a candle to Milosevic. He is a man with visions. No one else has visions like these. Leaders like Clinton and Blair, they are not statesmen, only bureaucrats employed by vast financial consortiums.'

'Doesn't Milosevic feel cornered?'

'In no way. He's supremely confident. He is an optimist, just like me. America ought to be ashamed over what it's done to us. We'd like nothing better than to collaborate, but it has to be on an equal footing. America is the source of all wickedness in the world,' Branko asserts, and fixes me with his young eyes. He reminds me of the comic-book character Tintin, with his parted, slick hairdo, crisply ironed shirt and V-neck sweater. His favourite subjects – Slobodan Milosevic and American imperialism – flow out of him like water. It's like turning on a tap.

Branko was elected chairman of the Socialist Youth in the spring of 2000 and has ambitions of a career in politics. Slobodan Milosevic does not enjoy any great popularity among young people. To the extent that Serbian kids are politically involved, it is mainly on behalf of the opposition parties, or Otpor. I'm curious to learn what drew Branko to join the Socialist Party. But it proves tricky to get anything personal out of him: he tends to answer any question with a minor variation on several themes, regardless of what he was asked. He enrolled in the SPS when he was twenty because he wanted to do his part in the Serbs' battle against the US and to maintain the nation's border. 'Besides, I wanted to try to solve some of the issues young people deal with here. And, of course, the party has an excellent platform all around,' he adds. 'It's the only party that actually wants to help young people. We've got plans to build a hundred thousand new flats for young people. Look at all the bridges we've built this last year alone, without a single cent of aid from the US or the UN.

'Our goal, in contrast to the American-funded

opposition, is to keep our country intact. Look at Montenegro, for instance; this is a republic run by the CIA, counter to its own national interests. President Milo Djukanovic is just like Noriega in Panama, a puppet of the United States. And I believe that all young Serbs think as I do,' Branko adds after a pause. 'There's a conspiracy in place against us because we love our liberty. Every other country has submitted to the American world order, but we have refused, and that is why we are being punished. We're the only nation in the Balkans that still have our independence. The whole world is prejudiced against Serbs. We are portrayed as an irrational people, like killers and rapists. You've been here for a while, so you've seen that we're normal people.'

Those innocent eyes again. 'I doubt that you've met any criminals here, right? Or any rapists?'

The Americans are to blame for the conflict in Kosovo as well. It started because the US wanted a military base there. 'The Albanians took to terrorising the Serbian population, refused to work, refused to attend schools. With American help they were able to destabilise the whole society. Their leaders are paid from abroad. There was never any ethnic cleansing of Albanians, I can assure you. The only ones who were ethnically cleansed were Serbs. But if you say that to an American he'll disagree, because all he knows is what he's seen on American television, and they consistently accuse Serbs of ethnic cleansing. The Americans fake their footage to trick the audience. And when a regular Joe in America hears all day long that the Serbs are murderers and rapists, then he'll eventually believe it.

'Kosovo is still a part of Serbia. But conditions won't be normalised again until we can move our forces in. Only then can we protect the Serbian population,' he emphasises. 'KFOR has to leave, and we have to enter.' Branko orders another vodka and interrupts his river of words to ask me what the title of the book is to be. 'What about *False Prejudices?*' he asks. 'Or *Fake Prejudices?* You're writing the book in order to go beyond the preconceptions, right? And all the stereotypes and preconceived notions of Serbs are false.'

I tell him I appreciate his suggestions. He offers to help me have the book translated into Serbian. 'The party can surely help you get it published here,' he thinks. I imagine a book cover with a discreet SPS logo in the corner.

Branko travels a lot in Serbia, visiting the local chapters of the SPS. I ask if I can come along. 'Of course,' he answers. 'Next week, I am going to Nis and Uzice. I just have to run it by the party office first. Have you hit the town, by the way, seen any nightclubs and discos?' He invites me to join him and his friends. 'Then you can get to know me a little better. It is my duty to ensure that your stay in Serbia is a successful one. We might have a barbecue this weekend – would you like to come?'

I'd be delighted to. 'Care for some pizza?' Branko asks. I accept this offer as well. 'Despite the sanctions, there is no actual poverty here. Nobody is starving. There are those who can no longer afford to travel abroad, yes, but everyone has money for food, to visit friends or throw a party. Well, perhaps two per cent or so of the population can't afford meat these days,' he admits, when I bring up the presence of soup kitchens and studies that show two-thirds of Serbia's retired people live beneath the poverty line.

'People in the West always insist that the standard of living is so low here. But look at the US – there's poverty for you! Why don't you ever talk about the poverty in the US, or about all the blacks that fill their jails? You are always on China's case about human rights. But consider what you yourself did last year – you bombed us! Isn't that a violation of human rights? We've shown that we are strong. No other nation in the world would have survived what we've been through. I'm not saying that there isn't a crisis here, only that we're working our way out of it. If not tomorrow, then in two, three or five years. Nobody can say that we don't belong in Europe, geographically or cultur- ally. Nikola Tesla was Serbian. The batteries in your tape recorder wouldn't have worked, and we wouldn't have any electricity, if it wasn't for Nikola Tesla.'

The volume of the pop music climbs. The Siesta is apparently a watering hole for Milosevic's youth. Branko says hi to several, and the tables become crowded with young, well-dressed men. Branko fits in perfectly with his classic, almost posh style. He is a child of privilege. His father is a retired diplomat and the family spent a few years in Australia. The aspiring politician tells me that Yugoslavia was a great country to grow up in. 'We were the most advanced country in the socialist bloc, we could watch American movies and listen to music from England, in contrast to places like Czechoslovakia, Bulgaria or Romania. We could travel where we pleased, didn't need visas anywhere. Now we are being treated as pariahs, but we're just as democratic as any other nation in Europe. We will have elections this autumn and they will be con- ducted with the same integrity as the international community's,' Branko says, expressing his confidence in a socialist victory. 'We've shown that we are able to take care of people, even as the US commit murder to desta- bilise this country. One of their tools is the student organisation Otpor, who do the killing and the terror for them. The leaders of Otpor are paid by the Americans, even though their members are just ordinary students. You know, young people always like to criticise – not just the regime, but their parents,' the twenty-four-year-old confides to me. 'We are trying to show who Otpor's puppet masters are. The leadership includes, among other things, a large number of criminals.'

'What sort of criminals?'

'Does that really matter? Criminals of all stripes, of course! And when the student population is infiltrated by criminals, things are bad. These kids are not promoting sound values like sport or culture. They insult their own mother, because what is a country if not your motherland, and you cannot disgrace your motherland.'

It's late afternoon by now. The heat is oppressive and we stagger outside in the glaring sunshine. 'It's because of the war that the weather is so hot,' Branko tells me as we look for precious shade on the pavement. 'Throughout May the temperature has not dipped below thirty-five degrees, and not a drop of rain. Half our crops have already been burned up by the sun. And to think that we once exported food to all of Europe. But the bombs destroyed the ozone layer,' he tells me. 'Not just here, but over Bulgaria and Romania as well. But our neighbours have only themselves to thank for supporting the Americans.'

Branko abruptly halts his stream of words. Suddenly his face looks tired.

'I work from early morning to midnight. It gets me a little depressed sometimes.'

'Depressed?'

'When I come back from a trip at midnight and have spent my whole day smiling, shaking hands, being charming, I'm so worn out that I can only go straight to bed. And that makes me depressed, because I know all my friends are out partying. But I just can't do that and get up again in the morning. I'd like nothing better than to party, get a girlfriend, but there's just no time. Not even for a girlfriend,' he sighs, and adds, 'I had a girlfriend, for three years. We broke up three years ago and that'll have to do until I get married. But the Yugoslav girls are the prettiest in the world.'

Before Branko disappears into the SPS building, he promises to let me know when I can accompany him on a trip. He never does, so I get in touch with him again myself. My coming along to Nis or Uzice isn't going to work out, I'm told. 'Those are somewhat special trips,' he parries, but promises to contact me later.

It never works out that I follow Branko around Serbia. Most likely the party won't let him bring a Western journalist to their meetings. Nor do the invitations to dinners, discos or nightclubs ever go beyond the hypothetical. The barbecue keeps getting postponed. Branko always has to check his calendar or with his secretary first.

In the summer Branko leaves for a youth conference in Cuba, joining delegates from Serbia, Cuba, Vietnam, North Korea, Libya and Iraq. 'There were representatives from the US and the UK as well, from their communist parties,' he tells me on his return. I'm surprised to see that he is just as pale as he was when he left. 'The conference ran from eight in the morning till late at night, so there was never time to get a tan,' Branko explains, and admits that the whole thing was rather dull. They'd split into groups and brainstorm slogans, which they eventually voted on. 'What sort of slogans did you come up with?' I ask.

'Well, for instance, "Resist American Imperialism",' he answers. I ask if he had a chance to sample a *mojito*, Cuba's national cocktail, consisting of rum, mint leaves, lime and brown sugar. Branko has never heard of it. 'We never really went anywhere at night. You can't go drinking when you have to get up at six or seven in the morning.'

Branko is probably the only person I've met who has spent a week in Cuba without sampling either sunshine or nightlife.

Branko remains loyal to the party, despite its loss of power following Milosevic's fall. In the autumn of 2000 he is re-elected chairman of the Socialist Youth and in December he wins a seat in the Serbian parliament. I leave a dozen messages with his secretary, others on his answering machine, and try dropping in on him in parliament. He never gets back to me and doesn't answer his mobile when I call. Just as I'm about to give up the chase I hear on the radio that the SPS is arranging a demonstration the next day in support of the former TV boss Dragoljub Milanovic. He has been arrested and charged with killing sixteen of his former employees. They lost their lives during the NATO bombings. Milanovic is alleged to have learned that the station would be bombed that night, but never passed the warning on to his staff. Some even claim that he said anyone who left would lose their job. Milanovic is a prominent member of the SPS, and the party's defence is that it is NATO who should be on trial – they are the ones who dropped the bombs.

Branko will be there, I think to myself.

The following day I go looking for him among the roughly one thousand demonstrators. I find him on the edge of the crowd, wearing jeans and a navy-blue duffel coat, engaged in polite conversation with a pretty young girl.

'I've had you under surveillance,' I tell him, trying to put a gloss of charm over the awkward fact that he's done everything possible to avoid me.

'I've gathered as much,' he responds suavely. He explains that he's been extremely busy. For months on end.

Around us the crowd shout slogans and wave flags. Branko just stands there and I try to imagine him shouting or engaging in the demonstration in any way. The youth leader is always poised, clearly saving himself for bigger things.

Someone hands me a leaflet. 'Hague Tours,' it says, over a drawing of a huge, terrifying spider waiting for its prey – an unsuspecting family about to walk into its clutches. 'The Hague takes you to freedom – special rebates for Serbs – pay only the one-way fare,' reads the text. On the other side there's a picture of a heart wrapped in barbed wire, then shot through with a NATO missile decorated with a skull. The very heart of Serbia is under attack.

The slogans grow louder. The new government is referred to as 'Hague's choirboys'. Branko seems increasingly uncomfortable to be spending this much time in my company and tries to shake me off by inviting me to come by the office the next day. The party's new headquarters is in Novi Beograd, on the other side of the Sava, and looks like a fortress made of green and black glass. Its old offices, in the centre of town, were looted during the revolution.

Branko is, as always, impeccably dressed, in a dark-green suit and a burgundy tie. His secretary brings a glass of water for him and a double espresso for me. The tiny packets of sugar bear the red, white and blue SPS logo, Serbia's national colours. I look around. The portrait of Milosevic

has gone. It has been replaced by an SPS calendar and a portrait of Branko himself speaking at a podium. Can we
deduce that Milosevic is not the hero he once was?

Branko is unequivocal: 'Oh, he's the boss – he's the
leader of the party.'

'Then why don't you have his picture on the wall any
more?'

'The demonstrators burned all the portraits we had.
Only one survived; it's in the office of the general secretary. But these days it's not really imperative,' the young
politician says about the formerly omnipresent portraits. I
perk up, thinking he might have lost faith in the man with
the visions. But his answer remains in character: formal and
void of passion. 'He is still the president of the party, but
no longer President of Yugoslavia.'

Despite this, Milosevic's visage is everywhere in
Belgrade. As part of a campaign titled '*Ko je kriv?*' – 'Who
is to blame?' – Otpor has covered the city in posters of
Milosevic superimposed on a background of war, fleeing
people and poverty. Almost every wall in the Serbian capital demands the arrest of Milosevic. After a few weeks
the '*Ko je kriv*' concept is replaced by '*Kriv je*' – 'He is
guilty' – with a huge picture of Milosevic smoking a cigar.
This time the background is made up of empty shelves.

'Otpor's campaign is demeaning and sleazy. It's an attack
on our national honour, presuming that the Serbs alone
are to blame for the Balkan wars,' says Branko, visibly
angry. 'But just you wait and see – if they arrest Milosevic,
this whole nation will rise in protest.' Finally he looks me
in the eye. Usually he gazes right past me when he speaks,
out of the window, up at the ceiling, towards the door.
The direct Tintin gaze disappeared when the leader fell.

'I meet him often,' Branko says. 'He stops by several

times a week. He's actually in the building now. To meet a delegation from the Ukraine, communists from the Ukraine.'

'So I might have passed him in the lobby?'

'No, he doesn't enter through the main lobby,' Branko smiles. 'He gets out of the car in that parking area over there and then walks in the back door.'

Branko points out of the window. 'He's deeply wounded by all these lies and false accusations. Particularly those about his family. These lies about his son being a common criminal are particularly painful.'

Branko often attends the support demonstrations outside Milosevic's villa in Uzicka Street. These demonstrations are meant to function as a human shield to protect Milosevic from getting arrested, but it's usually a purely symbolic position – they rarely number more than ten people.

Branko finds it puzzling that the SPS lost the election. 'We must have made some mistakes, but I'm not sure what. We rebuilt roads and bridges after the bombing, people began to see that our policies yielded tangible results – and they still turned their backs on us. Of course, the opposition was backed by the US and could throw money at everything. And it was far cheaper for the Americans to pay for the opposition's coup than to have to pay all those billions in reparations that we would have demanded of them.'

For all this, Branko claims to enjoy being the opposition for a change. 'Now we are left with the cream of the crop – our members today are those who truly believe in the socialist idea. It used to be that a lot of people joined the SPS because we were in charge of everything, and they thought they could get a job if they joined,' he explains, and admits that times are not what they used to be. 'We no longer have companies funding our activity; they now give their donations to the Democrats instead. But we shall return,' he assures me. His gaze sweeps across at the portrait of himself on the wall, and then out of the window again.

It is a sad and downcast Branko that greets me two hours after the arrest of his beloved party president. He hasn't slept for three days, having followed the negotiations by phone from the SPS building. Branko's belief that the population would rise to defend Milosevic did not come to pass. Only a few hundred demonstrators stood guard outside the compound in the brief two days it took to arrest the ex-President.

It's six in the morning on 1 April and the SPS is holding a press conference. The party makes a frontal attack on the government that arrested Milosevic. 'Well, at least we managed to avert a civil war,' says Branislav Ivkovic, the parliamentary leader of the Socialist Party, who was with Milosevic as the drama unfolded.

Branko sits in the conference hall. His gaze is dull and his hands are in his lap. I approach him once the press briefing is over. 'I can't bear to talk to anyone,' he says, and turns away, the weight of the world upon him. His narrow back disappears around a corner.

A few days later the Socialist Youth conducts a planning meeting. 'Slobo, come back,' reads a poster in the conference room, which is soon filled with strapping young men and a few girls. 'Petrol's gone up by thirty per cent after Milosevic's arrest,' a young man states triumphantly. 'By the time they catch me it'll have doubled,' he adds. Another complains that the bus fares have increased as well. Then I am ushered outside.

'We will fight to defend him and to prove his innocence,' Branko tells me afterwards. 'Milosevic will emerge from this an even greater hero than ever. For the first time he is the victim. We will become incredibly popular once people understand what has happened. We're about to become a formidable opposition party,' he adds, and delivers the final proof that the arrest was stage-directed by the Americans.

'On the first night the action began at around two a.m. – prime time for US television. On CNN, Madeleine Albright and Richard Holbrooke were in the studios already, ready to comment on Milosevic's arrest. When he was taken into custody, on Sunday morning at four-thirty, it was still evening in the US,' he crows. 'So the authorities haven't won – the US has. It goes against all sense of national honour and dignity, of course. The government here just did what they were told. They ought to be ashamed. They say they're not going to send him to The Hague, but that is the goal of the Americans, and in turn that of our own government. They're brainwashed, that's the main problem.'

I notice that the sugar packets no longer bear the SPS logo and that the juice is served in plastic cups. 'We're the opposition now – we can't afford to be extravagant,' Branko replies.

I ask who he thinks will replace Milosevic as the party's leader. 'Milosevic will always be this party's president,' he shoots back, as if finding the question deeply offensive. 'At the very least he will serve as the honorary president. I think we'll see a collective leadership with several vice-presidents, and then Milosevic consulting with us from jail.'

For his own part, the now twenty-five-year-old has great

hopes and plans. 'In ten years I might be Foreign Minister. Maybe in fifteen.'

He's convinced that the Socialist Party will return to power. 'Prices will go up, unemployment will rise and social problems will increase. People will return to us, because we, as socialists, are the only ones who have the best interest of the average citizen in mind,' Branko tells me, as usual without any tangible passion, and while looking out of the window.

None of us says anything for a while, until Branko arrives at his conclusion: 'Nobody thinks of themselves as Milosevic's successor. It can't be done – no one has his charisma. There is only one Milosevic.'

Branko picks up the phone after just one ring.

'You want to see me? How nice! Come to the office tomorrow.'

What's this, then? Three years go by and Branko is no longer trying to avoid me?

When I enter his office I am met by a ramrod-straight Branko, his handshake firm, his head held high. It's as if he's recovered his equilibrium after the long fall of his hero and the initial election defeats. The SPS tried to get back to the seat of power following a fairly bad election result in 2003,* and the governing coalition relies on its votes in parliament. 'A lot has changed, cabinets have come and gone, we've been out, now we're back in.'

Branko Ruzic has become one of the party's four vice-presidents, and definitely the youngest of the bunch. The twenty-eight-year-old sits, knees apart and full of good

---

* The SPS received 7.61 per cent of the vote in the parliamentary elections of 28 December 2003.

cheer, on the sofa of an office in the centre of Belgrade; the
SPS has recovered its former headquarters after the looting
three years earlier.

The party has gone through a painful transition following its fall from grace. The big issue has been what to do
with Milosevic.

When the deposed leader was sent to The Hague he still
held the presidency of the party. In theory he would have
the last word on any decisions made. After a few years of
consulting with an imprisoned president, several prominent party leaders moved to dump him – including Branko
Ruzic.

'We changed the statutes. The new rules say that if the
president of the party is unable to perform his duties, the
chairman assumes his tasks. This means that Milosevic no
longer has a formal role in the party any more; he's sort of
an honorary president,' is how Branko puts it, as diplo-
matically as he can. And with his customary logic, cool
and efficiency. His desk is a marvel of order. His appoint-
ment book, his mobile, the charger, a notepad, a calendar.
Nothing else.

'We support and help his case in The Hague. We have
several teams working with his defence, including a group
of volunteers called Sloboda – Freedom. But ultimately
we had to put the party first and make sure that we would
be able to survive the so-called revolution that swept the
country. We decided we needed to be pragmatic and retain
our command here in Belgrade. This does not at all mean
that I think Milosevic is guilty of war crimes. I was in The
Hague myself, visiting him. Well, I didn't get to see him
personally, but I could hear what he said in court. He sat
behind a glass wall and he waved to us in the audience.'

Despite his inherited gifts for diplomacy, Branko isn't

entirely able to cover his disappointment in his former idol. 'When he was stripped of his formal title in the party he became so agitated that he denounced us and encouraged his supporters to vote for Seselj instead. That was a fatal move. I'm sure we lost several hundred thousand votes because of it. And I am disappointed because the party has always been his most loyal supporter. I couldn't count all the hours I have demonstrated on his behalf, protested at his arrest or his extradition, defended him to the media, in debates and at meetings. And then, in the end, he is the one who lets us down.'

Branko refuses to put it any more harshly than that. When I ask if he feels betrayed he says, 'No, not betrayed. You can write "disappointed".'

Branko falls silent for a minute.

'I think Milosevic based his decision on information from someone who doesn't have our interests at heart – perhaps his wife. Someone who doesn't quite get the big picture. For instance, he was led to believe that the entire population would take to the streets and demand his release if he only asked them to – that the whole country stood behind him. It did not. I understand that he's under pressure – he's in jail, he can't see his family – but when he tried to excommunicate key members of the party leadership, like the new president, Ivica Dacic, he simply went too far. Don't misunderstand – he's still a great man, and he's got incredible charisma. I'm sure he's disappointed in us as well; he probably expected the party to do anything he asked of us, as before. But now he simply doesn't act as a party leader.'

'You've taken his portraits down?'

'Nah – I believe there's one left.'

'Where is it?'

'In his office.'

'Which office?'

'Milosevic's office. Nobody uses it. It's just as he left it.'

'Wow. Like a museum. Can we go and look at it?'

'No, I don't have a key. I don't know who has. Personally I'd rather see someone who needs an office use it. I don't think we should treat him as a deity. I mean – he's no Tito.'

Branko shakes off the past and smiles at me.

'I think we'll have a great shot at becoming a strong, leading force on the left once we profile ourselves as a modern party and focus on workers, students and farmers. I would like to remake the party into a social-democratic entity; we need to rid ourselves of the nationalist tag we were branded with. But during the last campaign a lot of other parties stole liberally from our platform. Suddenly everyone wanted a socially oriented message. The voters became confused and Seselj's people lied without compunction. For one thing, they said that a loaf of bread would cost three dinars if they were in power, knowing full well that's just not possible. But, because the population is so disappointed at the lack of any sort of improvement, we're seeing a radicalisation of the electorate. People will latch on to anything. The economy is going badly and we are unable to attract any foreign investments. The US recently withdrew an aid package of a hundred million dollars because they said we weren't collaborating with the tribunal in The Hague. As if we would sell any of our countrymen to The Hague for a hundred million. Can't they see for themselves that hunger and unemployment only serve to radicalise the population further? Which in turn will lead to a new level of isolation and sanctions!'

Branko exhales. Then he suddenly smiles.

'I've got married since we last met.'

'Congratulations!'

'Right after you left, really. I have a son now, Milutin. He was two last week.'

'Where did you meet her?'

'In the SPS. She was the leader of a local chapter in Belgrade. But she's retired from politics now. We certainly won't be the next Milosevic and Mira! One politician in the family is plenty. But she's an incredible support to me, because she knows what being a politician entails. So she's always behind me; kind, sensitive, beautiful – everything I need. Besides, she's an excellent adviser. She can follow the debates on TV, and when I get home she coaches me on getting better at smiling and being more relaxed on camera. And she's good at picking out clothes for me – matching ties, choosing which suit . . .'

'I couldn't help but notice that you laugh and smile a lot more than before.'

'Yes, I think I'm happier these days. But we live in a closet – our flat's thirty-five square metres. It's all we can afford for now, though it's typical for a young Serbian couple, and I wouldn't want to be any different. As a leader of a social-democratic party I have to live like the people do.'

'Last time you said you wanted to become Foreign Minister?'

'I'm well on my way. Or at least, I'm on the right way. I have a seat on the foreign committee in parliament. But in order to make the cabinet, we have to be the governing party first. We need more votes.'

'What would you do if you were Foreign Minister today?'

'First, I would tell the world the truth about Kosovo and the ethnic cleansing there. Then I would begin negotiations to get an agreement that would give Serbs autonomy over certain areas there. But now the international community couldn't care less about Kosovo. They can't see that the Muslims there support bin Laden and international terrorism. The Albanians were very adept at manipulating the American politicians even before the Kosovo war. Furthermore, I believe Serbia has to join the EU. We can wait; we need to develop further, I don't want us to join as a poor nation. But perhaps as a semi-developed nation?'

I note that Branko's desk doesn't include a computer. Is this perhaps a consequence of his being a politician in a semi-developed country?

'We just don't have that many,' Branko explains. 'It costs a lot when you lose power.'

Flown Bird

'How can I remain the same?
How can I save myself from the changes?
Only through changes.'

Milan Mladenovic, *Blue and Green*

Snezana fights her way on to the route 41 bus. As always, it is chock full and requires a special boarding technique. You have to make your way to the front of the crowd waiting to get on, establish a foot on the lowest step and then force yourself forward. This is not the time – and there is no room anyway – for manners. The struggle is long, as the bus won't depart before it's able to close its doors and the mêlée at the bus stop is over. Once on board, you're squeezed until it's time to get off. You reach your destination bruised and battered, having fought to remain upright when the bus turns, from coping with the potholes along the way, from getting shoved and pushed by strangers getting on or off.

However, it's a free ride, as there's just no way you'll be able to make your way up to the driver to buy a ticket.

'It didn't use to be like this,' sighs Snezana when we finally disembark at Republic Square, exhausted and drenched in sweat. 'The buses are fuller, because people can't afford petrol any more. On top of that, they never replace buses when they break down, so there are fewer of them. And there's no such thing as a schedule any more. The bus arrives when it arrives.'

'It didn't use to be like this' is something Snezana says often. Because nothing is like it was when she left. Snezana is among the thousands of young people who've given up on a life in Belgrade to try their luck abroad. For the past seven years she has lived in Frankfurt. This Easter holiday she's come home to visit her mother and brothers.

'I can afford to take a taxi now, but I used to take this bus all the time. And when I'm here I seek out the life that I used to have,' she explains. 'If I were to take a taxi to town I would feel even more alien here than I do already.'

Her appearance indicates a higher degree of comfort and familiarity with taxis than with buses. Snezana is wearing Gucci sunglasses and black designer clothes. Also, there's a vast psychological gap between her and her fellow bus passengers, as Snezana has not yet got used to seeing the bombed-out buildings we drive by. Just half a kilometre from her mother's house in the Senjak area we see a literal parade of ruins. Everything was targeted – the Interior Ministry, the Foreign Ministry, the Defence Ministry, the government's quarters, those of the army chiefs of staff. A year after the bombings they cut through the landscape like deep wounds – black craters, burned-out windows and collapsed walls.

'Every time I see these buildings it makes me want to cry. They represent everything Serbia has become – an enemy of the West. Even if these buildings and departments stood for everything I fought against, and left behind, they still feel like "mine". It hurts to see them like this.'

This is not the only stab she receives on the way into the city centre. 'That's the Radio Beograd building,' Snezana points out. She hasn't been inside for seven years.

'Everything changed with the war in Croatia, in 1991, when the regime began interfering in what we broadcast. The whole mood changed. Even I, who worked with programmes on film and music, received politicised editorial directions. We were told what music we could play and which films we could review. The editor was fired and the regime installed a puppet in his place. Professionalism and expertise meant nothing any more; the only thing that mattered was the degree to which you were loyal to the regime. When our boss was fired we organised a strike. It went on for several weeks, and when the union board got word that the puppet wouldn't be left in charge of the station after all, we thought we'd won. We called off the strike and the next morning I went back to work. The guard asked for my access pass, which was weird, because he'd never done that before, and he knew me well enough. He checked my credentials against a list of names. Then he confiscated the pass and told me there was no need to come back. I didn't have a job any more,' Snezana recalls.

'I went through something of a personal crisis after that. I didn't know what I wanted to be, or what to stand for. I'd never been interested in politics, but suddenly our whole lives were politicised – everything was a matter of your loyalty to Milosevic. Any job I applied for involved making political compromises. I refused, and remained unemployed. I was twenty-seven years old and thought it was not too late for me to start again somewhere else. I had an aunt in Frankfurt, so I went there, and learned German at the Goethe Institute. And I've been there ever since.'

This exodus of highly educated young people leaving the country for good is commonly referred to as a brain drain. They may be artists whose liberties have been curtailed by the regime's restrictions, journalists who refuse to be censored, young men who fear being drafted into the Yugoslav army, engineers who can't find work because of the crisis. The fields of science and electronics have been particularly hard hit. At the turn of the millennium the average Serbian salary was about twenty-five pounds a month. Of those who leave, some get well-paid jobs abroad, while others wash dishes or drive taxis.

Snezana belongs among those who've done well, even if the life of an immigrant isn't always easy. 'People ask me where I'm from when they hear my accent. If I say "Serbia", the conversation ends right there, as if I were a war criminal. So I've taken to telling people I'm from Belgrade; for some reason that carries less stigma,' she says with a shrug. It took her a long time to make new friends.

'I had an odd experience when I visited the new Jewish Museum in Berlin. It includes a narrow path that you can follow – "the stream of emigration", which takes you through a labyrinth where the pathway goes around huge blocks in every direction. The blocks appear to be straight, but they're actually tilted. They lean in or out, in optical illusions. You end up feeling nauseous or seasick, and I wandered through this thing and thought to myself, yes, this is actually how it feels to be an emigrant – a bit seasick, a bit nauseous, always awkward, never on safe ground.'

Still, Frankfurt is now home for Snezana. She lights up when she tells me about the nice flat she has fixed up, with a balcony and a view of the city's skyline. 'I'm always going to be a stranger there. But I think I've settled for good. I can't think of anything I could do in Serbia. Everything's coloured by politics. I could work with the opposition, but I really don't care about politics. I want to do my own thing, and be free. Here I can't even breathe.'

Once she'd learned German, Snezana looked for work and was lucky. She got a job as an assistant and a translator for the well-known German theatre director Alexander Bril, who was in the process of producing Slobodan Schneider's play *Snakeskin* at the Schauspiel Theatre in Frankfurt. The play was set against the war in Bosnia, and Bril wanted a bilingual production in German and Serbo-Croatian. Three weeks before the premiere his lead actress withdrew because of pressure from her family. They didn't approve of her, as a Serb, being called on to play a Bosnian woman raped by Serbian soldiers. The director decided that Snezana was the only possible replacement at this late stage of the process. And so she walked on stage for the first time in her life. She won rave reviews.

'I became an actress, completely by accident,' she laughs. The whole cast were from the former Yugoslavia, but everyone was cast as a different nationality than their own. The director wanted to demonstrate that there are no significant national differences between the peoples of Yugoslavia, but that this was a war in which ordinary human beings were made to hate each other, fed by a sequence of atrocities. To me it makes no difference whether someone is a Serb, a Croat or a Muslim. Atrocities were committed by every side, so I just played a woman who was raped – not a Muslim woman raped by Serbs,' Snezana says.

These days she is starring in a new production of the musical *Hair*, a box-office phenomenon. It is no longer the Vietnam War but Kosovo in 1999 that serves as the political backdrop. The songs are the same, but the plot has been altered. Snezana plays a Serbian woman who serves as the mistress of ceremonies. She is always alone on stage, and talks to NATO spokesman Jamie Shea, who appears above her on a video screen. Or she recounts Serbian myths, speaking of bridges, angels and princes. At the musical's conclusion she sings 'Sunshine' with the rest of the cast.

Sometimes she is booed when she accepts her curtain calls. 'I can't tell whether it's Serbs who are angry at their negative portrayal, or Germans who are upset that Serbs are portrayed too positively. It's a pacifist musical,' she says. 'My guess is they are Germans. Nationalist Serbs probably wouldn't go to see *Hair*,' she reasons.

Snezana was shocked at the massive support among Germans for the NATO bombings. 'Very few Germans spoke up against it; there was hardly any kind of debate. When the author Peter Handke declared himself against the war he was treated as if he were crazy.'

The actress herself doesn't think the bombing solved anything. 'Milosevic is still in power.'

If Snezana is a stranger in Frankfurt she feels the same way in Belgrade. 'Once I knew everyone and I was always in the thick of things,' she remembers. We're in an outdoor café while a hot April sun beats down on the pedestrian street, Knez Mihailova, where Belgrade's urbanites enjoy their espressos and watch the street scene. Many of them are noticeably well dressed, even though the stores are rather meagerly stocked. The shelves seem full and you don't really notice a shortage of anything until you actually need something specific and wander from store to store looking for it.

Just down from the café is a grocery shop with a long queue outside. The customers are allowed entry in groups. Most likely they've just received a shipment of cooking oil, which is one of the most in-demand items in Belgrade these days, along with sugar, flour and milk. If you turn away from the queue you're looking right at a glittering Versace store. You rarely see anyone enter; the outfits inside cost several years' worth of salaries for the people in the queue for cooking oil.

Snezana is on her way to meet her younger brother, Srdjan. He runs a production company that makes commercials and music videos. On her way there she suddenly stops in front of a run-down building. 'Akademia,' she says, by way of explanation. 'Once this was one of the hottest clubs in Europe.'

She tries to go inside to see if Akademia still exists in the basement of the art academy. A brusque manager stops us, but once Snezana has explained her nostalgic urge he is more than happy to give us a tour of the place that he assures us was the fourth hottest club in Europe at some point in the eighties. Once we get down into the basement, both the manager and the former clubber get lost in reveries of the past. This is where they all came – the best bands and the hippest jetsetters. A membership card was the epitome of happiness. 'Back then we were a normal nation and Belgrade was a required stop for stars on tour. These days no good bands come here,' Snezana says. Sasa, the manager, is a few years younger than the former VIP and listens intently to her stories. 'Some bands do stop by, but it's hard to make any money from it.' He points out a water leak in the corner, as if it symbolises this fall from grace.

Back out on the street Snezana continues her stories of the happy eighties. At seventeen she got a job on the teen magazine *Mladost* – Youth.

'I think it was published by the Socialist Youth, but nobody bothered with politics back then. It was a really cool magazine and I worked there for five years. In 1988 I became a DJ on Radio Beograd and later I had my own movie show. I played whatever music I liked and talked about the most recent movies,' she recalls, losing herself in memories. 'Those were the best years of my life. I ruled the world and I was at the centre of everything that went on.'

A lot of young adults in Serbia share her nostalgia for the eighties. Even if the economy was in crisis already, it seemed to Snezana that things could only get better and anything was possible. Tito was dead, the country enjoyed its new-found freedoms and people had money to travel, shop and enjoy life. Those halcyon days ended abruptly when the wars of the nineties crushed both the freedom and the personal finances of regular citizens.

'The past is my best friend and worst enemy,' Snezana sighs. 'I escape to it when everything else gets too depressing. But it's dangerous as well, because it keeps me from living in the here and now. Especially when I'm in Belgrade, I tend to dive into sentimentality. We Serbs are a pathetic people, we really are. We're trying to forget a miserable present by recalling some glorious past.'

We've reached her brother's offices. The siblings haven't seen each other for a year, but we have to wait: Srdjan is in the middle of casting nude models and strippers. He's making a commercial for Hotline, a phone-sex company. We sit down next to the girls waiting to audition their loveliness. Three made-up, long-legged girls with ample cleavages regard us with disdain and triumph as they go past us to the audition suite. They must have assumed that we're the competition, and feel pretty sure of having us beat.

'You understand why I left?' Snezana asks. 'Here getting cast in a commercial for Hotline constitutes success. People sell themselves for nothing,' she says. 'I don't want to get this dirty. I just want to be free.'

Her little brother has opted to stay. It's hard to make ends meet for a young director, and he's got to take whatever jobs come his way. A soft-core commercial is as good as any other job, and pays better.

The majority of Snezana's friends have gone. Many of them have left the country, others are dead – from disease, an overdose or another means of suicide. But some still remain, and one evening I meet a couple in a café. I ask why they've stayed in Belgrade. 'I've stayed 'cause I stayed,' is Sanja's curt reply. Someone else just hums the Clash's 'Should I Stay Or Should I Go' by way of an answer.

'There was a time I was invited to parties almost every night, which would have been great if they all hadn't been *bon voyage* parties for friends leaving the country,' the Clash guy explains. An anthology of essays has just been published here: *Why I'm Still in Serbia, and What My Hopes Are*. Young artists, writers and musicians were asked to write about why they had stayed. Most of them focused on roots and family and the hope for changes. A journalist took issue with the question itself: 'As if it is abnormal to live in one's own country,' she wrote.

'In a way I feel guilty that I didn't stay to fight,' Snezana tells me when we walk home that night. 'We all share a responsibility – for not seeing what was coming and for not doing anything now. Here most people are apathetic and tired. I'm not, but then I don't live in Belgrade any more. I left. Now there's nothing for me to do here and I do like my job in Germany. As an immigrant you have to create a whole new identity once you're removed from your customary surroundings and environment. It's as if you've fallen ill and then have to discover the things you genuinely appreciate about being well. You have to build a life from the bottom up. I had a happy childhood and an even happier time in my teens – and then, *pff*! Suddenly there's nothing at all. Now I'm neither happy nor unhappy,' a listless Snezana concludes. 'Not that happiness is a goal per se. It's not happiness that drives a human being, after all.'

Snezana is in Frankfurt when Milosevic is toppled, and follows the unfolding events on TV. Even if she's happy about the changes in her homeland, the change of power doesn't make any discernible difference for her. Snezana's life takes place outside Serbia now, beyond the reach of any regime. To return would mean starting all over again. Snezana has grown accustomed to her little flat, the challenging work and the perpetual vertigo of the emigrant.

Three years later I get a letter:

Amsterdam, 30 May 2004

Dear Åsne

How nice to hear that you are back in Serbia and haven't forgotten about us. I'm so pleased that your book is still developing! You invested both time and effort in it at a time when we were 'world enemy number one', and hardly anyone bothered with the underlying issues. I myself have spent a lot of time thinking about my homeland and what my feelings are for it.

When I was in Belgrade last year, I heard on the radio that the borders between Croatia, Serbia and Montenegro had been opened for the first time since the wars began, and that you no longer needed a visa to travel there. My immediate thought was: I have to go there . . . I have to go back . . . I have to go back to Dubrovnik . . .

They still didn't have any kind of organised transport, so I flew from Belgrade to Tivat in Montenegro, and from there by bus to Herceg Novi, where I took a taxi to the border with Croatia. I had to get out of the car there, because the Montenegro cab drivers didn't yet have permission to cross the border, and vice versa. I got out of the taxi on the Montenegro side, picked up my suitcase and began walking towards 'the other side'. It was around noon, and really hot. The sun burned my cheeks and the heat spread throughout my body. I walked with the smell of the cypress trees in my nostrils, and heard the cicadas sing, surrounded by these wonderful, dangerous and beautiful mountains. In this no man's land I sat down on my suitcase for a spell, just so I could take in the fantastic view around me. Memories of childhood summers welled up within me, and I recalled a poem by Jure Kastelan.

Lijepa si zemlo moja, meni najdraza . . .

You are so beautiful, my beloved country . . .

I sat there, within these few hundred metres of no man's land and felt – or rather, I knew – that this was my country! The country I was born in, the country that was always on my mind, the country I will love no matter where I am. The country that once had no borders, but which is now carved into six pieces.

After having lived abroad for almost twelve years, I had begun to believe that the only 'homeland' I had was my mother's tongue. As I generally spoke another language, I felt like my 'homeland' was slipping away from me. Language is something you can lose as well. Not entirely, not completely . . . but when you begin to dream and think in a foreign language – then your homeland is somewhere else.

Sometimes I thought that the only 'homeland' I had managed to keep was my friends, no matter where I was or they were. The older I get, the more apparent it is to me that when I think of 'home', I think of my mother, my brothers, my aunt, my friends; I thought of all the people I've loved, everyone I've met along the way that I now carry in my heart. I thought they were the only country I had.

And then . . .

That moment in no man's land made me realise that even I come from someplace. From a beautiful place. I had repressed that for twelve years. I had denied that I had roots, because I was always going somewhere else, fleeing, moving away. I thought: Even I have a place where I can sit down and feel that I am home. At long last.

Snezana.

The Valley of Hunger

'If you fail at everything else in life
at least try to live honestly.'

Serbian proverb

The Zaric family sit in their run-down, overflowing living
room and wait for lunch to be ready. At three o'clock
Branka will return home with the leftovers from the student canteen. That's still a few hours off. But there's not
really anything else to do except wait. Branka is the only
member of the family who has a job.

Her husband, Milos, lost his job when NATO bombed
the Zastava car and arms plant on 9 April 1999. By then he
had worked there for more than thirty years. 'Zastava is a
state factory, and they only kept on those that openly supported the SPS. I opposed the party, and had to go,' Milos
tells me. He was never formally fired but, like thousands of
others in the industrial town of Kragujevac, he is on an

extended 'compulsory holiday'. The market for Yugos, the car that they produced, has gone anyway, and Milos is under no illusion that he'll ever get his old job back.

'Good riddance, with that lousy pay,' he says. 'A dog in the West costs more to feed than I got paid a month.' As a phone operator at the plant he belonged to Yugoslavia's middle class. There is no middle class any more. A few are rich and the vast majority are poor. Kragujevac is called 'the Valley of Hunger'.

It wasn't always so. Once this was one of Serbia's most vital cities. These days it is estimated that 80 per cent of the population is without work. Only remnants survive of the city's former main employer, the plant that once was the biggest factory in Yugoslavia. The bombings gave the authorities an excuse for the downsizing and the resultant decline, and they used this relentlessly in anti-Western propaganda. The bombed-out, wretched ruins are displayed ad nauseam to anyone who expresses the slightest interest.

'It was like shooting a dead man,' notes Milos. Production had ground to a halt well before the bombs fell.

In 1989 a quarter of a million cars rolled off the assembly lines at Zastava. By 1999 the number had shrunk to a mere 1800. South Korea's Hyundai considered investing in Zastava, but wrote in their report that the factory was a museum and that there was no possible way it could be modernised. One would have to rebuild from the ground up. 'It's all Milosevic's fault,' says Milos. 'Anything he touches dies. He's thrown us into four wars for no reason; thousands have been killed because of his madness.' Milos thinks the West should be much tougher on Milosevic and that the sanctions should remain until he resigns.

'Better people freeze for a spell, so they can understand what Milosevic's policies get them. But as long as they have a bit of heat and a bit to eat, so the country just staggers on, arse backwards.' Milos was among the very few in Kragujevac who supported the NATO actions. 'They shouldn't have stopped with the car plant – they should have bombed Milosevic's house, his wife and his corrupt kids. And why wasn't his hometown, Pozarevac, obliterated? His son owns half the town!'

Milo is quite passionate on this point and shouts from the sofa, a cigarette and an overflowing ashtray at hand. His son Milan and his daughter-in-law Biljana sit in silence. Like many young adults in Kragujevac, they have never had a job.

The living room testifies to a glorious past. The family haven't bought a piece of furniture for at least ten years, since the economy started to collapse in earnest. Now three generations of Zarics share three rooms. There is no way the son and the daughter-in-law could afford a place for themselves and their five-year-old daughter, Milena.

Milan is a mechanic. He's been registered as unemployed for fifteen years. 'I'd take any job I could get. But in this country you have to know someone in order to get hired anywhere.'

Ideally he would have become a musician. Sometimes he plays drums in a dance band, but it doesn't happen that often any more. People just don't have that much to celebrate. At one time he could earn good money during the summer. Last summer he had just one gig a week and this winter it was even less. 'The worst thing about being unemployed is that you lose your self-respect. You feel inadequate and useless. A lot of people start drinking or take pills. You are no longer in charge of your own life. Without money you can't plan for anything,' he says, and lights another cigarette. The whole family are heavy smokers.

We can hear the ticking of the clock. It's still an hour until Branka brings lunch. Milos breaks the oppressive silence. 'My son destroyed Vukovar,' he suddenly offers. 'Look at what this regime has made people take part in – killings and looting.'

Milan was in the artillery during the war against Croatia.

'I didn't kill anyone. I merely secured our positions. But it was terrible; none of us knew what we were fighting for, and I was scared, scared I'd never get home again. I did four months there, returned home, only to be sent right back again. Every time the military police were at the door I just had to put my uniform on and go along. When the war in Kosovo started I went to hide; I couldn't fight another pointless war for a regime I opposed.'

Biljana sits on a stool, listening. She's pretty, with fake-blond hair, but for a twenty-eight-year-old her face is drawn. One of her front teeth is a bluish grey and has a hole straight through it. Biljana dropped out of school ten years ago and has never had a job either. Sometimes she sells make-up from a catalogue. People tick what they want and she orders it. She earns a 30 per cent commission, but she hasn't made a sale in months now. People in Kragujevac don't have money for make-up any more.

'I would love to have my own shop, with clothes and make-up. I know just how I'd want it to be. But in order to get that I'd need money – and I've never even worked in a shop,' she says, feeling her life slipping through her fingers. 'When I wake up in the morning I know that this day will be just like all the others,' she sighs. 'I've never had a lot and I don't ask for much. But I would like to have had a job. Got up in the morning, dropped Milena off at nursery school, gone to work, had a bank account . . .'

Like many Serbs, Milena dreams of moving abroad. 'I'd be a street-sweeper, anything, just to get away from here. Most of all, I'd like to go to Australia. As far away as I can get.'

A framed picture of Vuk Draskovic, the opposition leader and monarchist, looks down on us from the wall. 'Only he can save Serbia,' says Milos, and asks about Norway's monarchy. He wants to know the responsibilities of the Norwegian King and is curious about the rules of succession. He fetches a picture of Crown Prince Aleksandar, who has become a British citizen and lives in exile in London. 'He has to return. We have to get rid of our President and become a monarchy, like Norway,' he says, and takes me into their bedroom. Behind the door hangs a full-figure poster of Vuk Draskovic. 'One for all, all for one,' the poster reads. 'He is the first thing I see every morning,' laughs Milos. 'He's our last hope.'

Finally Branka makes it home, huffing and puffing under the substantial weight of the shopping bags from the canteen. Her daughter-in-law rushes to help with the bags and her coat, gets her slippers and seems to strive to anticipate her every need. The family's sole provider plops down on the sofa, complains of back pains and the February freeze and lights a cigarette. She keeps her family alive, but she's hardly a breadwinner in any other respects. She hasn't been paid for four months. 'I'm hoping they'll pay me soon,' Branka says. 'But luckily I am allowed to take food home; we wouldn't be here without it. Of course, the food gets worse and worse; everything is rationed, like after the Second World War. The students get twenty grams of meat each day, potatoes, cabbage or macaroni. They come to me with grey faces and scold me because the food isn't any good,' she says, and adds, 'They're a scrawny bunch, really. When they yell at me I just tell them, "Take your plate to the director, and ask if he'd be willing to eat what's on it." Nobody has risen to the challenge so far,' she says, and tells me about the corrupt director of the student canteen, who sells off the best meat to hotels and private customers and has all sorts of delicacies brought up to his office every day.

'Why don't you report him?'

Branka just stares at me in wide-eyed wonder. 'Report? To whom? To Milosevic?'

The canteen is run by the state. Nobody dares to report or criticise. 'Five years ago the corrupt director arrived at work like a pauper in rags,' she tells me. 'Today he's dressed like a prince and has three cars, four secretaries and a grand house. All paid for by the money he's stolen from the students' food budget. Oh, this country has fallen so far,' Branka sighs, and begins to cry. 'Who would have ever thought this could happen to us? It's terrible; my husband can't get a job, my son can't get a job, my daughter-in-law can't work. I love my country. I was happy here. Now I haven't bought myself anything to wear for ten years. They've taken everything from me and sent my son to a pointless war. Luckily he came back alive, but there could be other wars and they might take him again.'

Branka moved to Kragujevac when she was fifteen, and married Milos a few years later. 'Those were the days. We went to the movies, to the theatre, restaurants; we could travel to Belgrade or go on holiday along the coast. Now there are no parties anywhere and people don't even have anything to talk about. It's devastating to see that my kids live far worse than I did when I was young,' she sighs, and tells me stories from her own youth, when she would go straight from parties to work. 'I just needed a sip of mineral water and I was good to go,' she tells me, drying her tears.

Biljana heats up the food Branka has brought home: sauerkraut with bacon bits. Along with this, she serves tinned fermented cabbage, which generally is the only vegetable that poor Serbs eat in the winter months. In addition a plate of fried meat patties is put on the table today, most likely in their guest's honour. I'm invited to join them at their table. The food tastes like what it is – from a Serbian student canteen, reheated, slightly past its best-by date.

After lunch we gather in the living room for coffee. The TV is on. Milos fiddles with the remote. In Belgrade Serbia's industrial leaders are meeting to discuss the future of Zastava. The Minister of Industry outlines a new plan of action: 'The first item on our agenda is Zastava, the most important plant in Serbia,' he says. Nobody pays him any attention; they've heard it all before. 'Not even a child would believe that stuff,' Milos says. 'The minister doesn't even believe it himself – he's just reading the script they gave him.'

The phone rings. Milos is called out on a little job. 'I've picked up one or two things after thirty years as a phone operator,' he chuckles. These days he helps people rework their phone lines and power supply, so that their usage isn't registered. 'The state has been stealing from us our whole lives, so it's just proper to get a little payback,' he reasons, and gets ready to go. He throws an apologetic glance up at the saint's image on the wall: 'There are bigger sinners than me in this country.'

If the Zarics have little faith in the Belgrade government, the local city administration enjoys their unwavering respect. The dynamic Mayor of Kragujevac, Miroslav Marinkovic, has found ways to build roads and bridges and to establish a few small businesses. Branka mentions that aid from Norway has been earmarked for a new bridge near by. But the city council can't do much about the local economy; last year their operating budget was just a fifth of what it had been two years earlier.

I call in at Marinkovic's office after I take my leave of the Zarics. His figures prove to be depressing reading.

'Industry in Kragujevac is running at two–three per cent of capacity. Only a few businesses, those who bake bread or make other consumer products, are operating. Tens of thousands here have never had work, an even greater number is officially employed somewhere but never do any work, because there's nothing getting made there,' he explains. 'Yugoslavia is ailing. It's a serious illness. But the government is only trying to deceive people. The Vice-Prime Minister, Vojislav Seselj, says that if we would only sell the artworks in Tito's residence we could save the economy. That's like telling a dying cancer patient that he'd get well if he'd only drink some orange juice,' sighs Marinkovic. 'We live within a maze of myths, just to keep the unpleasant present out of sight.'

In contrast to his fellow citizen Milos Zaric, Marinkovic is highly critical of the sanctions. 'Without Western aid there is no way we can institute reforms, and without reforms there is no Western aid. We have vast industrial complexes and a large market, but we need money. The West does nothing; it just sits and watches as the sanctions benefit Milosevic, and at the same time complains that we're not doing anything to get rid of him. Did anyone ask the Germans to get rid of Hitler in 1943?'

Miroslav Marinkovic once again refers to his arch-nemesis Seselj, who thinks it's just great how Serbia's international isolation has given the authorities new levels of control. 'We don't need anyone's help; we have mush-rooms and raspberries for everyone in this country,' was his recent remark. Rather, it is the grey market that keeps the 180,000 inhabitants of Kragujevac alive. One might be fooled by the teeming street life of the former industrial city, as it seems everyone is busy with something. But people are driven outside by poverty and unemployment. They offer wares for sale everywhere you go. One man has a bag of clothes pegs, another sells saplings. Elderly ladies sell old slippers, home-knitted socks, an almost brand-new lampshade, a wall socket. But, most of all, people sell cigarettes.

It's June 2000 and four months have passed since my first visit to the Zarics. They all await me in the potholed court-yard outside their tenement building. All except for Milan. 'He's asleep,' says Branka. 'You see, he had a gig last night,' she proudly reveals. Then Milos takes the floor. 'Everything's got worse, worse than last time.' He displays the front page of today's newspaper: 'Djukanovic to Lisbon, Jovanovic to Hanoi,' reads the headline. 'That says everything about our two countries,' he snorts. 'Milo Djukanovic, the President of Montenegro, is strengthening the ties to Europe, which invests vast sums in his country. Meanwhile our Foreign Minister, Zivorad Jovanovic, trav-els to Vietnam, North Korea, Sierra Leone and Cuba! Before Milosevic came to power we all thought Yugoslavia would move closer to the West. But it's the exact opposite that's happening – we're becoming the pariahs of Europe! We're living in a reservation, we can't go anywhere and nobody wants us.'

Branka is on sick leave owing to a back injury and can no longer work or bring home any food. She's due money on her recovery, but given that her last payment was for the month of February, it stands to reason that dole money for June will be a while coming. Now Biljana and Milan support the family. Biljana finally found work in a kiosk, selling magazines, sweets and cigarettes, and she earns close to fifty pounds a month. She beams over her new job, even if it's all off the books. She has no rights should she become ill or get fired. 'But it's just an incredible feeling to earn your own money,' she says.

This last couple of months Milan's band has got more gigs and he takes home about five pounds a night. The gig lasts from eight in the evening until four or five in the morning. Most of his income goes on the regular expenses.

'Everyone in the family does their bit to make sure that there's always something in the fridge,' Branka says. 'After all, it's more economical to live together,' she adds, half discouraged, half encouraging.

'We rode in open trucks, like cattle!' Milos shouts with delight. 'We just drove on, nobody could have stopped us! When we left Kragujevac we said we wouldn't return before Milosevic was gone. They flew their helicopters right above us, but none of us were afraid.'

It's late spring 2001 when I meet the Zaric family again, on Milos's birthday. But it's 5 October that is the big day. Milos recounts the heroic deeds, tells of the farmers who arrived on their tractors, the bulldozer driver who'd had just about enough of Milosevic and bulldozed his way to Belgrade.

The whole family is gathered for a birthday lunch, except for Biljana, who's at work in the kiosk. 'She's five months pregnant now,' Branka says with a proud smile. She's cooked a feast of beef patties, fried potatoes and fermented cabbage. The celebration begins with the obligatory *rakija*. We toast Milos, the revolution, the new President and Prince Aleksandar. Where the picture of Vuk Draskovic used to hang, there is now a picture of the Yugoslav prince.

Biljana's pregnancy is the only major news in the family. Milos is still out of work, Branka is still on sick leave and Milan gets the odd job here and there. 'We can't expect improvements overnight,' a forgiving Milos says of the new government.

He is still hoping that foreigners will buy Zastava and rebuild the whole plant from the ground up. 'The Yugo can't compete with foreign cars,' he says.

Branka generally listens to Milos talk. When she's not ladling more fried potatoes on to my plate.

Over coffee the phone rings. Once again someone wants Milos to fix his power lines so that his electricity consumption remains a mystery. Milos leaves, more reluctantly than before. 'It is a bit of a fraud,' he admits. 'Before, I was delighted to deceive our corrupt regime when I could, but these days the state needs all the money they have coming to them, so they can institute much-needed reforms.'

Milan is playing tonight and we all decide to go to the café. It's been a year since Milos and Branka went out anywhere. I get a chance to catch up with Branka. She's increasingly worried about the family's living situation. 'Yes, there'll be more of us soon,' she says. 'Milena can't remain in her parents' room for ever, of course, and what will happen when they have more kids? I have an old aunt and an uncle who live in a flat of sixty square metres; when they die Milan could take over the flat.'

'How old are they?' I ask.

'Seventy,' Branka replies.

'Well, they could live for another fifteen years,' I say.

'Yes, they could,' Branka sighs and stares at me. 'They very well could.'

Short beeps greet me down the line when I dial the Zarics' number three years later. Have they moved? Is the number out of order? I try directory enquiries. They list a number of Milos Zarics in Kragujevac, but none of them is my Milos.

I can only go and see for myself. I should be able to retrace my steps back to their flat, just as I found Verica and Radovan in Adrani. Again I take Drago along. After the requisite fumbling we find their block. We park the car, and as I cross the courtyard a girl comes running up and throws herself into my arms.

I see Biljana coming down the stairs.

'Milena saw you from the window!'

'I can't believe she'd recognise me – she can't have been more than five when I was here last.'

'When was that?'

'It's going on three or four years now.'

'Well, come inside, come inside.'

Biljana makes coffee. Milena stands in the doorway stealing glances at me. Drago and I have taken our seats in a pair of recliners in the living room. Nothing has changed here; everything is just more worn.

The child Biljana was carrying when I was here last

must be about three now. But I can't see any trace of a toddler.

Biljana joins us. 'Here everything is as it always was,' she says. 'Everyone pitches in as best they can.'

'Are things getting better?'

'Worse. We're worse off now. I still work in the kiosk. Milos does what he can. Branka is back at work at the canteen and Milan plays. But there haven't been a lot of gigs and they don't pay well. He's playing for tips more often than not. For two weeks he played all night without making more than twenty euros, but suddenly, the other day, this huge party paid the band several hundred euros to split between them.'

I enquire about the other child.

'There is no other child,' Biljana says. 'We just have Milena.'

She gets up and goes into the kitchen, where she stays for a while. When she returns it is with a packet of cigarettes, which she offers us. Biljana inhales hungrily, as if she's sucking on life itself.

'We tried to call you but couldn't get through,' I say, trying to gloss over my painful question.

'Well, we haven't paid the phone bill. We had to help pay the expenses for the funeral of one of Branka's friends, so we couldn't afford it.'

'Oh, I'm sorry to hear that.'

'No, no, he was old.'

'But the phone bill? Isn't that what Milos does — help people hook up their phone so that it doesn't count their minutes?'

'That was before, that was before. It's a new system now,' she says, and gets up again. 'Branka and Milos should be here any minute now. I have to get lunch ready.'

Milos comes through the door, wearing a dirty shirt and worn-out trousers.

'Oh!' he shouts when he sees me, shakes my hand and laughs. Branka returns from the canteen. Her eyes well up with tears.

'*Ima nas.* Here we are,' says Milos when he has cleaned up. 'Just like before.'

'We don't give up,' Branka laughs.

While Biljana is of the opinion that life has got worse these past three years, Branka and Milos maintain that it's 'a bit better'.

'Expectations, expectations,' Branka explains. 'The young ones had sky-high expectations about what their lives would be like. We old ones know that nothing changes overnight.'

'How have things improved?'

'I get paid on time now. Once a month it's pay day – not like before, when it came months later.'

'But the transition has come at a price,' Milos says. 'Our Prime Minister got killed. And we won't see the likes of a man like that for a hundred years. No one can fill his shoes. Zivkovic made a miserable job of it, just as Kostunica is doing now. But we only have ourselves to blame. If the people aren't good, their governments won't be either. We Serbs can't handle being confronted with the truth – we're blaming others for all eternity. It's a never-ending story. Take this issue of the new government not wanting to cooperate with the tribunal in The Hague. Let them try him there, I say, and if he's not guilty they'll give him back to us, if it's so important to everyone,' says Milos. 'Nationalism is coming back in a hurry. Just look at these Radicals, and their crazy notion that anywhere Serbs live should be incorporated into some sort of Greater Serbia.

All that means is another war. Is that all we know how to do? Make war?'

Milos has worked himself into a lather. Branka does her best to calm him down. Milos gets up and retrieves the *rakija* from the cupboard over the TV.

'This one we've made ourselves, from the plum trees at our cabin,' he says, and displays the bottle.

'If we hadn't had the cottage I don't what would have become of us,' Branka says. 'There we grow vegetables and fruits. Just enough to make it through the year. And it's so beautiful out there; you'll have to come with us some time. It's quiet and peaceful – everything there is as it used to be, in a good way.'

After a supper of meat, fried potatoes and handpicked tinned mushrooms with coffee and fifty-odd cigarettes, we say our goodbyes to the Zarics. Branka discreetly hands me a small glass and a bottle. Cherry jam and plum brandy. The Archangel Mihajlo is painted by hand on the bottle, and he looks at me with a virtuous face. The clear liquor wobbles behind his eyes. 'My cousin painted that,' Branka tells me. 'He certainly knows his stuff,' she sighs. 'Come back soon. You know you always have a home with us!'

'What do you think?' I ask Drago once we're back in the car.

'Nice bottle.'

I'm sitting with the Archangel Mihajlo in my lap. Tender brushstrokes have left him with a golden aura illuminating his head, while his wings envelop the bottle's contents. He looks at me with lenient eyes.

'I meant about the family,' I clarify.

'Milos is a wise man,' Drago replies.

'And Branka is a wise woman.'

'Besides, they have each other,' says Drago, with far-away eyes.

The God-fearing one lowers his eyes and smiles. The cork leaks a little and the smell of plum brandy fills the car.

Roots

'I closed my eyes and imagined her in a long, black dress.
She turned and looked towards the sky.
She raised her arms upwards to catch
the air, the sun and the clouds. Her arms turned to wings,
and it looked as if she was about to take to the air.
But when the wind lifted her heavy, black dress,
I saw that she had roots in the place of feet.
Powerful roots reaching deep into the earth.
I realised that she would never fly.'

Excerpt from Ana Rodic's *Roots* (2000)

"If it only survives, if it only survives," cries Empress Irina, drenched in sweat from her labour. She has given birth to many children, but they all died soon after their births. "Are the icons in front of me?" the Empress asks fearfully. The women surrounding her answer yes. Candles are burning in front of every icon. The last candle to go out will tell which saint will save this child's life. "The child will be named after the saint who saves it," one of the servant girls whispers. The girl child survives, and the candle in front of the Apostle Simon burns the longest.'

Ana curls even further up in her chair. 'Simonida was a genuine Serbian princess, but the stories of her birth, her childhood, and her love life I've made up myself. I've heard so many legends in my life that it's the easiest thing to make up a few of my own,' she says with a laugh. When I meet her, Ana Rodic has just received rave reviews for her latest novel, *Roots*. It's the twenty-eight-year-old's third book and, in her opinion, her best work so far. This last week she has gone from one interview to the next. The night before I meet her she has taken part in a TV programme on literature, along with 'an old aunt who'd written a book about Ivo Andric'. Ana showed up in a little black dress and heels that went on for ever, in order to 'look thin'. She was nervous and responded with single syllables to each question posed to her. Her mother called her after the programme went out, in order to tell her how terrible she had been. 'The other authoress had written a serious tome about Ivo Andric and gave proper answers, while you, who've written a book about an adulterous princess and fucking in Belgrade, just sat there and vamped in a miniskirt,' was the gist of her mother's message.

Ana laughs and is relieved her televised ordeal is over. She's far more comfortable curled up in a chair, a glass of whisky in one hand and a cigarette in the other. Of everyone I meet in Serbia, no one seems to enjoy life as much as Ana – at least as long as it involves a drink, cigarettes, wine and good food. When the first bombs fell on Belgrade she went to an antique store and bought herself a gorgeous necklace, then put on her fanciest dress and organised a dinner party. 'I thought that if it was my fate to die that night I'd rather die with a glass of wine in my hand. We ate ourselves through the war,' Ana recounts, and admits to having inherited her rather unusual survival skills from her 'crazy mother'. Said mother was once stopped on the street by a foreign TV crew and asked to comment on the war. 'Do be so kind as to stop your bombing immediately,' she said. 'I've already gained five kilos due to this, and unless you cease soon I will be rolling into the bomb room!' Ana laughs and claims that the only way to survive in Serbia today is through dark humour and the belief in a better future.

It is, however, Serbia's past that has a hold on Ana's imagination. 'There is no present. This very moment exists only because it's where the past meets the future. Serbia is in a deep crisis; we are isolated, we're regarded as rank barbarians and we've lost faith in ourselves. The only thing we are left with is to recover that time when we were strong and the land was in bloom. Maybe that will inspire us to rebuild our country – because Serbia has a proud heritage. Extremely proud,' she emphasises, in case I didn't catch it.

Heroics are Ana's chosen subject. The plot of her novel centres on the women in Serbia's only dynasty – the Nemanjic Dynasty – which lasted from 1168 to 1371. During the Nemanjic era the Serbian feudal state came into its own, financially, militarily and culturally. In one period, under the rule of Tsar Dusan, around 1350, this was the most powerful nation in south-eastern Europe. At that time Serbia was about the size of the territory Milosevic controlled for a few months in the winter of

1992. The empires covered different areas, though. Dusan's included Greece but not Bosnia. And Tsar Dusan held on to it for a bit longer – some twenty years. But the constant infighting between the various Serbian feudal lords made it far easier for the Turks to emerge triumphant from the decisive battle on the Kosovo plains in 1389. This battle gave birth to the legends of Tsar Lazar and the myths surrounding the Serbs' divinely ordained empire. And even with the fall of the dynasty it was that great legacy of the founder of the Serbian Orthodox Church, the Nemanja St Sava, which served to create a Serbian identity that survived half a millennium of Ottoman rule and moulded the Serbs and Serbia into what they are today.

In Ana's novel past and present are intermingled. Thoughts of characters from the past appear in the minds of the contemporary protagonists. They become inspired through dreams in which the Nemanjas speak to them and provide them with signs. The main character in the book is a historian who participates in a book project about Serbia's women and is put in charge of the Middle Ages.

Ana decided early on that her main character had to be male, to counter the preponderance of medieval women, 'Otherwise it would have been classified as feminist literature,' she explains. 'Besides, I needed a love interest, so while at the library he meets Masa, with whom he falls in love. This in turn creates problems because he is married, but they manage to work together, after a fashion. Of course, their book never materialises,' Ana laughs. 'Here in Serbia nobody ever manages to complete anything. People have all sorts of splendid ideas, but they rarely yield results. And his love for Masa remains unfulfilled as well. But at least they're able to learn something about the Middle Ages.'

The story takes place in contemporary Belgrade and provides a glimpse of what life is like in the Serbian capital, with its refugees, black marketeers, cash crunch, disillusionment, drug overdoses, suicides and infidelity – lots of infidelity.

'What – you haven't noticed?' Ana marvels. 'Affairs are rampant in Belgrade. Everyone is betraying everyone. We're such a passionate people to begin with, and now, with times so bad, marriages and relationships fail all the time. Nobody trusts anybody any more.' Ana gives me an inquisitive look and asks if I've acquired a Serbian boyfriend yet, and what I think of Serbian men, if I'm familiar with Serbian stamina and virility.

'Bah – it's just another myth anyway,' she says. 'But you won't get far with a book on Serbs if you insist on studying us like animals in a zoo. You have to live here, fall in love, make friends with us,' Ana says, and generously invites me to a party on Saturday and a dinner on Sunday, with further weekend plans over the months ahead.

'Perhaps I might introduce you to some interesting men. What sort of men do you fancy?'

The door opens and Marko enters. Marko is Ana's boyfriend of five years. He is a computer designer and Ana's complete opposite: quiet, organised and systematic. Their biggest fights are about housekeeping – who, how often and how meticulously. Ana's mess drives Marko nuts and Ana can't stand it when their flat is spotlessly clean. But whether clean or messy, their one-bedroom flat is filled beyond its capacity. All it can hold is a kitchenette, an alcove for sleeping, a writer's desk, a sofa and two easy chairs.

Marko is tired and goes to sleep in the bed a couple of

metres away. I get ready to leave, but Ana is in rare form. 'Shall I read my book to you?'

We sit up all night. Ana reads and explains in her Balkan English, with interjections of French and Serbian sayings, between puffs on her cigarettes and gulps of whisky. By five in the morning she has finished the book. 'Let me know what you think in the morning,' she says, and expels me into Belgrade's dawn. In the taxi home I recall a line in Tim Judah's book *The Serbs*: 'The Land of the Living Past'. People are obsessed with the past and unable to move beyond lost battles or vanished empires. It is never too late to avenge misdeeds and injustices committed centuries ago.

The next evening Ana picks up where she left off. 'There's nothing wrong about being proud of your country, and right now it is crucial for Serbs to know that we have a great history. During the Nemanja Empire princesses came here from France, Hungary and Byzantium in the hope of marrying our kings. Painters and artists made pilgrimages to Serbia and we were a part of the rest of the world,' she tells me, clearly unhappy about Serbia's current standing in the international community.

'These days we have to travel to Budapest to get a visa anywhere, and most likely it will be rejected, because the West is terrified that we won't leave once we're there; we've become a pariah state,' she snorts, and recalls her trip to Greece with a girlfriend a few years earlier. 'We were detained in immigration and they called Belgrade to determine who we were. And in front of the whole passport control queue we were made to show that we had enough money for a two-week holiday in Greece. It was humiliating and almost deprived me of the desire to travel anywhere ever again.'

Ana wasn't always an ardent student of history. She

scraped through her secondary school exams and had to choose her university from the bottom rung. In the 1990s that meant Kosovo: the university in Pristina was the only one willing to accept a student of her dubious ability. 'I knew even then that I wanted to be an author and wanted to study world literature, but in Pristina they taught only Serbian literature and history. So I majored in that. Although most of my time there was spent in love with someone or other, and I hardly did anything beyond sitting in cafés looking cool. So I failed my exams in medieval literature – twice. But once in a while life leads you to a place that changes you for ever. I visited the monastery in Gracanica, in Kosovo. There's a fresco of Simonida there and I suddenly remembered the songs and poems that my father used to sing to me about her. Something happened within me and I began to cry. I was staring at this woman and it looked to me as if she was crying as well. Everything was so sad and gorgeous. I went outside the monastery and sat down. A few chickens ran around and it was like being back in the Middle Ages. Suddenly this huge BMW pulled up with the speakers going full blast; the chickens scattered into the air, and when the dust finally settled I could see a man coming up in a cart pulled by a horse. It all became this strange moment where the past and the present became one. It's strange being in Kosovo, because you can feel the energy of the past everywhere. It hits you right across your head – this is where most of our proud history took place. You really feel that this is your land, Serbian land,' says Ana, who refuses to talk about the fact that Kosovo is presently lost and that Serbs risk their lives by even visiting.

'After the incident in Gracanica I began to study the Middle Ages with a whole new level of interest, and I passed the exams. I wrote some short stories of various women of that era, and began with Jefimia, Serbia's first female writer. These stories became the foundation for *Roots*.'

My first spring in Belgrade includes a multitude of café visits, shopping sprees and parties with Ana. Each time I meet up with her she appears to have all the time in the world. She delights in her reviews and generously invites me into her life. At first glance Ana's life might seem identical to that of most young Europeans, but a decade of war and crisis has left its mark on her. 'I've learned that anything can happen to you. That we, living in the middle of Europe in the twentieth century, can look out of the window one evening and see the skies lit up by exploding bombs. That you can become your neighbour's enemy overnight, that you can become outlawed, excommunicated. I'm just the same as you; it's just that my life is much harder.'

Ana never thought her life would turn out like this. 'I went to a good school, we learned French from the first year onwards and I remember thinking we'd make a splendid generation. But it didn't turn out that way; none of my classmates are doing anything serious. They spend their days in cafés, make a few deals, do odd jobs. A lot of them started using drugs, some died,' Ana notes sadly. 'This is a nation where the abnormal has become normal. It's quite normal here to be neurotic, melancholic or apathetic. We've got used to the fact that we can't travel anywhere else, and if we do make it abroad, people there stare at us and wonder where we've got the dagger hidden. Or they pity us, thinking we are refugees. We've grown accustomed to living among one million refugees. Just yesterday

I saw this cashier yelling at a Serbian refugee from Croatia, calling him all kinds of names and telling him to go back where he came from. As I walked out it struck me that I hadn't reacted. I just stood there, waiting for it to be my turn,' Ana says, thoughtfully.

'I'm twenty-eight and I've lived with my boyfriend for two years. Normally this would be a time to consider having kids, but then I think of how much nappies are and that the shops don't have any milk, and then I think we can wait. Our options are shrinking all the time. The only thing I know is that I have to write. I have so many stories in me; right now I am working on three different novels simultaneously. One is about claustrophobic love, about a couple who no longer love each other but don't dare leave each other. The second is a love story from the Middle Ages and the third is a mythological story of a knight who is the son of a dragon and a woman. Right now I'm working on the part where the woman makes love to the dragon; it's getting quite erotic, really. I'll have to watch myself so I don't descend into rank vulgarity,' Ana laughs, between saying hi to friends as they stop by our table.

It's not easy to make a living as an author in Serbia. It's hard to get your books published and the publishers pay little. So Ana has to take on a few extra jobs. She writes scripts for TV series, advertising texts and radio jingles. She has a wide range of talents to draw on. 'I recently worked on two jobs at the same time – a script for a TV show called *Erotica* and a play about St Sava. The play was to be written in a very archaic language and convey the faith of the most important individual in the Serbian Orthodox Church. At the same time I had to make the deadline for the erotic texts – so one instant I'm writing, "Father, help my people!" and the next, "Be careful when using whips and handcuffs!" When I was done my head was about to explode, and I had to clear my mind with a stiff drink. But both pieces turned out rather well!'

Ana says she wouldn't be able to pursue her writing if it wasn't for her boyfriend and her family. 'I'm blessed to have so much help. One writer I know is married with a kid, and he has to take any odd job he can get and never has time to write any more. That's sad. A lot of people live like that and not a lot of good books are being written in Serbia now. This is a madhouse, a wild country – so inspiration should be the least of one's problems.'

Ana is fully committed to a life of writing, but her original dream was to become an actress. 'In school, we had an audition for a part and I didn't get it – the prettiest girl in our class did. And the boy I had a crush on had a crush on her. So I swore I'd never audition again. I went home and studied myself in the mirror. All the while I went through everything I wanted to say to the boy. I wrote it down and showed it to a girlfriend. She liked it and asked me to write a love letter she could send to her boyfriend. Soon I was writing love letters for all my friends, like a regular Cyrano de Bergerac. Later I began writing little stories. I got a job as a translator for a woman's magazine, translating articles from *Cosmopolitan* and *Elle* and the like. One day I went to the editor and asked if I could show her some stuff I'd written myself. She liked it enough to print it. It was just a stupid article about the various emotional stages of getting dumped – classic *Cosmo* stuff,' Ana laughs, as she spots someone she knows and once again tries to fix me up with one of her friends.

A few weeks later I meet Ana again, at Gaudí. She looks depressed and tired. It's the miserable present that's weighing her down and she can't seem to muster the energy to escape back into Serbia's glorious past. 'I can't get a thing done, I'm just going around in circles, I don't do anything, I'm a complete failure. I never finished my studies, I can't write at all and I don't have any money.'

'What about the three novels you're working on?'

'I've hit a wall. I turn the PC on in the morning and just sit there and stare at the ugly letters for a while. Until I turn the damn thing off and go outside. Then I go to a café and maybe I'll meet someone I know. But I can't afford more than a single cup of coffee,' she sighs. 'I commiserated with another author and he told me it's always like this after you've published a book. You're left feeling spent and lethargic, but it's normal, according to this guy. So all I really have to do is just wait for this depression to pass,' a listless Ana decides.

'How's your book coming on, by the way?' she askes me. 'You think you'll get anywhere with this Serbs-in-the-zoo idea? Well, you may start worrying about the period after publication. That's when this depression sets in. You should dread it!'

During the thrilling days of October 2000 Ana sits in front of the TV drinking whisky. She watches the parliament being stormed and sees the police fire tear-gas canisters into the crowd just a few streets away from her flat. It never occurs to her to participate in any of it. 'I couldn't get that excited about politics,' she says. 'Although I'm happy of course that Milosevic is gone.'

We're strolling around inside Kalemegdan, the fortress of Belgrade. It was originally built by the Romans but has been extended by later rulers. Ana wants to show me her favourite church, Sveta Petka.

'Go all the way down, stand in front of the Virgin, cross

yourself three times, kneel and pray for something. If you see her smiling back at you, your wish will come true. After all that, drink from the holy water in the font; it will protect you.'

It sounds like a stage direction for one of her plays. She waits for me outside the church, because she's got a new puppy that shrieks whenever she is more than two steps away from him. 'I'm practising for the mummy part,' she laughs.

I go inside and face the Virgin, who seems to be smiling already. But I forget to formulate some sort of wish.

After this we take a seat on a bench in the park, resting our legs on the railing facing the Danube. We enjoy the view and exchange news. Ana's got a lot more work lately, so she's no longer as broke. 'I write ad copy, scripts for TV shows and series,' she says. 'Just crap, really.'

The three novels have been put aside for now. 'I'm waiting to be inspired,' she says. 'At least things are better here now – people are happier, life is easier. But maybe I could only write within the chaos,' she worries. 'All I do these days is fluff.'

Ana's bout with writer's block does pass, though, and as spring turns into summer she gets back to work on her novels. And she's getting married to Marko in May, so she has her hands full with the wedding preparations. But despite her personal happiness, Ana remains dubious about Serbia's future, regardless of Milosevic's arrest.

'The Serbian earth is full of blood,' she says, balancing her espresso cup as she looks at me. 'With all this blood beneath our feet, we'll never see peace.'

Three years later we meet on Tsar Lazar Street, of all places. You'd be hard pressed to find a more symbolically

burdened street name, even here in the Serbian capital.
Ana is waiting for me in a café on the second floor of a
bookshop specialising in spiritual literature.

The author sits and reads as I enter. She looks tired and
worn.

'Yeah, I'm tired,' she says, reading my thoughts. 'I'm not
getting anywhere. I feel trapped here.'

We're the only customers in the café – in the whole
shop, for that matter, not counting the sales assistant, who
doubles as our waiter. He serves tea with milk and cinna-
mon cookies.

Ana has put her myths aside for the time being and
focused on the present. She has written an ambitious TV
series based on the lives of four young women which has
made her both famous and controversial. The eighteen
episodes became a phenomenon throughout Serbia, but at
a price. Ana was dragged over the coals by the press.
'These people don't exist in Belgrade – nor do these cafés,
conversations, clothes or problems,' went a typical review.
'A *Sex and the City* rip-off!' read another. Others support
Ana's version of life in the big city and have called her show
the first modern series on Serbian television. Finally, they
say, someone who takes the lives of young women seriously.

'The very same day that the war in Iraq began, one of the
news magazines here ripped me apart over four pages.
Makes you wonder whose perspectives are out of joint,'
Ana shrugs.

Back at her flat she shows me more clippings. She has a
whole folder full of interviews with her and the actresses.
Ana became a celebrity overnight and suddenly found herself in the gossip pages. 'It was an ordeal,' she says. 'I made
something absolutely everyone insisted on having an

opinion about. In the end I just locked myself in my flat and brooded.'

But, all in all, the experience was a positive one.

'The four main characters are all looking for love, but always in the wrong places. They end up running in circles. The series says something about how difficult life is here. Ultimately it's a series about being alone. I wanted to create an ode to solitude. And I wanted to portray regular people. The protagonists are not dynamic or ambitious – they're lazy and scared. That's something everyone can relate to, no?'

The name of the series is *Lisice*, which means 'Foxes', but it can mean 'Handcuffs' as well.

'Is that what Belgrade feels like?'

'I feel it more strongly every day that goes by – that I have to get out and breathe, draw fresh air, smell the world. Belgrade is just a vast village. I have to get out before I lose my mind! It's tough to be young. But maybe it's even worse getting older,' she wonders.

'You have to be as clever as a fox to survive here – but even then, we still live our lives in handcuffs.'

Don't Happy, Be Worry

'Musician, poet, philosopher, sailor, father, husband
– looking for a job.'

rambadeus@yahoo.com

Rambo stands in the stern of the boat and paddles with a
wooden plank. 'Give me the row,' he says in his Rambo
English, and means I am to hand him the oar. We're in a bay
next to one of Belgrade's major motorway interchanges,
and our little boat putters out towards the River Sava. The
tiny dinghy drifts helplessly out towards the swift currents,
and even though we can hear the noise from the motorway
we feel rather anxious as the splint of our propeller has
broken off and between us we have one oar and a plank.
Oh, and it's snowing. Heavily. The snow melts on the
bamboo roof that covers half the boat. Rambo the rock
star and Nebojsa the philosopher are paddling furiously
against the current to stay out of the Sava's imposing waves.

Suddenly we spot our salvation – a man building a terrace on to his houseboat on the shore. 'Nice terrace!' Rambo hollers.

'I'm starting an open-air café,' the man explains before throwing us a lifeline.

In no time at all he has found a piece of wire to fix our propeller, and it suddenly works like a charm. 'Nothing is made well in this country, so people are good at fixing things,' chuckles Nebojsa the philosopher. His name means 'He who is without fear' and our vessel, built of welded metal sheets, takes him at his word by heading straight for the Sava again.

I've just met Antonio Pusic, better known as the rock star Rambo Amadeus, one of Serbia's most innovative artists. When I requested an interview with him he responded with an email listing the four main reasons he didn't give interviews:

1. When I am interviewed by foreign journalists, I am always left feeling like a weird insect carrying a rare disease put on a cold glass plate and studied through a microscope while I wait for the scalpel to dissect me.
2. Why would you want to include me in a book about Serbs? I'm not a Serb, but a multi-ethnic mutant – Montenegrin-croatserbian. And before I would even begin to consider letting you have an interview, you would have to familiarise yourself with the last thousand years' worth of history of my birthplace in Montenegro, Boka Kotorska, and its traditions within shipping, trade, warfare, conquest and art.
3. And about our current situation? I think we've got exactly what we were looking for. You should have been here in 1989; then, everyone hailed our beloved dictator.

4. If you still want to meet me for a drink, then call me on
   my mobile. With the utmost respect for your country and
   people,

Rambo Amadeus

'I think we should get to know each other first,' Rambo
said when I called. 'And then I'll think about whether I
want to do an interview or not. And in order to get to
know me better, you'll have to go boating with me. I've
won fifty competitions in sailing in the former
Yugoslavia, and I'm one of the best sailors in Boka
Kotorska.'

Once we're in the middle of the river, and the engine has
cleared its throat enough times to inspire some kind of
confidence, Rambo reveals that he'd happily give up his
career in order to be a full-time fisherman. 'But you can't
turn your back on the world when you live in chaos. You
can't shut your eyes to the injustice of this country. I certainly can't, at least. But if I could strike a deal with God or
the Devil for some peace of mind, and it meant me never
singing or playing a note ever again, I'd do it.'

Rambo Amadeus emerged on the scene in the late 1980s
with a new kind of music and satirical lyrics about Yugoslav
society. His first CD became a popular antidote to the
techno-inspired folk music that held Yugoslavia in a death
grip at the time, with its nationalistic, warmongering, sen-
timental lyrics. You heard this odd hybrid wherever you
went: in bars, kebab stalls, taxis and on the street. On TV
the videos were in constant rotation, with nationalistic
iconography stirred into a syrupy musical hodgepodge.
Rambo ridiculed the whole phenomenon, calling it turbo-
folk – because a turbo never stops – and rode his disdain to
the top of the charts.

'My first two CDs were mostly a joke, but they were intended as an attack on the stupidity I saw sneaking into everything,' he says. To align himself with this trend of inanity he needed the silliest stage name he could think of. He decided on Rambo Amadeus over Rocky Chopin. 'The name isn't even pathetic – it's exploding the pathetic. It's like having two TVs in your living room, both of them tuned to the same episode of *Cassandra*,' he explains. Rambo Amadeus was an instant success. This was before the wars started and Yugoslavia split apart, and he toured for sold-out audiences in Croatia, Slovenia, Bosnia, Serbia, Macedonia and Montenegro.

'I toured a lot throughout Yugoslavia and came into contact with a lot of different people. When I was putting out my third CD, in 1990, I knew we were heading towards war. "We can't let the others get us!" I heard wherever I went. Everyone started checking their bloodline to determine what nationality they were. If someone had asked me, before 1990, what my nationality was, I'd have been at a loss for words. My mother and father never talked about it. I was baptised as a Catholic, my brother as Orthodox. Today I know full well that my mum is Serbian and my dad half Croat and half Montenegrin.'

Rambo is interrupted by some moaning and groaning from the metal can, as it bobs out into the Sava, passing houseboats, fishermen and the odd piece of rusting scrap metal in the shape of a boat. I've brought along a bottle of Norwegian Linie aquavit to keep the snowstorm at bay. We're headed for Bole Kornjaca's – Bole Turtle's. We dock next to a collapsing wharf and seek shelter in Bole's shed. Inside, a casserole's simmering on the stove. According to Rambo, Bole makes the best soup in all of Belgrade, from fish freshly caught from the Sava. Bole has three tables on his houseboat. A group of guys sit around one of them playing cards. At regular intervals one of them emits a soft roar and slams a winning hand down on the table. Bole stands by and keeps an eye on things, serves beer and soup and puts more firewood in the stove. We order fish soup, bread and beer, and warm ourselves next to the oven.

One of the men from the other table comes over to ours. The stranger and Nebojsa the philosopher begin to discuss the future of Kosovo. They're both of the opinion that Kosovo is a part of Serbia and has to be reunited with the motherland, and that Kosovo is the heart and soul of Serbia. 'The Serbs have to win back that which has been lost to us,' the stranger concludes. 'Kosovo is ours.'

Rambo doesn't say anything. When I ask his opinion he shrugs. 'I don't understand what they're talking about. I can't relate to any of it. I'm sick and tired of listening to talk of nations and territories and who has the right to which area. My country is where I feel content,' he says. 'In this country all you ever hear is that we're stronger and better than anyone else. But why is everything going to hell, then? I'll tell you, it's the five hundred years of "negative selection". When the Turks came into power here, the more cowardly ones converted right away, while the more resilient ones were killed off. And so it has continued. The herd mentality triumphs and the original, individual perspectives are obliterated. That's what it was like under Tito and that's the way it is now. In order to be heard you can only parrot what the authorities have said already.

'And look at all these myths and heroic epics. It's just to cover up the fact that this is a nation, a culture, of cowardice. We've lost every battle we've been in, but refuse to acknowledge it,' says the anti-nationalist. 'I'm endlessly disappointed in my people. All I really want to do is leave, and forget everything. But I have my family here, and my kids. I don't know that I'd be able to provide for them any better somewhere else,' he sighs.

Rambo is married and has two sons, one and three years old. 'God created a perfect world; everything was perfection, except for man. We ruin everything.'

It's starting to get late and it's high time to see if our little boat is able to carry us back to Belgrade. Bole receives a goodbye shot of aquavit before we get the engine going and putter off. Rambo and Nebojsa strike up a song. Do I know any Norwegian songs?

'*Eg rodde meg ut på seiegrunnen*' – 'I Rowed Myself Out to the Fishing Banks' – seems to fit the chilly occasion. By the time we tie the dinghy to a tiny dock in Belgrade, it's dark.

Rambo gives me some homework before we part. 'Find out how many boys in Serbia have been baptised Slobodan these last two years. If there are any, then find them for me,' he requests. I check with those of my friends who might have connections within Serbia's central statistical office – without any luck. It doesn't release data related to names. The only other response came from Nis, Serbia's second-largest city, where nobody has been named Slobodan these past two years. 'Good work,' Rambo says when I present my research data. 'I'll give this interview some thought.'

While I'm waiting I manage to see Rambo Amadeus in action. The basement bar of the technological institute is filled to the rafters. Rambo sings, plays guitar and cracks jokes. The crowd sings along when they know the lyrics, but some of the material is brand new. Rambo likes to try out his songs on an audience before he records them. He has a devoted fan base that follows his work through his website – Rambo refuses to promote his CDs in any other way. 'If people like them they'll buy them. If they don't, then I don't want to be the one tricking them into buying one,' he says. The students laugh at his joking around. The main thrust is a sustained mockery of Milosevic, the authorities, the mentality and the dreariness of living in Serbia. 'Just think, if I were born in Scandinavia!' Rambo shouts at one point, and everybody laughs, as if the very thought is absurd. The musician lets no opportunity to ridicule the government pass him by, whether he's on stage, doing interviews or writing songs. He's also involved in G17+, an opposition network of people from various sectors of society – economists, politicians and artists. 'They call on me for ideas, but never listen to my advice. Mladjan Dinkic, who runs the network, called me last night, wondering what to do next. I suggested they buy the seventeen leading Gypsy fortune-tellers in the country, round them up in Republic Square and have them pro-nounce all manner of wicked curses on Milosevic. Diseases, accidents, what have you. If they were to pool their nefarious abilities simultaneously it just might work. Or at least work as well as anything else,' he reckons.

Ideally Rambo just wants to focus on the music. He calls his stuff acid-horror-funk. These days he is in the process of recording his new songs with a full band in a studio. I drop in quite often to see how things are going. Once in a while he'll come up with something that sounds like an incoher-ent mishmash of sounds and beats on a loop. The studio is filled with instruments of every kind, a stable of musicians and a dog who barks in perfect time.

'This is the hit,' Rambo says, and plays me what will be the first track on the CD, 'Shepherd, Come Back'. 'It's about the mentality of this people, about a nation that can't do anything unless it has a strong leader to follow. First it was Tito, then Milosevic, and now people are just waiting for the next one to come along. Since the opposition fails, time and again, to come with a serious alternative to Milosevic, the need in the people for a leader who can rescue them grows exponentially.'

A few lines in the song are repeated over and over: 'Shepherd, come back/your sheep can't live without you/we thought the grass was greener elsewhere/we thought you wanted the grass for yourself/Shepherd, come back/Your sheep can't live without you'. Another track on the CD is called 'Don't Happy, Be Worry'. According to Rambo, this song summarises the prevailing mood in the Balkans these days: the joy is gone, only the worries remain. And on 'Balkan Boy' Rambo comments on Balkan men with a self-deprecating eye:

I'm clever, I'm not a fool
I learned English in elementary school
My grandfather was a Partisan
He died in a car-accident like a hero man
In my country was an ethnic war
I don't want to shoot
I want to play electric guitar
I am Balkan Boy
and I search for employ
I can wash the dishes faster than a machine
I can babysit your baby older than sixteen
I have no money I have no friends
But God gave me intelligence
big dick and a couple of eggs
to put some happiness between your legs
People, people vote for me

> *to present me always on TV*
> *to earn lots of dollars and marks*
> *to sleep in hotels, not in parks*
> *I am Balkan Boy*

Late one evening my phone rings. 'Rambo here. Let's make a deal,' he says. 'I will be in your book if you will be on my CD. Could you come to the studio now?' It's almost midnight, but the studio's not far away, so the prospect of a singing career in Serbia sends me scurrying through the streets. 'Sing that fishing song of yours,' Rambo tells me, and orders me straight into the booth. I sing, *'Eg rodde meg ut på seiegrunnen'* in myriad versions. High, low, light, dark, slow and fast. 'Tell me a fairy tale of a lighthouse that falls in love with an oil platform,' Rambo tells me next. And I launch into a rather incoherent storytelling session in Norwegian. After this Rambo wants me to act out the two fishermen from the song – first the angry one who hits the other, then the scared one, his victim. All in all, it takes less than half an hour.

The next morning Rambo sets off for Slovenia to mix his record. He keeps me continually updated on the progress of 'our' song and plays me snippets of it over the phone. Two months later he calls me with the good news: 'Our song is finished. Come and listen!'

I take the night train from Belgrade to Ljubljana. I was woken no fewer than seven times during the night by an assortment of passport controllers, border police and luggage checks. The train runs from Belgrade, through Zagreb in Croatia to Ljubljana in Slovenia, and every one of those countries remains deeply suspicious of each other and their respective citizens. By the time the train reaches Ljubljana, at seven in the morning, I am completely exhausted.

Rambo waits for me at the station. My song is the second track. He's named it 'Laganese' – '*Lagano* means calm,' Rambo explains, laughing. 'A laganese is a calm, romantic ballad. Except this one. It is about the lack of communication between people, and between East and West.' To my ears the song is about as kitsch a pop song as I've ever been subjected to. My fishing song has been set to shrieking seagulls and waves and is mixed in with my oilrig fairy tale and the fighting fishermen. My voice is mixed against Rambo's, and he is trying to make contact. 'Are you a foreigner? From Hungary? England? Don't you want to talk with me?' I just keep on singing and telling stories. Rambo is visibly pleased with his mix and grows even more delighted when I describe the effort as utterly pathetic to Norwegian sensibilities. 'Cool!' he says. 'Pathetic is good.' He gives me a copy. 'You can play it on Norwegian radio,' he suggests. 'It'll be a smash here! Maybe we'll become famous in Norway as well!'

We take a stroll through Ljubljana. After six months in Belgrade the contrast is palpable. The mood is lighter, people seem happier and, not least, the city is more modern. 'Of course it is,' Rambo explains. 'While we were part of the Ottoman Empire for five hundred years, the Slovenes were part of the Austro-Hungarian Empire. Look at the cars – they're just ordinary cars. In Belgrade all you see is either these huge Mercedes that the Mafia drive around in or the old, crappy Yugos that regular people drive. The mentality here is totally different. This is not the Balkans. Maybe I'll move here,' Rambo thinks.

We go out to celebrate the completion of his CD. Rambo is off to Montenegro the next day. 'I dread going home. In Montenegro all everyone can talk about is politics, and in Belgrade people are just unconscionable these days. I've asked my parents not to tell me anything related to politics – I'm just sick of hearing everyone complain while nothing happens,' he says. 'The Balkans have become a prison for me, a prison I cannot escape from. People have no dignity left. If they see a chance to make some cash they take it. If it means stepping on someone else they couldn't care less. People only think about themselves and nothing at all beyond that. Just like sheep. Sheep don't care about other sheep,' he sighs. 'Spending these last few months in Slovenia has given me a lot to think about, and I've concluded that I have to get out.'

Rambo escaped once before. A few years ago he worked as a builder in Amsterdam for six months. 'I was just one of the guys, made friends and had the time of my life. Nobody knew who I was. It was like I'd spent my first thirty-five years within a black hole and had finally come out of it. Nobody misunderstood me, like they do here, and nobody bothered me. Unfortunately after six months they threw me out. I couldn't get visas for my family, who were supposed to follow me,' says Rambo, and tells me that none of his new friends or co-workers believed him when he said he was a famous rock star in Yugoslavia. 'Before I left I called my manager back home and got him to put together a concert. He set a show up in Slovenia and I brought along one of my Dutch friends, whom I'd fooled into promising to play saxophone with me on stage. He never believed for a second that I was a huge star – until we got off the plane and were met by my manager and a horde of journalists,' Rambo laughs. 'That I'd spent half a year doing minimum-wage work in Holland was a good story for the Yugoslav press,' he chuckles.

Rambo soon grows serious again, and tells me he's committed to not having his sons grow up in the Balkans. 'I don't want them to start school in Serbia and meet kids who're just the mirror image of their parents,' he says. 'My sons are pretty bright already and it won't take them long to figure out that the smart money's on crime. The criminals are the only ones who have money, status and fun in the Balkans. This society's just too much for me,' he says. He'd like to look for work in Holland or Denmark or Norway. 'I'm an expert on sailing boats – I can refurbish them, paint, rig, work on an oilrig, whatever,' he suggests.

'But you're a singer,' I protest.

'Yes, a singer who sings in Serbian,' he replies.

With the fall of Milosevic, Rambo decides to stay anyway. The new CD comes out in October and Rambo is planning a tour throughout the former Yugoslavia. I meet him a few days after the revolution and he's in rare form. He's editing his latest video and proudly shows me the clip for the shepherd song – a flock of sheep, intercut with a crowd hailing Tito, who limps around waving to his people. Then back to the sheep, then more Tito footage, and then footage of demonstrations from the past few years' events in Serbia, with the cops tearing into the crowds, and then more sheep. At the end we see Rambo clapping along as he sings, 'Shepherd, come back/we can't live without you' in front of screaming fans.

And just as Rambo predicted, the song is a huge hit in the autumn of 2000. The video's in constant rotation on TV and becomes the number everyone shouts for during his live shows. At football matches, entire stadiums break into spontaneous renditions. In Croatia the head of the broadcast network refuses to show it. When I ask Rambo what the explanation is, he just says that the broadcasting boss probably recognised a sheep when he saw one.

Later, even 'our' song makes an appearance in the charts. In the wake of the shepherd song's momentum, it climbs and climbs and lingers for a long time in the middle of B92's playlists. For a week in May it holds the number-one spot on Belgrade's most popular radio channel! At some point during the spring of 2001 '*Eg rodde meg ut på seiegrunnen*' achieves cult status in Belgrade.

Following the first heady days after the revolution, Rambo falls into a deep depression that lasts three weeks. 'I used to spend ninety per cent of my energies trying to figure out how to get rid of Milosevic, and how I could exclude him from my life. Once he fell, all my anger suddenly had nowhere to go and I suddenly didn't know what to feel any more. But now I feel totally energised; I've got ideas for a whole bunch of new songs and my goals are no longer global – but intimate. It feels fantastic, because I feared that my life would never be about my own, personal sphere – my family and my children – but always to do with Milosevic,' Rambo admits. 'Have you heard that there's been a wave of suicides? People see that Milosevic is gone and their lives are still shit.

'I want to make the world more clever. I am trying to find the weak parts in our mentality and make songs that can put pressure on the tender spots, like acupuncture. Our weak spots are demagoguery, masochism and obstinacy. This people have been seduced by demagogues throughout the ages, and these demagogues have said idiotic things so often that people have ended up believing them. I've written a song about this, and the chorus goes: 'It's better with one warm beer than four cold ones/it's better with an old grandma than a young girl,' chuckles a visibly pleased Rambo.

'We're masochists. People here will work for pocket lint, as if they feel doomed to eternal suffering, instead of looking around for something better. Your typical Serb will tell you: "Maybe I don't make a lot of money – but at least I sleep well at night." And when it comes to the obstinacy, you'll find that Serbs will automatically gravitate to the opposite side of what everyone else wants, just to be contrary. For instance, I'm completely unable to understand the problem with Kosovo. Let them go, I say. The underdeveloped south wants to separate from the developed north. Good riddance, I say.'

Rambo worries that nationalism remains an important factor in Serbian politics, particularly when it comes to the Yugoslav President, Vojislav Kostunica. 'I can only picture Kostunica waking up in the morning; he'll look at himself in the mirror and say, "Serb!" Then he goes to the bathroom and thinks, "Serb going to the bathroom,"' Rambo mimics. 'It's beyond me, perhaps because I'm fortunate enough to live in a multi-ethnic body. To me Kostunica is an old-fashioned relic who thinks it's the territory people live in that determines their quality of life. He's an anachronism,' he concludes.

We're sitting in his new office. Rambo has rented an office in town, in order better to separate his private life from his business. His hours are from two to six. Rambo is behind his desk; I'm in an old, soft easy chair. The furniture was given him by various friends: a radio from the fifties, a suede sofa, Chinese curtains, a Gypsy woman on the wall. Rambo fingers his guitar as he speaks, accompanying his many points as they roll out of him.

'I can't understand why they haven't arrested Milosevic yet,' he says. 'They say they don't have sufficient proof and have to follow the letter of the law. But the law is just a tool in the service of justice, and sometimes it can even get in the way of justice. When that happens, justice must supersede the law. The Germans had a law that said Jews were to be burned. What is moral, what is law and what is justice then? Here they say they don't have a case against Milosevic. That's like spitting in the faces of those who lost their families in the war,' says Rambo, angry now. 'The Hague Tribunal came into being because some countries don't have the authority or moral credibility to prosecute criminals. It would have made me very proud if we were able to try him here and sentence him to jail for life – and then, if The Hague still wanted him, lend him out to them for a while. I'd like to see him punished for starting the wars, even if most people here are more concerned with what he did to the Serbs themselves – that he stole, and ruined the economy. In Germany school kids visit Auschwitz, and I'd like to see our children see and learn about what we did; the same goes for Croatia and Bosnia. The most beautiful thing would be if we cared about our own crimes and they about theirs, and not like it is now when everybody just cares about their own victims and the others' crimes, so that nothing moves on in people's minds.'

Drummer Trut, bassist Mihajlo and keyboardist Pancevac arrive to finalise the details of this weekend's show in Sarajevo. Rambo and his band were the first Serbian act to play Sarajevo after the war and the three-and-a-half-year Serbian siege of the town. Rambo had become popular in Sarajevo when he suddenly stopped in the middle of a live broadcast of one of his concerts and delivered a fiery speech in support of the besieged town. 'This is a pointless war!' he shouted. That was the last time Rambo performed live on TV.

I join the band on the tour to Sarajevo. It takes us an hour to reach the Bosnian border. The process of checking passports seems to take for ever on each side of the border. The musical instruments have to be meticulously registered. 'It was never like this when Tito was alive,' offers a laconic Rambo, and then explains, very politely, that he's not carrying any CDs when the immigration official wants one. 'There must be more immigration officials and border guards in the former Yugoslavia than in all of Europe combined,' he snorts. 'No way am I giving a CD to a policeman.'

We drive into Bosnia. In the Serbian part, Republika Srpska, quite a few people wave to the car, which carries Belgrade plates. Once we cross into the Croatian Muslim area, some shake their fists at us. The sufferings of the war are still visible along the road as we drive by hundreds of houses where only the foundations remain. Five years have passed since the peace treaty was signed, but in many places whole villages are still empty after their inhabitants fled or were forcibly removed. 'I hate the term "ethnic cleansing",' Rambo says as we drive through the skeletal remains of the war. 'If something is dirty it needs cleansing. It's a terrible word to use about the madness of war.'

In Tuzla we drive through an open-air market where people sell anything from washing powder to second-hand shoes. The roadside is lined with women selling black-market cartons of cigarettes. 'It was never like this when Tito was alive,' says Rambo. 'He wouldn't have allowed it.'

He says the same thing about the litter along the road: 'It was never like this when Tito was alive.'

The river we drive alongside is full of rubbish, bottles and cans; even the bushes and trees along the riverbank are riddled with litter; as if someone has decorated them all with plastic bags.

I ask Rambo what his constant references to Tito might imply. 'I just mean what I say. Tito would never have allowed this. A lot of things were better under Tito,' he states. 'The country was cleaner, we didn't hate one another. As everyone worked in state-run companies, nobody had to chase money – everybody had just what they needed. Whenever someone did run after money, people would laugh at them.'

On the road down to Sarajevo things get quiet. We drive by one graveyard after another. Entire hillsides along the road are covered in crosses and white stones. Crosses for Christians, white gravestones for Muslims. In the war, no other town was hit as hard as, or suffered greater casualties than, Sarajevo. The last cemetery we pass is inside the city itself, on a former football pitch. Even in public parks people have been buried. Until the war began, Sarajevo was the epitome of a multi-ethnic community. Now mainly Muslims live here, but people of other faiths can still be found.

We're running late and head directly for the press conference. Rambo hits the 'on' button, jokes and plays the fool for the journalists. 'Before, I was only famous in Yugoslavia, but now I'm an international star,' he beams – and lists Serbia, Bosnia, Croatia, Slovenia, Montenegro and Macedonia. The young urban music critics laugh, as if worrying about nationalities is a thing of the past. Rambo is asked what the shepherd song is really about. He replies that it's about the shepherd needing to return.

'And who is your shepherd?' the journalist wants to know.

'Josip Broz Tito,' Rambo responds earnestly. 'You can

interpret that song any way you like,' he continues. 'You could take it to mean that we made a mistake when we divided Yugoslavia. We thought it would make our lives better, but as it turned out our lives got worse and we feel like sheep abandoned by our shepherd.'

'Since you're from Montenegro, how do you feel in Belgrade?' asks another reporter.

'At home,' Rambo answers.

'Nobody used to ask things like that before, but now that Montenegro wants to separate from Serbia I'm constantly asked how I feel in Serbia, as if I were a stranger,' Rambo tells me later. He thinks it's an impulse borne of sheer stupidity that Montenegro now wants to leave Yugoslavia and separate from Serbia. 'Montenegro has always been subsidised by Serbia, and they will be a lot worse off if they secede. But the politicians there aren't clever enough to master the new game of Yugoslavia. I'm beyond caring at this point. I had my heartache in 1991, when Croatia and Slovenia broke off from Yugoslavia. Now it's all the same.'

Despite his stardom, Rambo hasn't got rich from his music. The tour budget requires the band to stay in a borrowed flat while in Sarajevo. They eat for free in a local restaurant, provided they play a jam session there.

The next day Rambo prepares for the concert, and shows me his morning workout, which consists of breathing and muscle exercises. This has just been taught to him by a Tibetan martial-arts master whom Rambo has hired for a month to work on him and the band. The exercises consist of standing very still for a long time and then slowly flexing muscles and changing positions as you grow weary. The rest of the band shows little interest in the new regimen.

Then there's coffee, a bit of guitar picking, a sound

check and lunch – a very late lunch which ends up with us running through town to make the nine o'clock show. There are a lot of people outside the venue who couldn't get tickets. Rambo and the band take the stage for a two-hour show. Rambo plays and clowns around; people were calling for the shepherd song from the moment he took the stage, and when he finally does it the whole audience joins in. He plays a number of songs with political or social subtexts, like the one about the man who collects scrap metal for a few Deutschmarks a day; or the one about how Yugoslavia was partitioned so many times that in the end there was nothing left; or about the car fetishism of the nouveau riche and the ensuing battle between a Mercedes and an Audi A8. People double up with laughter when Rambo acts out the two car owners. At the end the audience demands the shepherd song again, in lieu of encores.

In Belgrade I often drop by Rambo's during his office hours. There's always someone there; the Tibetan martial artist does his exercises in a corner, drummer Trut smokes hash and plays Indian music and a young female fine-arts student wants to paint the rock star's portrait, while a hotel owner wants advice on how to market his hotel and a classical composer stops by for a chat with musical colleagues.

'I've become known in rather new circles. All kinds of different people, even businessmen, seek me out to collaborate. All of a sudden I'm respectable. I'm even on TV now. People have taken to asking me for favours, because they think I'm important. But I was more important before, due to my long tongue. Now everybody's got long tongues,' he mocks.

'I'm offered all kinds of assignments, including scoring

a movie in Slovenia – a Serbian–Slovene co-production, of all things. It's good that we've started collaborating again; it's promising. The partitioning of the country began with Slovenia, and the reunification will grow out of there as well. They were always a few years ahead of the rest of us. But it's like physics: once something begins to split, it doesn't stop until everything has divided itself down to the very last particle, and we probably have some way to go yet. Montenegro, Kosovo, Vojvodina and Sandzak will tear away from Serbia; Dalmatia from Croatia. And then we can start thinking about putting it all back together again. I wouldn't mind living in a country with two hundred million people in it; then I could sell a hundred thousand records instead of a few thousand!'

Rambo still won't peddle his music at any price. During one of my visits he's being interviewed by Serbian TV, with the requirement that they never show his face on screen, only footage of an aquarium. 'I don't want to wear out my welcome,' he explains. 'Besides, I'd like to maintain my freedom of movement and be able to go and buy some peppers at the market without getting recognised. The people who dig what I do and come to my shows know what I look like, of course, but there are not that many of them. If I splash my face on TV all the time, all of Serbia will recognise me and start yelling things on the street.'

One fine afternoon we sit in his office and drink whisky. The café below brings us glasses and ice. All in all, Rambo is more content with his life these days, but he still feels a frequent urge to leave Yugoslavia behind. 'Although when I lived in Holland, I noticed very quickly that Europe doesn't need my mind for anything – only my muscles. I can very well imagine an iron curtain being dropped around the EU and the rest of the world pretty soon. Only if you're remarkably intelligent, or have something else they need, will you be allowed inside. My dream is to live in a country in north-western Europe, by the Atlantic, where I can sail and be the resident composer for some small, obscure theatre company. But I do feel that we now have an opportunity to get on the right track in the Balkans. I don't think the people have improved measurably, but if we can set up a fair and just system it will allow the good people to rise upwards and the dumb ones to fail. It's about time.'

Rambo still wouldn't mind an international career. 'But it's not really tempting to be one of a thousand unknown artists in London; I'd rather wait to be discovered by someone here,' he says, and illustrates his reasoning with a joke:

Two maggots, father and son, live in shit.

The son: 'We live in shit – is that good for us?'

The dad: 'Yes, it's good – we've got food, and it's warm.'

The son: 'But I heard that some maggots live in apples?'

The dad: 'I've heard that, too. Apparently lots of maggots live in apples.'

'Isn't that much better?' the son asks.

'Yes, I would think so,' the father responds.

'But then why don't we just move into an apple?' the son wonders.

'Because it's very hard to leave your fatherland,' explains the dad.

'Vancouver.'

It's been three years and I'm back in Rambo's basement studio.

'Vancouver,' Rambo repeats and looks at me with sleepy, tired – but steady – eyes. He looks like a man who's finally come to an important decision, after a long binge. The musician has just returned from a tour of Slovenia and is due to get back on the bus again in the morning.

'I don't feel great at my concerts any more. I feel good, but not great. It's time to move on.'

Rambo was in Canada a few months earlier, invited to play at a festival. He says he's never felt so relaxed.

'People walked around with smiles on their faces. All day long. The Canadians are the friendliest people I've ever met. Besides, I liked the climate there: damp, humid and cold – but still some sunshine, and then, of course, the ocean. They have everything they need there, except a sailing coach. I can lie by the docks all day and wait for people who want lessons. Kids, adults, whatever. What do you think?'

Rambo once told me he didn't want his sons to grow up to become 'mirror images of their parents'. Now he has a third son and the two elder ones are growing up.

'Children should be raised among smiling faces. Not among people who kill their Prime Minister. One day they'll kill him, the next it's me.'

Rambo grows pensive when he talks about Zoran Djindjic. 'The killing was yet more proof of how abnormally diseased this society became under Milosevic. A medieval logic governed everything; the legionnaires conquered land for their ruler. Then they were unable to accept his fall and the changes it incurred. Like the great statesman he was, Djindjic should have realised this and played a safer game. His first move should have been to educate himself in demagoguery. Only populist charlatans have ever succeeded in leading, or better misleading, this country. He played a high-stakes game and it cost him his life. Unfortunately Kostunica, on the other hand, has learned every demagogue trick in the book. He knows the power of the feudal mentality of Asia Minor that Milosevic dug out from deep down in the recesses of our consciousness.'

Rambo drums his fingers on the table, then gets up to put on another jazz record.

'It's rare that it's the smart ones who govern. That's a universal problem, is it not? The quick ones go for business and the wise ones are content to sit home and think. So it falls on the less gifted, whose ambitions nevertheless are on a par with the businessmen's, to deal with politics. We're witnessing a global absurdity: corporations are growing more powerful than nations. Capital, and its need for pro-creation, is the most perfect social creation. Look at sharks: ruthless predators – and one of the oldest organisms on earth. They have endured and survived everything, precisely because of their brutal simplicity. Another absurdity awaits us in the future: we will not have any other fish than sharks. There will be wars, in utterly unknown and unexpected forms, where the sharks, having run out of all other prey, will begin to devour each other.'

Rambo adjusts himself in the chair before continuing.

'I'm not really convinced that *Homo sapiens* is the best effort of our Creator. The universe is endless, but our ruthless egocentricity has us convinced that everything orbits around us. If you look at the massive destruction humanity has perpetrated upon itself, it could appear that the evolution of our consciousness runs counter to that of the universe. If you look at us from this perspective, Serbia is no longer the exception to the rule.'

The musician leans forward, resting his elbows on his knees. 'The banks here have started lending money to people,' he tells me. 'That is probably a promising development. The best way to shake people out of their inertia is to put them in debt. Then you give them the power to realise their dreams overnight, while ensuring that they'll spend years paying for their dreams. This is the principle upon which the stability of the Western world rests.'

Rambo Amadeus rouses himself, as if shaking off all thoughts of politics. He's just recorded yet another album and is hard at work designing the cover, a video, a remix and other details. He plays his latest songs for me. I crack up over 'Good Morning, Mr Popovic', which is a mix of a cassette course in Serbian. The new album is called *17 Pickles*. Rambo is about to explain the title when he suddenly interrupts himself.

'Did you ever stop to think that Mona Lisa doesn't have any legs?'

'Uh, no . . .'

'These days I am drawing Mona Lisa's legs.'

Rambo proceeds to show me several sketches of the beauty's legs in various poses. 'I think it's a damn shame that the world has never seen Mona Lisa's legs. Da Vinci chose to cut her body in half. It's about time someone gave her back her legs! When I'm finished I will go to the Louvre, approach the administrator and present him with her long-lost legs. What do you think?'

From up on the wall, Mona Lisa smiles down on us. Two half-naked women in black and white try to copy her seductive glance, whereas an Oriental mask is content to stare blankly from two empty eye sockets.

'Nationalism,' Rambo bursts out. 'It's back in the saddle, riding us again. After the wars were over, and Milosevic was gone, we thought, in our naïve enthusiasm, that we'd turn into Switzerland overnight. Those days are gone. We still have a miserable standard of living, are poorly educated, saddled with a pathetic health-care system, lots of pollution and a marginal standing in the eyes of the world.'

Rambo begins to hum something that sounds like a kids' song. Bright, metallic, the words come into being:

> *Ko to kaze, ko to laze, Srbija je mala?*
> *Nije mala, nije mala, tri put ratovala!*
> *(Who says, who lies Serbia is small?*
> *It's not small, it's not small, it has fought three wars!)*

Rambo repeats the chorus, faster and faster. 'Listen, this harmless ditty is probably the most nationalistic tune in the world. It was banned under Tito, but it was a huge hit during the Milosevic era.'

Rambo has recorded the warmongering tune for his new CD:

> *Who says, who lies Serbia is small?*
> *Who says, who lies that the planet is small?*

'The new nationalism is of a different breed. It's not hateful and vindictive, like it was ten, fifteen years ago. All this talk of "strong, Greater Serbia" is a sort of comfort-nationalism; it's no longer aggressive. But it still stunts our growth.'

Who says Serbia is small? Who says the planet is small?

Rambo sings faster and faster. His voice sounds like a turbine.

Suddenly he pauses.

'This is how it all starts,' he says.

Thank You

to all those who shared their lives and thoughts with me so I could write this book about them.